Gods
of the
Mississippi

Religion in North America

Catherine L. Albanese and Stephen J. Stein, editors

GODS

of the

Mississippi

◆

Edited by
MICHAEL PASQUIER

Indiana University Press
BLOOMINGTON & INDIANAPOLIS

This book is a publication of

Indiana University Press
601 North Morton Street
Bloomington, Indiana 47404-3797

iupress.indiana.edu

Telephone orders 800-842-6796
Fax orders 812-855-7931

© 2013 by Indiana University Press

Cataloging information is available from the Library of Congress

1 2 3 4 5 18 17 16 15 14 13

To our teachers

CONTENTS

FOREWORD

This engaging collection of essays assembled by Michael Pasquier explores and exploits the manifold diverse ways that the Mississippi River and the Mississippi River valley have impacted historical, religious, geographical, social, and cultural realities in mid-America and continue to do so today. After working through these essays, one will never again be inclined to limit the Mississippi to any one single category of experience. These essays collectively challenge the standard simple definitions of "the Mississippi."

Pasquier has brought together a selection of historians whose expertise ranges widely across the subfields of American history. Most also possess focused research interests on specific religious traditions, geographical regions, and/or cultural patterns with some link to the Mississippi or to the regions surrounding the river. These scholars bring their expertise to bear upon those waters and the religious contexts of this great river as well as upon the diverse ways the river has impacted our understanding of American history, especially the portions of the national narrative dealing with the religious experiences of Americans. The nature and character of those relationships form the substantive center of this collection.

The authors of the essays in this volume, for example, challenge a number of the older ways of organizing American religious history, a narrative that rather standardly moves on an east/west axis. The river's path, however, flows from north to south and features religious stories located in the Midwest, a neglected area in the nation's history, including its religious history. In these essays we encounter the religious traditions held by African slaves in the Mississippi River valley in the antebellum period, the religious changes introduced into the worlds of the Choctaw and Chickasaw Native American tribes when Christian missionaries entered the river valley, as well as the tensions and conflicts that surrounded the members of new religious movements who settled in the valley, including the Mormons at Nauvoo, Illinois. In the case of the Latter-day Saints, they experienced dramatic empowerment from the river but also ultimately tragic conflict with others in the region and the murder of their prophet and founder, Joseph Smith.

Another part of the Mississippi River valley was the delta region which in the decades following the Civil War became a shaping force on Christian worship and liturgical patterns within the expanding holiness and Pentecostal movements as well as a productive context for African American fraternal orders and societies. Religion in the lower Mississippi River valley and in the New Orleans region also included the powerful presence of Roman Catholicism, which was involved in the construction of racial boundaries, the formation of the culture of Jim Crow, and the empowerment of laywomen in the genesis and transmission of Catholic piety.

This rich account of Mississippi religion and culture takes a turn to the contemporary with an essay on Johnny Cash. It is an account of the inner life, the public career, and the biographical twists and turns that this prominent performer and entertainer experienced and the diverse ways in which he responded to religion at various times during his career. Mississippi culture clearly figured in his life at times in very troubling ways.

As he introduces the essays that follow, Pasquier speaks of "the collision and coalescence of religious peoples and ideas" shaped by and shaping the world of the Mississippi. He is correct to underscore the shaping character of the Mississippi upon the religion and culture of the people who moved to, across, or up and down the river. Thus the river becomes a rich metaphor for the process of cultural mediation carried out by religious people who were in the region of the river. The net result of the religious forces operative in the Mississippi River valley was very mixed. Some of the traditions prospered precisely because of the advantages—geographical location, abundant resources, expanding population, and the like that the context provided. Other religious communities were the victims of problems as a result of their presence in the valley. Pasquier did not intend that this collection would be an uninflected tribute to the Mississippi.

This volume closes with an important afterword by Thomas A. Tweed, a set of reflections subtitled "Repositioning the Narratives of U.S. Religious History." Tweed uses the occasion of the publication of this collection of essays to praise the contributors who have expanded the substance and complexity of the narrative of American religious history by means of the attention they have directed to a region that has received too little attention in the conventional histories of American religion. This instance of a new narrative, in his judgment, holds the promise of other historians also expanding the geographical scope of the narrative of American religious history to a global tale, tracing the stories of religious Americans back to the locations across the globe from which they came. Such a perspective also invites informed comparisons between America's religious life and the host of geographical locations across the globe from which religious Americans came. In other words, Tweed judges that the essays in Pasquier's volume are highly suggestive about a possible variety of valuable expanding future moves by historians of American religious history. The mighty Mississippi leads to an even larger world.

Catherine L. Albanese
Stephen J. Stein
SERIES EDITORS

ACKNOWLEDGMENTS

Those responsible for supporting, organizing, and writing this collection of essays are many. I started soliciting contributors to *Gods of the Mississippi* in 2007. I was a visiting assistant professor in the Department of Religion at Florida State University at the time. John Corrigan, Amanda Porterfield, and Amy Koehlinger were very kind to support my scholarship in Tallahassee. In 2008–2009, with backing from the American Academy of Arts and Sciences, I continued to solicit and edit essays from a growing number of scholars interested in expanding our understanding of religion in America. I am grateful to Jon Sensbach, Richard Callahan, Tracy Leavelle, Sue Ann Marasco, and Arthur Remillard for participating in a roundtable discussion of "Religions along the Mississippi River: Region and Space in American Religious History" at the Annual Meeting of the American Society of Church History in 2009. The rich conversation that followed our presentations on that wintry day in New York City convinced me that we were onto something important.

The final pool of contributors crystalized in 2009. Many thanks to all of you—Jon Sensbach, Sylvester Johnson, Arthur Remillard, Thomas Ruys Smith, Seth Perry, John Giggie, Alison Greene, Justin Poché, and John Hayes. It is because of your patience and diligence that Thomas Tweed agreed to write the afterword to our book. Thank you, Tom. I am also grateful to my colleagues associated with the Young Scholars in American Religion Program and the Center for the Study of Religion and American Culture at Indiana University–Purdue University at Indianapolis—especially Ann Braude, Linford Fisher, John Hayes, and Quincy Newell—for reading a draft of the introduction. And thanks to Dee Mortensen, Sarah Jacobi, and June Silay at Indiana University Press for your incredible editorial insight, along with the copyediting skills of Elaine Otto and the commentary of Catherine Albanese, Stephen Stein, and the anonymous reviewers.

Final manuscript preparation would not have been possible without the support of my home institution, Louisiana State University, especially Delbert Burkett, Chair of the Department of Philosophy and Religious Studies, and Gaines Foster, Dean of the College of Humanities and Social Sciences. The same goes for each of the institutions that supported those who contributed essays to *Gods of the Mississippi*.

This book is dedicated to our teachers, including Rodger Payne, Chair of the Department of Religious Studies at the University of North Carolina Asheville. Rodger introduced me to the study of religion in America while I was an undergraduate at Louisiana State University. Were it not for Rodger, this book would not have been written. Thank you, Dr. Payne.

Gods
of the
Mississippi

INTRODUCTION

◆

Religious Life on the Mississippi

Michael Pasquier

The gods on their thrones are shaken and changed, but it abides, aloof and unappeasable, with no heart except for its own task, under the unbroken and immense arch of the lighted sky where the sun, too, goes a lonely journey. As a thing used by men it has changed: the change is not in itself, but in them.

—William Alexander Percy, *Lanterns on the Levee,* 1941

In 1833, at age thirteen, James Buchanan Eads moved to St. Louis, Missouri, with his family. They arrived by steamboat. Before everyone could disembark, the watercraft exploded, leaving eight people dead and the Eads family alive. As a young man, Eads worked aboard steamboats and started a riverbed salvage business. His fortune made, he spent the Civil War years designing and building ironclad gunboats for the Union. From 1867 to 1874, Eads led the construction of the first large-span bridge that supported railroad traffic across the Mississippi River in St. Louis. The following year, Congress rewarded Eads with a contract to build a jetty at the mouth of the Mississippi in order to improve navigability. Speaking before a crowd of four hundred men in St. Louis, Eads vowed "to undertake the work [of opening the river mouth] with a faith based upon the ever-constant ordinances of God himself; and . . . I will give to the Mississippi river, through His grace, and by application of His laws, a deep, open, safe, and permanent outlet to the sea."[1] He believed, like many people before and after his time, that "the improvement of the Mississippi"—the building of levees, dams, jetties, reservoirs, and canals in order to prevent flooding and ease navigation—"involves the contemplation of one of the sublimest physical wonders of the beneficent Creator," that "immense valley which is now justly known throughout Christendom as the 'Garden of the World.'"[2] Eads completed the jetty project in 1879, to which the *New Orleans*

Daily Times proclaimed, "There is no parallel instance of man's employment of the prodigious energies of nature in the realization of his aims."[3] Eads died in 1887, having engineered ways for people to cross the Mississippi by railroad from east to west and to travel unimpeded up and down "the old Father of Waters" to the Gulf of Mexico.[4]

Fast forward to August 2005, when Hurricane Katrina funneled a twenty-five-foot wall of water up the Mississippi River–Gulf Outlet, creating what some have called a "storm surge superhighway." Completed in 1968 and operated by the U.S. Army Corps of Engineers, the Mississippi River–Gulf Outlet (also known as Mr. Go) is a canal that provides deep-draft ships with a shorter navigation route from the Mississippi River to the Gulf of Mexico. The twentieth-century construction of Mr. Go is in many ways a legacy of Eads's nineteenth-century attempt at mastering the Mississippi. It is a testament to the persistence of people to live in the vicinity of a body of water with both creative and destructive powers. Since Katrina, in a remote location of St. Bernard Parish on the banks of Mr. Go, thousands of pilgrims have visited a marble monument that reads, "In Everlasting Memory of Katrina Victims, St. Bernard, Louisiana, August 29, 2005," followed by 163 names, beginning with Bertha Acosta and ending with Gloria Young. Behind the monument, extending out of the waters of Mr. Go, stands a metal cross with an image of the crucified Christ's face at its center. Standing near the shrine on the sixth anniversary of Katrina, a thirty-one-year-old resident was asked how his community had changed, to which he replied, "It's funny to look back at where it is now and where it was before. It's funny because it is not what it was. It's different. But it's home."[5] It wasn't just a storm that changed this man's home. It was also a river that, for centuries, confounded those who call upon deities to control its waters and attracted those who need a place to call home.

There is much to be said about the history of life along the Mississippi River. It seems an obvious place to study the movement of peoples and ideas throughout American history. Mark Twain thought so, beginning his book *Life on the Mississippi* (1883) with the grand statement, "But *the basin of the Mississippi is the* BODY OF THE NATION." By extension, it went without saying, though Twain said it anyway, that "the Mississippi is well worth reading about. It is not a commonplace river, but on the contrary is in all ways remarkable."[6] Looking at the long-term success of his novels *The Adventures of Tom Sawyer* (1876) and *The Adventures of Huckleberry Finn* (1885), it is difficult to argue with the man. In each of his fictional narratives, the river is both a character in the plot and a conveyor of the plot. The river is Twain's vehicle for examining some of the most pressing moral questions facing a growing nation of readers from New York to San Francisco and from St. Paul to New Orleans. After all, it is on a raft near the banks of the Mississippi River that Twain has Huck choose hell over delivering the runaway slave, Jim, to his master.

During the nineteenth century, what set Twain apart from most Americans writing about the Mississippi was his interest in capturing the soul of a nation without the aid of belief in a Christian god. And yet, as historian Tracy Fessenden reveals, Twain's unbelief was an "ambivalent refuge" from that which he gained a reputation for disparaging at every step of his pseudonymous life.[7] Despite his formidable credentials as a skeptic and satirist of all-things-religious, Twain, at the very least, was moved to think and write at length about the river of his childhood, adolescence, and adulthood. He, like so many other Americans of his time, recognized the powerful enchantment of a watery artery pulsing through the heart of a reputedly chosen land. All jokes and jabs at American religions aside—and there were many—Twain represented the Mississippi as a significant body of water. The risk in writing a book about the Mississippi—and by starting it with Twain—is that we might also get caught up in the national mythologies of a river and an author. The purpose of *Gods of the Mississippi,* therefore, is to discover how a body of water like the Mississippi River has influenced the religious beliefs and practices of people on personal, local, regional, national, and transnational levels.

The life and works of Robert Baird, in addition to Twain's, represent the challenges associated with the study of religion and culture along the Mississippi. Baird was a graduate of Princeton Theological Seminary, a Presbyterian minister, a domestic missionary, and, perhaps most famously, the author of *Religion in America* (1844). He was also one of the earliest interpreters of what historians have called the "evangelical empire" and "evangelical surge" of the nineteenth century.[8] In the words of historian John Lardas Modern, Baird was an influential booster of the "systematic organization of mass media" used to leap, almost imperceptibly, the "categorical boundary between the religious and the secular" during a period of westward expansion in North America.[9] For Baird, the Mississippi was not only a body of water to be crossed in order to extend "Christendom" to a people of "mixed race—Americans, emigrants from all parts of Europe, and natives of the islands in the Pacific Ocean."[10] It was an enormous valley encompassing a territory "whose influence will soon be felt to be favourable, or disastrous, to an extent corresponding with its mighty energies, to the cause of religion."[11] In other words, before spreading "America's God" across the entire continent, Baird believed it was necessary to establish a physical and metaphysical order in the great space between East and West.

Over a decade before the publication of *Religion in America,* Baird was already attuned to the evangelical Protestant penchant for draping ideas of secular progress over Christian missionary initiatives. He was the anonymous author of an 1832 travel manual entitled *View of the Valley of the Mississippi, or the Emigrant's and Traveller's Guide to the West.* In it, Baird treated religious matters almost as an afterthought, devoting a mere six out of more than three hundred pages to the subject of "Religious Denominations and Sects." He counted sixteen denominations in the Mississippi valley, chief among them Methodist (800,000), Baptist (700,000), Presbyterian (550,000), and "Papal" (500,000). Following his brief statistical breakdown of Christianity, Baird included twenty-two pages on "The Steam-Boats of the West," in which he discussed the history and mechanics of steamboating alongside warnings about the pervasiveness of profanity, gambling, fighting, drinking, and other "scenes of shocking depravity." In response to such "evil practices" aboard steamboats, Baird assured his imagined readers that "if he perseveres with a heart bent upon doing good, (and every Christian ought to make this a *primary* object in all his journies, whether on business, or pleasure in other respects), his hallowed influence will pervade the boat, and produce a lasting impression."[12] Such overtly moralistic asides of the kind made in reference to steamboats appear throughout Baird's book written (or masked) as a practical guide for travelers to the Mississippi valley.

Indeed, much more can and ought to be made of Baird's complicity in the development of evangelical Protestantism in the American West. But it is equally important to take seriously the content and implications of *View of the Valley of the Mississippi* and hundreds of other books, pamphlets, and articles written during the nineteenth century about the past, present, and future of the Mississippi. Baird's exhaustive, if not a bit embellished, geographical, statistical, and historical description of the states, territories, cities, economies, institutions, and communities of the Mississippi valley should be an indication of the region's potential for innovative inquiry into the history of religion in the United States. To focus entirely on the missionary objectives of Baird, however veiled in secularism, is to overstate the impact of a coalition of westward leading, still proceeding evangelical Protestant leaders on the everyday lives of millions of Americans and non-Americans who settled along, traveled down, and ferried across the Mississippi. Buried in some of Baird's most fleeting observations are questions about the collision and coalescence of religious peoples and ideas in a region known for its cultural shapeshifting. Describing "One of these large [steam] boats, filled with passengers," Baird imagined "almost a *world* in miniature." Surveying the "Character, Manners, and Pursuits, of the Inhabitants of the Valley of the Mississippi," Baird began with the assertion, "The population . . . is exceedingly heterogeneous, if we regard the very great variety of nations of which it is composed."[13] The task of this collection of essays is to begin where Baird and so many others have stopped, namely, with the simple recognition that the Mississippi valley was a real and imagined space of incredible commotion and diversity throughout American history.

Furthermore, the reason for laboring through the books of Twain and Baird is to stress that the study of religion and culture along the Mississippi is as much about national identities as it is about regional trends and local particularities. It is as much about conflicts over the grand narrative of religion in America as it is about people who rarely exhibited concern for books and Bibles. Twain and Baird were neither the first nor the last people to lay claim to the meaning of the Mississippi for national audiences. In his book *The Frontier Spirit in American Christianity* (1923), Peter Mode took inspiration from Frederick Jackson Turner's "Frontier Thesis" when he described the Mississippi valley as "far removed from the strifes of Europe and large enough to cradle its millions." The valley's 1.3 million square miles, according to Mode, "had been set by God as the stage for this process of race development" in the West and a catalyst for the "Americanization" and "frontierization" of Christianity.[14] In similarly dramatic fashion, William Warren Sweet prefaced his book *The Rise of Methodism in the West* (1920) with the contention that "The heart of Methodism lies in the Mississippi valley; there live the bulk of her membership, there she has performed her greatest achievements, and there perhaps lies her most brilliant future."[15] Edwin Gaustad wrote more generally of those who "saw across the Mississippi—America's Jordan—a land to be redeemed, a people to be won."[16] In Gaustad's *Historical Atlas of Religion in America* (1962), as with other surveys of American religious history, the Mississippi was to be reached and then crossed in ultimate fulfillment of "*the conquest of the West.*"[17] The river appears as a static physical barrier dividing the trans-Allegheny West and the trans-Mississippi West; it did little to transform the religious landscape of the United States.

Such overwhelmingly Protestant, nationalist, and frontier narratives of the United States have directed the attention of historians away from the study of religion and culture along the Mississippi. Lessons can be learned, however, from Sydney Ahlstrom's critique of Turner, Sweet, and those he called "frontier enthusiasts." "The 'frontier' in America," he warned, "is not a region, but a process. . . . The creativeness of the frontier, or rather, the power of the frontier to alter or refashion whatever came into it, must not be exaggerated."[18] Following in the revisionist footsteps of Ahlstrom, Thomas Tweed and contributors to the edited volume *Retelling U.S. Religious History* (1997) stressed the diversity of American religions while at the same time articulating "coherent stories . . . that make sense of the religious past yet draw on new motifs and plots and include a wider range of settings and characters."[19] Particularly in the case of Catherine Albanese's work, the motifs of contact, boundary, and exchange became a form of narrative emplotment that avoided the determinative classification scheme running through American religious historiography from Baird to Ahlstrom and beyond. Moreover, their emphasis on social and geographic sites—from bedrooms and theaters to the Louisiana coastline and the Mexican border—has had a sizable effect on the manner in which historians have interpreted American religious history since the publication of *Retelling*. The study of religion in the Mississippi valley is in many ways a contribution to the ongoing conversation about how historians tell stories about religion in America.

A book about the Mississippi River challenges regional approaches to American history. One of the unique features of this particular river valley is its reputation as a space to be crossed as much as a place to be settled. The Mississippi River contributed to the movement of people—to it, across it, and along it—like no other riverine system in North America. It divided East and West, connected North and South, and functioned as a physical and metaphorical force driving people together in ways that were sometimes beneficial, sometimes destructive, and always demonstrative of the notion that space, place, and motion matter when it comes to understanding religion as something lived. Moreover, the transregional qualities of the Mississippi valley test traditional regional categories such as New England, the Middle Atlantic, the Old Northwest, the Old Southwest, the Midwest, the Mountain West, the Pacific Northwest, the Pacific Rim, the Southwestern Borderlands, and the South.[20] Arguing specifically about non-evangelical Protestant "others" in the South, but no less relevant to the study of transregional experiences in the Mississippi valley, historian Donald Mathews spoke of "the tendency of religious expression and sensibility to flow over boundaries—and at the same time to be fastidiously insistent upon them."[21] Perhaps it is this paradox of place—this sense of local particularity, geographic fixity, cultural impermanence, and social mobility—that is at the heart of regional studies of religion in the United States. Peter Williams hinted at this paradox by describing regionalism as "a powerful, if fluid and somewhat imprecise, category of the way in which Americans have experienced and interpreted their collective lives." The study of religion and culture throughout the Mississippi valley, because of its tendency to defy traditional definitions of region, functions as a cautionary reminder of the "regional mystique" that can sometimes lead to overly determined interpretations of American religious history.[22]

Historical examinations of river societies in the United States are many, though few concentrate on the role of religion in the development of distinctive cultures that crossed state lines and confounded regional identities. The Ohio River is one such waterway that captured the imaginations of Americans, white and black, as depicted in Harriet Beecher Stowe's illustration of Eliza, "weary and foot-sore, but still strong of heart," standing before the Ohio River, "which lay, like Jordan, between her and the Canaan of liberty on the other side."[23] Indeed, "the contrasts and continuities along this shared waterway," according to historian Darrel Bigham, made the Ohio River into "America's first interstate highway and arguably the most vital tributary of the Mississippi."[24] Keith Griffler, in his study of the Underground Railroad, included chapters entitled "No Promised Land," "Home over Jordan," "Band of Angels," "Egypt's Border," and "Prelude to Exodus" in order to demonstrate how African American Christians conceived of the Ohio River and its position between slavery and freedom.[25] Writing about the Potomac River, Joel Achenbach referenced the "key psychological role" and the powerful symbolism of a waterway dividing North and South during the Civil War.[26] Still other historians have paid less attention to the symbolic qualities of rivers, focusing instead on the tendency of religious adherents to organize societies around the environmental patterns of river valleys. Rivers, quite simply, were attractive places to settle, and the religious beliefs and practices of river communities were often influenced by the physical effects of living in close proximity to waterways.[27]

With its mouth extending into the Gulf of Mexico, the Mississippi River linked inhabitants of North America to the circum-Caribbean and Atlantic worlds, again weakening the rigidity of national and regional identities in the United States. Writing about the three key maritime regions of the world— the Mediterranean, the Atlantic, and the Pacific—historian Kären Wigen highlighted their "fractured, fragmented," and "intrinsically unstable" qualities, which connected people on a massive scale in "essentially contested" spaces.[28] By extension, religious beliefs and practices were made and unmade and remade in these watery worlds known for their high levels of spatial and temporal fluidity. Without overstating the case, it is instructive to compare some features of these oceanic arenas to life along the Mississippi. Moreover, if "Atlantic history . . . is a *slice* of world history," as historian Alison Games argued, then Mississippi valley history is a global history akin to Jon Sensbach's revision of the early South as "both a receiver and a generator of religious philosophies, a connector node for ideas and people in constant motion."[29] The same can and has been said of the religious diversity of other regions throughout American history, and yet regional designators persist, oftentimes for good reason. As historians follow the Mississippi, the goal is not only to understand life along a river, but also to follow lines of inquiry in other parts of the United States that might reveal alternative narratives of regional religions. Rivers represent only one way to study religion in the United States. Of course, there are others.

Comparative approaches to the study of river cultures are particularly useful for historians interested in understanding the development of religious landscapes throughout the Mississippi valley. Writing about the Indian city of Banaras, Diana Eck referred to the Ganges River as "important in both its particular and symbolic existence," as a place of settlement and a mover of people as well as a watery body to be contemplated and imagined and made meaningful.[30] Similarly, Vijaya Rettakudi Nagarajan recognized the "intermittent sacrality" of the Ganges, or how people may believe a river to be sacred while at the same time interacting with that same river in a manner that may seem profane.[31] Traveling up and down and across rivers can also take the form of pilgrimage, as was and is the case for the Ganges and so many other major and minor rivers of the world.[32] Furthermore, rivers can influence and sometimes dominate the lifeways of nearby inhabitants, as Jean-Marie Gibbal demonstrated in his description of the Niger River as "no less the axis of life in this region to which it gives meaning, history, [and] name."[33] Anthropologists have drawn similar conclusions about the cosmological creations of communities along the Orinoco and Amazon in South America.[34] Contests over the meaning of rivers have proven pivotal to the development of regional and national identities throughout the world. The riverine communities of Egypt and Ethiopia, for instance, have struggled to reconcile their Muslim and Christian traditions in a "Nile system [which] has remained," according to Hagai Erlikh, "a multicultural cosmos, a theater of ethnic diversity, of religious barriers, and of political dams."[35] In short, rivers appear, time and again, in the mythologies of ancient and not-so-ancient civilizations, thus highlighting the influence of rivers over the imaginative projections and demographic shifts of societies.

The Mississippi River, though rarely mirroring the obviously sacred attributes afforded the Ganges and other revered waterways by pilgrims, has functioned as a cultural conveyor belt for hundreds of years and for millions of people, exhibiting overtly holy qualities to some and powerful socializing forces for all. Another way to describe what is sometimes called "the sacred" is to begin with a question posed by the geographer Yi-Fu Tuan in his book *Space and Place*: "Given the human endowment, in what ways do people attach meaning to and organize space and place?" Fundamental to Tuan's understanding of the relationship between space and place is experience, whether direct or indirect, intimate or conceptual, or mediated by symbols or senses. Tuan loosely defined "space" as more abstract than but a constituent part of "place." Moreover, according to Tuan, "What begins as undifferentiated space becomes place as we get to know it better and endow it with value."[36] How, then, have people experienced space and place on or near or far from the waters of the Mississippi? The answer depends on whether historians are willing to challenge Mark Twain's romantic and playful characterization of life on the Mississippi. Few have done so. That being said, much can be gained from Thomas Buchanan's examination of "the hidden world of slaves and free blacks of the Mississippi River world" in his book *Black Life on the Mississippi* (2004).[37] Thomas Ruys Smith also provided original analysis of the literary representations and "symbolic meanings" associated with "the trope of the Mississippi" in his book *River of Dreams* (2007).[38] Together, Buchanan and Smith demonstrate the importance of understanding how rivers influence the thoughts and actions of individuals and how individuals influence the meaning and symbolism of rivers.

Gods of the Mississippi builds upon the insight of Buchanan and Smith by attempting to explain how the physical and imagined features of the Mississippi contributed to the development of religious ideas and communities throughout American history. Jon Sensbach opens the volume with an investigation of the religious entanglements between Africans and Europeans in colonial Louisiana during the seventeenth and eighteenth centuries. Specifically, Sensbach tracks the transmission of African beliefs and practices from the Black Atlantic to North America via the Mississippi River, with New Orleans functioning as a kind of rupturous gateway for the disassembly and reassembly of African religions in the New World. With the poetic aid of Langston Hughes's "The Negro Speaks of Rivers," Sensbach considers how enslaved Africans left a cultural imprint on the Mississippi River and how the Mississippi River impressed the cultural constructions of enslaved Africans in early America. The cultivation of novel creole religions and a distinctive black consciousness in colonial Louisiana, according to Sensbach, translated through the centuries to Hughes's conclusion that "My soul has grown deep like the rivers" Euphrates, Congo, Nile, and Mississippi.

The next four essays focus on religious developments of the nineteenth century. Sylvester Johnson writes about the partnership between American Protestant missionaries and the United States government to create a white, Anglo-Saxon, imperialist dominion in the Mississippi Territory. In contrast, Johnson illustrates how Mississippian Indians like the Choctaw and Chickasaw viewed American encroachment as a foreign imposition of "civilization." Arthur Remillard attends to the geographic and symbolic contests over the source of the Mississippi by recounting the expeditions of Zebulon Pike, Giacomo Beltrami, and Henry Rowe Schoolcraft. Competition over the meaning of the Mississippi's source, according to Remillard, demonstrates how the sacralization of the river depended on the civil religious discourse of American and European explorers. Thomas Ruys Smith looks at the development of new religious movements throughout the Mississippi valley during the Second Great Awakening. In the cases of the Millerites, Mormons, and Vermont Pilgrims, Smith explains how practitioners of new religious movements imagined the banks of the Mississippi River as the future site of the New Jerusalem and the American Millennium. Seth Perry extends the conversation about Mormonism by examining the rhetorical symbolism associated with the Mormon settlement of Nauvoo on the Mississippi River. Mormons, like so many other nineteenth-century residents, invested the river with such meaningful significance that over 12,000 people lived in Nauvoo by 1843 and an angry mob killed their leader, Joseph Smith, a year later.

The last four essays account for life in the Mississippi valley during the twentieth century. John Giggie tracks the transformation of African American religion in the Mississippi Delta after Reconstruction, paying attention to the innovative responses of Delta blacks to changes in technology, transportation, and commerce. The emergence of the African American Holiness-Pentecostal movement in the Delta, according to Giggie, was a consequence of the openness of Delta blacks to religious experimentation in the face of Jim Crow. Alison Greene also contends with the religious landscape of the Delta by concentrating on economic and environmental crises facing rural churches during the Depression. For outside reformers and local residents, the redemption of souls and soils became intertwined with denominational politics and labor activism, which, in turn, set the stage for future coalitions of faith and politics in a pocket of the South known as the Mississippi Delta. Justin Poché examines the bonfire celebrations of German and French communities along the River Road corridor connecting Baton Rouge to New Orleans. Rituals and stories associated with the bonfires, according to Poché, produced a moral geography of the Mississippi River that allowed German and French Catholics to cope with economic and environmental hardship. Finally, John Hayes connects the Delta roots of Johnny Cash to the unfolding religious themes contained in his music. Part biography and part musicology, Hayes notices an "arc of return" in the religious journey of the "Man in Black" from the folk religion of his youth, to a national evangelical Protestant stage alongside Billy Graham, and back again to his imagined home at the heart of the American Southland.

Taken together, the essays contained in *Gods of the Mississippi* provide readers with starting points for further investigation into the relationship between religious life and river life in North America. They take seriously the idea of "being lost at sea" in the vast region known as the Mississippi valley, which, according to philosopher Edward Casey, "means lacking place in an endless space-world." Some contributors to *Gods of the Mississippi* stress the inherent instability of place and its impact on the volatility of religious constructions in the sea-like world of the pan-Mississippi. Other contributors highlight the power of people to inhabit what may seem an uninhabitable place and transform, according to Casey, "a mere *site* into a dwelling *place*."[39] Thomas Tweed's theory of religion as "crossing" and "dwelling"—as the process of making homes and crossing boundaries—and as "confluences" and "flows"—as the process of emerging out of "the swirl of transfluvial currents"—illustrates why it is necessary to tell intentionally convoluted stories about religion and culture along the Mississippi.[40] Such a "polylocative" approach to the study of religion serves as a reminder that the methodological and theoretical orientation of historians influences the manner in which stories are told.[41] Correspondingly, the historical subjects of scholars are also in the business of collective orientation, of coming from somewhere, being somewhere, and going somewhere. The Mississippi River, as an aquatic metaphor and an aquatic body, is a space and place where scholars can observe the process of cultural mediation among religious peoples from around the world and around the bend.

NOTES

1. James Buchanan Eads, "Response to Welcome Address of the Mayor of St. Louis at the Banquet Given at the Southern Motel, March 23, 1875, in Honor of the Passage by Congress of the Jetty Act to Improve the Mouth of the Mississippi," in *Addresses and Papers of James B. Eads, Together with a Biographical Sketch* (St. Louis: Slawson, 1884), 48.

2. James Buchanan Eads, "Address on Behalf of the St. Louis Merchants' Exchange, to the Grand Convention for the Improvement of the Mississippi and Its Tributaries, St. Louis, February 12, 1867," in *Addresses and Papers of James B. Eads, 7, 8.*

3. John M. Barry, *Rising Tide: The Great Mississippi Flood of 1927 and How It Changed America* (New York: Simon and Schuster, 1997), 89. See also Pete Daniel, *Deep'n as It Come: The 1927 Mississippi River Flood* (Fayetteville: University of Arkansas Press, 1996).

4. Eads, "Address on Behalf of the St. Louis Merchants' Exchange," 15.

5. Benjamin Alexander-Bloch, "Hurricane Katrina Memorial at Shell Beach Honors St. Bernard Parish Residents Who Died," *Times Picayune* (New Orleans), 28 August 2011. See also "Through the Eye of Katrina," a special issue of the *Journal of American History* (December 2007); and "After the Storm: A Special Issue on Hurricane Katrina," in the *Journal of Southern Religion* (2009).

6. Mark Twain, *Life on the Mississippi* (New York: Bantam, 1981), v, 1.

7. Tracy Fessenden, *Culture and Redemption: Religion, the Secular, and American Literature* (Princeton: Princeton University Press, 2007), 137–60.

8. Robert Baird saw "the Anglo-Saxon race" as the driving force behind "the theoretical and practical mission of Protestantism for the world." Based on Baird's description of America's "evangelical Christianity," Martin Marty writes, "The United States was to be the base for that mission, but its internal empire had to remain secure and securely white Protestant." Martin Marty, *Righteous Empire: The Protestant Experience in America* (New York: Dial Press, 1970), 23. Speaking of an "evangelical surge," Mark Noll argues, "The central religious reality for the period from the Revolution to the Civil War was the unprecedented expansion of evangelical Protestant Christianity. No other period of American history ever witnessed such a dramatic rise in religious adherence and corresponding religious influence on the broader national culture." Noll, *America's God: From Jonathan Edwards to Abraham Lincoln* (New York: Oxford University Press, 2002), 165–66.

9. John Lardas Modern, "Evangelical Secularism and the Measure of Leviathan," *Church History* 77, no. 4 (December 2008): 820. Modern argues that "evangelical media practices helped make salvation a matter of 'national safety' rather than simply or solely a matter of faith" (805), which in turn made "evangelical secularism" into a "metaphysical solvent" (807) that permeated antebellum American society.

10. Robert Baird, *The Christian Retrospect and Register: A Summary of the Scientific, Moral, and Religious Progress of the First Half of the XIXth Century* (New York: W. W. Dodd, 1851), 194. For a standard, arguably definitive analysis of Baird's writings, see Henry Bowden's introduction to Baird's *Religion in America: A Critical Abridgment* (New York: Harper, 1970), xi–xxxvii. Bowden suggests, among other things, that "in many such instances Baird's prose sounds like a theological counterpart to the work of George Bancroft" (xxxvii). There is also good reason to link Baird with Philip Schaff, the founder of the American Society of Church History. See Jerald C. Brauer, "Changing Perspectives on Religion in America," in *Reinterpretation in*

American Church History, ed. Brauer (Chicago: University of Chicago Press, 1968), 2–4; and Klaus Penzel, ed., *Philip Schaff: Historian and Ambassador of the Universal Church: Selected Writings* (Macon, GA: Mercer University Press, 1991), 152–53. For more on the history of the field of church history, see *A Century of Church History: The Legacy of Philip Schaff,* ed. Henry Bowden (Carbondale: Southern Illinois University Press, 1988).

11. Robert Baird, *View of the Valley of the Mississippi, or the Emigrant's and Traveller's Guide to the West* (Philadelphia: H. S. Tanner, 1834 [1832]), iii. Robert Hubach suggests the possibility that Baird did not write *View of the Valley of Mississippi,* designating Lt. Robert (or Richard) Bache as an alternative author. Hubach, *Early Midwestern Travel Narratives: An Annotated Bibliography, 1634–1850* (Detroit: Wayne State University Press, 1961), 67. However, an 1832 review of the book states, "The author, . . . we are at liberty to state, is the Rev. Robert Baird, General Agent for the American Sunday School Union." In *The Biblical Repertory and Theological Review* 4, no. 4 (1832): 553. This particular journal was published by a Presbyterian organization close to Baird and his associates involved in the American Sunday School Union. Baird refers to the same *Review* in his book *Religion in America* (171). Henry M. Baird, the son of Robert Baird, also credited his father with writing *View of the Valley of the Mississippi* in his biography, *The Life of the Rev. Robert Baird, D.D.* (New York: Anson D. F. Randolph, 1866), 85. In it, he wrote, "The first, a duodecimo of about 350 pages, published in 1832, was entitled a 'View of the Valley of the Mississippi'; and appeared without the author's name."

12. Baird, *View of the Valley,* 346.

13. Ibid., 342, 99. After reading *View of the Valley of the Mississippi,* a Presbyterian reviewer wrote, "We fear to see the Valley of the Mississippi the strong hold of Popery; a prey to every fanatical teacher; wasted by infidelity, and DESERTED OF THE LORD!" *Biblical Repertory and Theological Review* 4, no. 4 (1832): 568. For more on Protestant American ideas about "popery" and what Lyman Beecher called "a plea for the West," as well as the influence of W. H. Prescott and Francis Parkman on the religious history of America, see Jenny Franchot, *Roads to Rome: The Antebellum Protestant Encounter with Catholicism* (Berkeley: University of California Press, 1994), 3–15, 35–82.

14. Peter G. Mode, *The Frontier Spirit in American Christianity* (New York: Macmillan, 1923), 35, 13.

15. William Warren Sweet, *The Rise of Methodism in the West, Being the Journal of the Western Conference, 1800–1811* (New York: Methodist Book Concern, 1920), 5. Sweet devotes a chapter to "Revivalism and the American West" in *Revivalism in America: Its Origins, Growth, and Decline* (New York: Charles Scribner's Sons, 1945), 112–39, although he stops short of the Mississippi valley in his description of the Second Great Awakening. Much the same can be said of Sweet's *Religion in the Development of American Culture, 1765–1840* (Gloucester, MA: Peter Smith, 1963), 97, 234–311. "The middle west," in his estimation, was an "'experimental laboratory' . . . unfettered by Old World patterns, [where] the term 'American' was to be given its meaning."

16. Edwin Scott Gaustad, *A Religious History of America* (New York: Harper and Row, 1966), 154–55.

17. Edwin Scott Gaustad, *Historical Atlas of Religion in America* (New York: Harper and Row, 1962), 37. Winthrop Hudson and Martin Marty, among others, followed Gaustad's vision of the Mississippi River, and by extension the Mississippi valley, as a vast rest stop for American migrants that bore little influence over the transforma-

tion of religion in American history. Hudson, *Religion in America* (New York: Charles Scribner's Sons, 1965), 132, and Marty, *Righteous Empire*, 47.

18. Sydney E. Ahlstrom, *A Religious History of the American People* (New Haven, CT: Yale University Press, 1972), 452–53. Kerwin Lee Klein provides a critical genealogy of frontier history and the history of the American West. Like many historians of American religion, Klein is mindful of the fact that "Stories are what we live in, and in them we find both our worlds and our selves. . . . As our traditions change, so do our histories; as our histories change, so do our worlds; as our worlds change, so do our traditions." Klein, *Frontiers of Historical Imagination: Narrating the European Conquest of Native America, 1890–1990* (Berkeley: University of California Press, 1997), 5–6. For more on contests over the moral landscape of the frontier West, see Amy DeRogatis, *Moral Geography: Maps, Missionaries, and the American Frontier* (New York: Columbia University Press, 2003), and Laurie F. Maffly-Kipp, *Religion and Society in Frontier California* (New Haven, CT: Yale University Press, 1994).

19. Thomas Tweed, ed., *Retelling U.S. Religious History* (Berkeley: University of California Press, 1997), 4.

20. The Religion and Region Series, edited by Mark Silk, is an eight-volume collection of books meant "to show how religion shapes, and is being shaped by, regional culture in America." Mark Silk and Randall Balmer, *Religion and Public Life in the Middle Atlantic Region: The Fount of Diversity* (Lanham, MD: AltaMira Press, 2006), 5. Each volume is based on a region traditionally believed to be distinctive from other parts of the United States.

21. Beth Barton Schweiger and Donald Mathews, eds., *Religion in the American South: Protestants and Others in History and Culture* (Chapel Hill: University of North Carolina Press, 2004), 2.

22. Peter Williams, *Houses of God: Region, Religion, and Architecture in the United States* (Urbana: University of Illinois Press, 1997), xi.

23. Harriet Beecher Stowe, *Uncle Tom's Cabin,* ed. Ann Douglas (New York: Penguin, 1981), 107.

24. Darrel Bigham, *On Jordan's Banks: Emancipation and Its Aftermath in the Ohio River Valley* (Lexington: University Press of Kentucky, 2006), 6.

25. Keith Griffler, *Front Line of Freedom: African Americans and the Forging of the Underground Railroad in the Ohio Valley* (Lexington: University Press of Kentucky, 2004). See also Joe William Trotter, *River Jordan: African American Urban Life in the Ohio Valley* (Lexington: University Press of Kentucky, 1998); Eric Hindraker, *Elusive Empires: Constructing Colonialism in the Ohio Valley, 1673–1800* (New York: Cambridge University Press, 1997); and Michael N. McConnell, *A Country Between: The Upper Ohio Valley and Its Peoples, 1724–1774* (Lincoln: University of Nebraska Press, 1992).

26. Joel Achenbach, *The Grand Idea: George Washington's Potomac and the Race to the West* (New York: Simon and Schuster, 2004), 273.

27. In his book about the Cape Fear River valley, Walter Conser argues that "by addressing this terrain as a region, one can display some familiar antimonies—urban and rural, Protestant and Catholic, Christian and Jewish—and explore how these boundaries were engaged, negotiated, and sometimes even modified. One can attend to patterns of collective identity across the region found in structures such as the sacred space of burials or the civic monuments to the Lost Cause. Finally, one can chart the persistence of issues, such as the interaction of religion and race or religion and gender, in a wider temporal and spatial perspective. In short, a regional examination

can tell us things that exclusive attention to congregational or denominational life may not capture." Conser, *A Coat of Many Colors: Religion and Society along the Cape Fear River of North Carolina* (Lexington: University Press of Kentucky, 2006), 3. For more examples of books about the history of religion in river valleys, see Paul R. Lucas, *Valley of Discord: Church and Society along the Connecticut River, 1636–1725* (Hanover, NH: University Press of New England, 1976); Randolph A. Roth, *The Democratic Dilemma: Religion, Reform, and the Social Order in the Connecticut River Valley of Vermont, 1791–1850* (New York: Cambridge University Press, 1987); Barry Levy, *Quakers and the American Family: British Quakers in the Delaware Valley* (New York: Oxford University Press, 1988); and Jon Butler, *Power, Authority, and the Origins of American Denominational Order: The English Churches in the Delaware Valley* (Tuscaloosa: University of Alabama Press, 2009 [1978]).

28. Kären Wigen, "Introduction" to AHR Forum "Oceans of Religion," *American Historical Review* 111, no. 3 (June 2006): 720. See also Wigen's introduction to *Seascapes: Maritime Histories, Littoral Cultures, and Transoceanic Exchanges,* ed. Jerry H. Bentley, Renate Bridenthal, and Kären Wigen (Honolulu: University of Hawai'i Press, 2007), 1–20.

29. Alison Games, "Atlantic History: Definitions, Challenges, and Opportunities," *American Historical Review* 3, no. 3 (June 2006): 748; and Jon Sensbach, "Religion and the Early South in an Age of Atlantic Empire," *Journal of Southern History* 73, no. 3 (August 2007): 641.

30. Diana L. Eck, *Banaras: City of Light* (New York: Knopf, 1982), 214.

31. Vijaya Rettakudi Nagarajan, "The Earth as Goddess Bhu Devi: Toward a Theory of 'Embedded Ecologies' in Folk Hinduism," in *Purifying the Earthly Body of God: Religion and Ecology in Hindu India,* ed. Lance E. Nelson (Albany: State University of New York Press, 1998), 277.

32. David Haberman, *River of Love in an Age of Pollution: The Yamuna River of Northern India* (Berkeley: University of California Press, 2006); Anne Feldhaus, *Water and Womanhood: Religious Meanings of Rivers in Maharashtra* (New York: Oxford University Press, 1995); and Kelly D. Alley, *On the Banks of the Ganga: When Wastewater Meets a Sacred River* (Ann Arbor: University of Michigan Press, 2002).

33. Jean-Marie Gibbal, *Genii of the River Niger,* trans. Beth G. Raps (Chicago: University of Chicago Press, 1994), 20.

34. Johannes Wilbert, *Mindful of Famine: Religious Climatology of the Warao Indians* (Cambridge, MA: Harvard University Press and Harvard Center for the Study of World Religions, 1996); and Allen Johnson, *Families of the Forest: The Matsigenka Indians of the Peruvian Amazon* (Berkeley: University of California Press, 2003).

35. Hagai Erlikh, *The Cross and the River: Ethiopia, Egypt, and the Nile* (Boulder: Lynne Rienner, 2002), 3. Thorkild Jacobsen, in his study of Mesopotamian religions, stressed the importance of the cosmic office of Enki, god of fresh water sources, and the centrality of the Tigris and Euphrates to the population and fertility of the region. Jacobsen, *The Treasures of Darkness: History of Mesopotamian Religion* (New Haven, CT: Yale University Press, 1976), 85.

36. Yi-Fu Tuan, *Space and Place: The Perspective of Experience* (Minneapolis: University of Minnesota Press, 1977), 5.

37. Thomas C. Buchanan, *Black Life on the Mississippi: Slaves, Free Blacks, and the Western Steamboat World* (Chapel Hill: University of North Carolina Press, 2004), 6.

38. Thomas Ruys Smith, *River of Dreams: Imagining the Mississippi before Mark Twain* (Baton Rouge: Louisiana State University, 2007), 7. For a survey of the history

of the Mississippi River, see George S. Pabis, *Daily Life along the Mississippi* (Westport, CT: Greenwood Press, 2007). For more on the significance of the Louisiana Purchase to American religious history, see Richard J. Callahan Jr., ed., *New Territories, New Perspectives: The Religious Impact of the Louisiana Purchase* (Columbia: University of Missouri Press, 2008). For an example of a work that considers how "a perceptual landscape overlaps the physical one," see Jared Farmer, *On Zion's Mount: Mormons, Indians, and the American Landscape* (Cambridge, MA: Harvard University Press, 2008), 6.

39. Edward S. Casey, *Getting Back into Place: Toward a Renewed Understanding of the Place-World* (Bloomington: Indiana University Press, 1993), 109, 116.

40. Thomas A. Tweed, *Crossing and Dwelling: A Theory of Religion* (Cambridge, MA: Harvard University Press, 2006), 54, 59, 60.

41. John Corrigan, "Spatiality and Religion," in *The Spatial Turn: Interdisciplinary Perspectives,* ed. Barney Warf and Santa Arias (New York: Routledge, 2009), 160–72.

1

"The Singing of the Mississippi"

THE RIVER AND RELIGIONS OF THE BLACK ATLANTIC

Jon F. Sensbach

In the summer of 1790 a barge carrying a group of enslaved Africans laboriously made its way up the Mississippi River from New Orleans, negotiating three hundred miles of bends before docking at the busy waterfront in Natchez. The captives were led off the barge, put up on the auction block for sale, and dispersed among farms and plantations in the region. Like the great majority of African slaves in early America, most left little trace in the historical record beyond, perhaps, a name in a plantation ledger. But through good fortune and persistence, one man had a remarkable chance to tell his story. His name was Ibrahima Abd-al Rahman, a Muslim from the West African kingdom of Futa Jallon, and he recounted a narrative of captivity, survival, and religious perseverance thousands of miles from home on the banks of the Mississippi.

His father was a king of the Fulbe people, in a predominantly Muslim region of what is now Guinea, where Arab traders had introduced Islam in the twelfth century. Educated in classical Muslim tradition, Abd-al Rahman learned to write Arabic and to study Qur'anic texts before being sent to the great Muslim university at Timbuktu. This life of learning was shattered by the slaving wars that ravaged West Africa to feed the insatiable Atlantic slave trade. Deeply enmeshed in these wars, Futa Jallon profited from raiding non-Muslim territories and selling captives to European traders. In 1788, in a campaign against a coastal opponent that had blocked Futa Jallon's access to the slave trade, twenty-six-year-old Abd-al Rahman was taken prisoner. His captors, he recounted many years later, "made me go barefoot one hundred miles

. . . to the Mandingo country, on the Gambia. They sold me directly, with fifty others, to an English ship. They took me to the Island of Dominica. After that I was taken to New Orleans. Then they took me to Natchez." There he was bought by Thomas Foster, a cotton and tobacco planter on whose nearby plantation the Muslim exile worked as a field hand and then foreman.[1]

By remarkable chance, Abd-al Rahman was recognized in the early nineteenth century by a physician who had traveled in West Africa and who now began a campaign to gain the release of the African prince. For years Foster refused to sell his slave, but in 1828 the case attracted public attention. Abd-al Rahman recounted his tale to several people, including a pair of Mississippi journalists, who published versions of it that brought his plight to the attention of the John Adams administration. The prince's memory for detail and his ability to write in Arabic proved convincing, and the intervention of Secretary of State Henry Clay secured his manumission. After unsuccessful efforts to gain most of his family's freedom, in 1829 he returned to Africa, where he died soon thereafter.[2]

Abd-al Rahman's rare tale of redemption and return was replicated by few Africans enslaved in the Americas.[3] Yet, as his experience shows, well into the nineteenth century people with direct memories of Africa lived along the Mississippi River, creating new lives in exile, adhering to African beliefs as persistently as possible but adapting to other faiths when necessary and leaving a dominant cultural imprint on the river corridor and beyond. Deep spiritual sensibilities underlay this legacy, sensibilities that survived the transatlantic slave trade, connected the river to Africa and the broader black Atlantic, and endured in the enslaved and free population of the region. From the periods of French, British, and Spanish colonialism to the age of American possession, the varieties of worship that derived from African religious traditions flourished in such creative abandon along the Mississippi River that collectively they emerged as one of the dominant North American contributions to global culture.

One of the great poets in American literature, Langston Hughes, paid homage to this connection in his famous poem "The Negro Speaks of Rivers." A native of western Missouri who spent much of his childhood in Illinois, Hughes was deeply influenced by the great river that cleaved those two states:

> I've known rivers:
> I've known rivers ancient as the world and older than the flow
> of human blood in human veins.
> My soul has grown deep like the rivers.

I bathed in the Euphrates when dawns were young.
I built my hut near the Congo and it lulled me to sleep.
I looked upon the Nile and raised the pyramids above it.
I heard the singing of the Mississippi when Abe Lincoln went
down to New Orleans, and I've seen its muddy bosom turn
all golden in the sunset.
I've known rivers:
Ancient dusky rivers.
My soul has grown deep like the rivers.

Born of romanticist yearnings for an idealized African past, Hughes's vision traces the origins of black America to cultural spores from the ancient civilizations that flourished beside African rivers. As Hughes saw it, one scholar has written, for the American of African descent "the muddy river is his race, the primal source out of which he is born anew, and on that 'muddy bosom' of the race as black mother, or grandmother, he rests secure forever." Hughes's lyrical understanding of the existential importance of rivers, especially the Mississippi, was entirely different from that of most African Americans of an earlier generation, for whom the Ohio River had far greater symbolic importance as America's River Jordan, the barrier and passageway between slavery and freedom. For Hughes, the deep timelessness of the Euphrates, the Nile, and the Congo in black consciousness had only one American counterpart: the Mississippi.[4]

This indelible African imprint, as Hughes knew, traced its source to powerful European imperial ambitions in the colonial period that stimulated the Atlantic slave trade, brought Africans to America, and transformed the New World. The French colonization of the lower Mississippi in 1699, anchoring France's territorial claim to the vast midsection of North America, linked the new colony of Louisiana to a circum-Atlantic imperial system stretching from France to West Africa, the Caribbean, and Canada. In the mid-seventeenth century, slave ships began bringing African laborers to French colonies in the West Indies for sugar production, and within a few decades, slaves from Senegambia, the Gold and Slave Coasts, Angola, and elsewhere outnumbered French colonists on Martinique, St. Domingue, and Guadeloupe, endowing those islands with heavily Africanized cultures. The same thing happened when enslaved Africans began arriving in Louisiana in the early 1700s.[5]

This essay will explore the transmission of African beliefs to the Mississippi River valley during the period of French and then Spanish colonization and into the early years of the United States. New Orleans and the lower Mississippi formed a vital gateway between the larger black Atlantic and growing African populations in towns upriver such as Natchez and St. Louis. A kind of capital of the greater Caribbean, New Orleans received influxes of enslaved Africans throughout the eighteenth century and after Haitian independence and the Louisiana Purchase in the early nineteenth century. From these well-springs emerged the city's famous Creole culture. At the same time, New Orleans and the river served as conduits bringing African Atlantic religious cultures deep into the heart of the continent, including voodoo and other forms of African worship, Afro-Catholicism, Islam, and, somewhat later, strands of evangelical Protestantism.[6] Recent scholarship on African-derived religions has emphasized the multidirectional movement and dispersion of religious ideas throughout the black Atlantic of the sixteenth through nineteenth centuries. The heart of this inquiry has been to determine how people of African descent assembled and reassembled religious systems ruptured by mobility. Accordingly, this essay will explore black religion at the intersection of two powerful water systems that by their nature constituted fluidity, change, and motion to the humans who traveled on them and lived along their shores: the Atlantic and the Mississippi.[7]

The African presence in the lower Mississippi valley region began soon after the founding of New Orleans in 1718. The French, eager to improve the profitability of Louisiana by cultivating rice in the low-lying areas downriver and tobacco further upstream around Natchez, began importing slaves directly from Africa. The trade was operated by the Company of the Indies, a chartered firm run by the Scottish financier John Law that administered Louisiana and had a trade monopoly on the Senegambian coast in West Africa. Because of these close ties, most of the approximately 6,000 slaves imported by the Company derived from Senegambia. Between 1719 and 1731, along with a final slave-trading voyage in 1743, the Company imported all the slaves to arrive in Louisiana during the period of French rule through 1763. Of those, two-thirds, or 3,947, came from Senegambia, while 1,748 came from the Bight of Benin and another 294 from Kongo and Angola.[8]

The largest of these source areas, the Senegambia region, encompasses a wide expanse of territory around the drainage basins of the Senegal and Gambia rivers at the westernmost edge of the continent, corresponding roughly to the modern nations of Senegal, Gambia, Guinea, Guinea-Bissau, and parts of Mauritania and Mali. Rice was cultivated heavily in low-lying coastal regions and, as in colonial South Carolina, planters in Louisiana valued enslaved Africans from these areas for their expertise in growing rice. In the eighteenth century, Senegambia was ethnically and religiously heterogeneous, peopled largely by diverse Mande, Wolof, and Fulbe speakers, many of them Muslim. Islam had penetrated the region as early as the eleventh century, and by the thirteenth and fourteenth centuries the great Muslim kingdom of Mali, centered in Timbuktu a thousand miles inland up the Niger River, had pulled Senegambia under its sway. In the eighteenth century, the French slave trade to Louisiana was controlled by coastal people who derived their slaves from the ceaseless wars of imperial consolidation and conquest that had long been a feature of West African life. About two-thirds of the captives taken as slaves from Senegambia to Louisiana were of the Bambara ethnic group, based several hundred miles inland, who, with their highly militarized warrior culture, were both participants and victims in this struggle. They were captured by other Mande peoples, mostly Mandinkas, and taken overland and downriver to the coast, an exhausting journey that no doubt proved fatal to many captives. The survivors were loaded onto ships at the infamous slave fort at Gorée for a transatlantic voyage of up to two months to the Gulf coast of Louisiana.[9]

Shipments of slaves arrived in the colony steadily for a dozen years, by which time Africans outnumbered Europeans in the lower Mississippi valley, though Indians still predominated heavily over both. In 1721, white colonists outnumbered Africans in New Orleans and the lower Mississippi valley by 1,075 to 580, but by 1731 Africans had reversed the proportion by 3,656 to 1,702, against some 35,000 Indians. The greatest density of this population was in the lower Mississippi valley, especially in the Bas du Fleuve region along the banks of the river below New Orleans, but small pockets of settlement also spread along the Gulf Coast to such towns as Mobile and upriver to Natchez, St. Louis, and the Illinois Country. New Orleans itself remained quite small, with fewer than a thousand people, and the French population outnumbered Africans 509 to 213 in 1737. But in the rural parishes where plantation agriculture was expanding, African workers formed a large majority of the population. In 1746, for example, one planter, Joseph de Villars Dubreuil, owned five hundred slaves, whom he used for public works projects, cultivating crops, and tending three hundred cattle. Other African laborers produced river boats, tobacco, lumber, and bricks, or sent produce and meat downriver to New Orleans.[10]

The African preponderance had at least two significant consequences for the region. First, African resistance to the plantation regime was a pronounced feature of life in the colony. The apparatus of patrols and enforcements by which the white minority controlled the slave population was not always secure, and Africans often escaped to the cypress swamps and other outlying areas, seeking shelter with Native Americans or in maroon communities. From these refuges, isolated and difficult to track, they built settlements and raised crops while waging a campaign of resistance against the planters with raids and other acts of sabotage. Controlling large sections of territory beyond the reach of the authorities, maroons remained an irritant for slave owners throughout the eighteenth century until the Spanish rooted them out. Africans also planned several large rebellions. In 1731, a conspiracy was uncovered in which four hundred Bambaras were set to rise up, massacre all white colonists, and enslave the other Africans. The leaders of the plot were executed. In 1795, another conspiracy was foiled at Pointe Coupee, northwest of New Orleans on the Mississippi, and twenty-three slaves were hanged. Though these planned revolts came to naught, they demonstrated that Africans felt sufficiently emboldened by their numerical advantage and their military background to conceive of overthrowing their colonial overlords.[11]

African superiority in numbers also meant that African cultures and religions flourished under slavery in a putatively European colony. Although Louisiana's African-born population in these early years was far smaller than that of longer-established colonies like Jamaica, Brazil, or Mexico, the same dynamic applied to African cultural persistence and renewal wrought by the thousands who emerged from the hold of slave ships year after year. That hold, in fact, as Kamau Brathwaite has written, became a "creative space" for cooperation, communication across linguistic chasms, and cultural sharing among captives at sea, giving rise to "the apparently miraculous transformation of imprisoned self in the New World." Gods and religious communities that were uprooted and sent into exile across the Atlantic remade themselves forever in the frenetic motion of the slave trade. African America was forged on the voyage across the Atlantic. When Africans arrived on Louisiana's Gulf Coast, as they did throughout the Americas, they brought with them traditions and ideas about spirituality that, while jolted by dislocation and enslavement, continued to serve as moral guideposts in an alien land.[12]

Among the several thousand enslaved Africans in Louisiana by the mid-eighteenth century, a variety of traditions and customs intermingled. Many—though likely not a majority—of the Senegambians were Muslim; many of the Kongolese and Angolans arrived in Louisiana as Catholics, because Catholicism had been practiced in their kingdoms since being introduced in the region by Portuguese missionaries in the sixteenth century. The numerically dominant Bambaras, like many West Africans, subscribed to a form of what scholars have generally termed *African traditional religions,* characterized by the belief in a cosmos created by a supreme god, inhabited and contested by a lively cast of lesser deities and other spirits, in which there was no dividing line between secular and sacred. Everything belonged to a spiritual universe. Bambara cosmology was ordered by elaborate creation stories that provided a basis for knowledge about the world, a code for ethical conduct, and a starting point for rich oral history recounted at length by *griots,* the storytellers of a village or clan. In Bambara religion, all life forms were believed to possess a vital spirit force which, upon death, roamed unmoored, unseen, and often in hostile fashion through the cosmos. Ancestors, in particular, closely watched human affairs and could become angry if not placated.[13]

To propitiate the ancestors, and to maintain equilibrium in a world poised between benign and malignant spiritual forces, humans sacrificed animals and wielded amulets and charms that were believed to encourage the spirits' good favor, protect the wearer, or cause harm to enemies. These charms, called *gris-gris,* were fundamental to Bambaras, who, according to a nineteenth-century French traveler in West Africa, "have some fetishist practices which include, among others . . . that of worshiping an enormous earthen vase, known throughout Senegambia under the name *canari,* which they fill with amulets of all sorts; they consult it before doing anything of importance." Indeed, some form of *gris-gris* was widely used throughout West Africa by Muslims and non-Muslims alike. Muslims typically wrote qu'ranic passages and other texts in Arabic and enclosed them in leather pouches worn around the neck, arms, and legs. The *gris-gris,* or "Gregories," as English traveler Richard Jobson described them in 1625, "Bee things of great esteeme among them," commanding "such a religious respect, that they do confidently beleeve no hurt can betide them, whilst the Gregories are about them."[14]

Direct evidence of the continued use of these amulets in Louisiana comes from the French historian and ethnographer Antoine Simon Le Page du Pratz, who lived in Natchez from 1718 to 1726, then in New Orleans until 1734. After his return to France, he published his three-volume *Histoire de la Louisiane* in 1758, translated and published in English as *History of Louisiana* in 1774. Though not specifically referring to any particular ethnic group, Le Page du Pratz wrote that Africans in the colony "are very superstitious, and are much attached to their prejudices, and little toys which they call *gris, gris.* It would be improper therefore to take them from them, or even speak of them to them; for they would believe themselves undone, if they were stripped of those trinkets. The old Negroes soon make them lose conceit of them."

While his description of "superstitious" "toys" reflects the condescension toward African practice common among Europeans, Le Page du Pratz showed both that Africans clung to long-standing tradition in the New World and that those customs were contested by diverse elements in Louisiana. Planters no doubt condemned what they saw as foolish heathenism, but Le Page du Pratz warned that confiscating amulets would prove too distressing to enslaved workers whose docility was essential. His observation that older Africans were already suppressing the charms suggests perhaps that elders were either counseling others to hide *gris-gris* from the masters or that they wanted white colonists to think that Africans were conforming to white demands.[15]

Other African customs flourished as well among the large clusters of enslaved people in river towns like Natchez and New Orleans and on plantations lining the river. As these practices survived the Middle Passage to be reconstituted in Louisiana, they became potent reminders of the connection between culture and resistance. "Nothing is more to be dreaded," Le Page du Pratz wrote, "than to see the negroes assemble together on Sundays, since, under pretence of Calinda or the dance, they sometimes get together to the number of three or four hundred, and make a kind of Sabbath, which it is always prudent to avoid; for it is in those tumultuous meetings that they sell what they have stolen to one another, and commit many crimes. In these likewise they plot their rebellions." Whether the enslaved were indeed plotting rebellion in these meetings is of course difficult to discern, but planters and officials considered African religions a fearful source of social disorder and rebelliousness.[16]

Even as African practices persisted in colonial Louisiana, covertly or openly, the Catholic Church increasingly entered the spiritual and social lives of enslaved people. As in the French West Indies, the church's attempted Christianization of Africans became an important vehicle by which clerical and civil authorities exercised social control and Africans negotiated the complexities of slave society. The *Code Noir* that applied in all the colonies required the baptism and religious education of slaves to "civilize" and domesticate them, but planters often resisted instruction as dangerous to social order, perfunctorily fulfilling only the baptism requirement. Clergy themselves, along with religious institutions like the Ursuline convent in New Orleans, were collectively the largest slaveholders in Louisiana, and their slaves had perhaps the greatest exposure to Christianity. By the end of the French colonial period in 1766, the majority of slaves in New Orleans had been baptized, though it is difficult to tell the degree of doctrinal knowledge or enthusiasm with which they did so. It is likely that many hoped baptism would bring a degree of social recognition and perhaps protection for marriages and families. The *Code Noir* required that slave marriages be consecrated by the church, but it did not give marriages legal recognition or protection, and the church was often reluctant to intercede its authority when masters sought to sell married couples apart.[17]

The Ursuline sisters, however, proved one major exception to this tendency by safeguarding slave marriages as much as possible. They bought and sold slaves like other slaveholders, but they sold family units together to maintain their cohesion. Unsatisfied with perfunctory baptism as a superficial index of Christianity, the nuns also emphasized greater awareness of the catechism and sacraments among slaves. The result of these measures was to produce a Christianized slave population with a deeper knowledge of Catholic doctrine and how to employ it to solidify and extend family formation. The essential building block in this strategy was godparenting, a basic component of the Catholic sacrament of baptism. During the baptism ceremony godparents attested to the spiritual state of the initiate and served as spiritual guardians thereafter. During the early years of black Christianization in Louisiana, in the 1730s and 1740s, most godparents were white, often the slaves' own masters and mistresses, including the Ursulines, perhaps signaling an effort by these new Christians to secure protections or privileges. In time, however, candidates for baptism, especially among Ursuline-owned slaves, usually chose black godparents, thereby creating elaborate webs of spiritual kin among African Catholics. For people violently uprooted by the slave trade, the strategy provided a new kind of community grounded in fictive kinship and spiritual leadership by godparents, and it prepared for the emergence of a new cultural identity among black Louisianans grounded in Catholicism.[18]

A similar process was at work in French colonial settlements to the north along the Mississippi River and to the east along the Gulf Coast. In the Illinois Country, enslaved Africans newly arrived from Senegambia and the Bight of Benin were transported upriver in the eighteenth century and became a visible minority in such river towns as St. Louis, Kaskaskia, Ste. Genevieve, and Fort de Chartres, which were founded to promote trade, agriculture, and mission work among Indians. The Jesuits were among the largest slave owners, as was a planter named Antoine Bienvenu, who owned sixty-five slaves in 1752. In 1732, out of a total population of 699 in the French settlements, enslaved blacks numbered 164. By 1742 their number had risen to 446, or about one-third of the population of 1,380, which included 785 French settlers and 149 enslaved Indians. More than 40 percent of Kaskaskia's residents were black. Consistent with the *Code Noir,* which pertained to upper Louisiana as else- where in the colony, slaves were required to be baptized and instructed in the principles of Roman Catholicism. Baptismal records show that almost all slaves in Illinois were baptized, though the registers are less revealing about whether extensive godparenting networks existed.[19]

Along the Gulf Coast in Mobile, however, where enslaved Africans had been brought in the early 1720s, sacramental registers show similarly high rates of baptism as well as complex godparenting connections among people of African origin and between blacks and Native Americans, both free and enslaved. Though the sincerity of native and African professions of Catholic faith cannot be judged by names in a register, along the coast and up the river through the enormous territory of Louisiana, the church proved a unifying, or at least a common, venue for the expression of some religious values by Africans and limited numbers of native peoples. Such spiritual connections indicate close social and sexual contact as well as mutual cultural influence between these diverse groups of people in Louisiana. Such moments of ex- change took place throughout the colony, and sometimes they led to coopera- tive militant efforts to resist white colonialism, as when, for example, Africans aided Natchez Indians in their unsuccessful uprising against the French in 1729. In quieter fashion, the cross-cultural contact suggested in church re- cords indicates the eighteenth-century emergence of a creolized mix of Afri- can, Indian, and European belief and practice.[20]

Between the end of French rule in Louisiana in 1766 and the first decade of the nineteenth century, a series of massive political changes fundamen- tally altered the demographic and social makeup of the colony and of river communities hundreds of miles to the north. These changes reflected the absorption of Louisiana in broader Atlantic upheavals wrought by revolu- tion and imperial rivalry, dislocations that underscored the colony's position at the crossroads of both Caribbean and continental circuits of exchange. The French surrender of Louisiana to Spain after the Seven Years' War, the arrival in New Orleans of refugees from Haiti between 1791 and 1809, and the Louisiana Purchase in 1803 permanently altered the political and social complexion of Louisiana and the cultural funnel mapped out by the river. Much of this turmoil entailed new movements of enslaved people into the Mississippi valley as well as transformations in the institution of slavery it- self, permanently altering black Atlantic culture in the region even as older patterns of continuity endured.

Soon after Spain took over Louisiana from French control in 1766, it reopened the Atlantic slave trade, which had been closed to the colony since 1743. By the time a census was taken in 1788, the number of slaves in the lower Mississippi valley had almost quadrupled from 5,600 to 20,673, representing 55 percent of the population. This increase undergirded the rapid expansion of plantation agriculture under the Spanish and more severe laboring conditions and heightening tension between planters and slaves. The increase in slaves was due mainly to imports directly from Africa and trans-shipments from the French and Spanish West Indies, a rapid population growth that historian Gwendolyn Midlo Hall calls the "re-Africanization" of Louisiana. Arriving in New Orleans in 1790 and sent upriver to Natchez, Ibrahima Abdal Rahman was part of this new demographic wave. Most of the new arrivals came from four main areas of West Africa—Senegambia, the Bight of Benin, the Bight of Biafra, and Kongo—giving the colony, in combination with the Afro-Creole population they now outnumbered, a richly diverse African cultural heritage.[21]

The end of the legal Atlantic slave trade to the United States in 1808 halted this feverish refueling of the slave labor force from Africa, but the revolution in St. Domingue and the creation of the independent republic of Haiti spurred a different influx of people of African descent into Louisiana from the Caribbean. In three separate waves—1791, 1803, and 1809—thousands of white and free colored colonists as well as enslaved blacks poured into the colony. The free people of color soon became part of New Orleans's Catholic, elite Creole social stratum, while the slaves, who adhered much more closely to African ritual practices, reinforced some of those aspects in Louisiana or introduced new ones. Most notably, *vodou*—widely considered a religious derivation from Dahomey in West Africa, mixed with Catholicism—is often attributed to these displaced West Indian migrants. With its panoply of spirits, strategies for propitiating deities, and ability to assimilate symbols and rituals from other religions, *vodou*, which became a dominant form of African-derived religion in the lower Mississippi valley, showed obvious Caribbean influence. But it is at least as likely that, since many of these elements were already present in the region before the arrival of the St. Domingue refugees, *vodou*, or voodoo, developed from a mingling of traditions in the cultural hothouse of Louisiana, becoming an indigenous and distinctive American religion.[22]

The interplay of all these forces appears vividly in descriptions of African music and dance in the famous Congo Square in New Orleans, a large open field at the western edge of the colonial town known in the eighteenth century as *Place des Nègres*. Originally a market square where slaves sold produce from their gardens, the plaza had become a sort of all-purpose site for African gatherings and festivities by the end of the century. The best-known depiction of Congo Square was written in 1819 by Benjamin Latrobe, the British-born architect and surveyor commissioned by the United States to design a waterworks for the city after the Louisiana Purchase. In this strange place where everything "had an *odd* look," he was transfixed by a sight "wholly new even to one who has travelled much in Europe & America." At a sprawling market on the levee he saw hundreds of people, "white men and women & all hues of brown, & of all classes of faces, from round Yankees, to grisly & lean Spaniards, black negroes and negresses, filthy Indians half naked, mulattoes, curly & straight-haired, quarteroons of all shades, long haired & frizzled, the women dressed in the most flaring yellow & scarlet gowns, the men capped and hatted," buying and selling a riotous assortment of produce, seafood, poultry, and dry goods. One Sunday, following a distant din that he "supposed to proceed from some horse mill, the horses trampling on a wooden floor," he came upon "5 or 600 persons assembled in an open space or public square," all of them black, dancing, singing, and chanting to the sound of percussion and plucked instruments resembling banjos. He had happened upon Congo Square.[23]

Fascinated by what he called the most "brutally savage" thing he had ever seen, Latrobe described the scene in some detail, writing in his journal that the crowd was divided into knots of onlookers gathered in a series of circles around musicians and dancers. Drummers pounded out propulsive rhythms on calabashes and wooden blocks while dancers performed a variety of steps. In one circle "a dozen women walked, by way of dancing, round the music in the center" as they "squalled out" a song; in another a man sang "an uncouth song to the dancing which I suppose was in some African language, for it was not French, and the women screamed a detestable burthen on one single note." Such dances "have perpetuated here those of Africa among its inhabitants." Indeed, dance and rhythmic music were integral to West African religious worship. In communal religious ceremonies common to the broad swath of territory that fed the slave trade, celebrants danced and clapped in circles to the sound of drums and other percussion as a ritual summoning of divine spirits. These performances often lasted hours as dancers entered a kind of trance or state of spirit possession that marked their complete metaphysical immersion in the supernatural world. Congo Square, it appears, was the public stage—culturally permissible under laissez-faire Catholic norms and flourishing as they did nowhere else in the American South—where the thousands of enslaved people who had arrived from West Africa and Haiti during the previous twenty years enacted powerful cultural memories that spoke of direct African religious transfers to the lower Mississippi valley. So strong was this continuation that specific African ethnic affiliations persisted in the square, "each nation taking their place in different parts of the square," according to one observer, who, describing the ritual facial scarification and filed teeth of the dancers, noticed that "the Minahs would not dance near the Congos, nor the Mandringos near the Gangas."[24]

That legacy left a deep imprint on American culture in several ways. Variations of the circle dancing, known as "ring shouts," became part of the spiritual vernacular of slave communities across the American South, often fused with elements of evangelical Protestantism to form a new kind of exuberant, even ecstatic Christian worship. The ring shout was not necessarily adapted uniformly from Congo Square. Rather, it reflected the broad lasting influence of African dance and worship through successive generations of enslaved people in different settings throughout the South. The African dances in Congo Square, however, did have a specific impact on American popular culture as the probable origin of American jazz. As the African-born population of New Orleans dwindled in the 1830s and 1840s, purely African forms of dance and rhythm gradually lost their specific religious connotations and absorbed French, Spanish, and other European sounds, instruments, and expressive dance stylings, along with those from American popular culture, to create new forms of music and dance in which one blended into the other. These kinds of "musical conversations," write historians Shane White and Graham White, "voice with voice, voice with instrument, instrument with instrument, instrument with body, and so on—were additive rather than disruptive." Congo Square can thus be said to be the incubator of a unique African American culture—fluid, improvisational, open to influences from anywhere. Though the Square itself fell into disuse as a market and dance ground after the Civil War, self-taught musicians in Storyville, the African American neighborhood adjoining the square, continued to play the music that once flourished there, the music that became the cultural hearth of ragtime and jazz and that quickly spread up the Mississippi River and outward to the rest of the nation. Though jazz is known as a profoundly secular music, its origins lie in the African religious diaspora to America.[25]

The Louisiana Purchase of 1803 wrought another major transformation to the African-derived religious culture of the Mississippi valley. Anglo-

American migration to Spanish Louisiana had begun in the late eighteenth century, and after the Purchase the flow of planters, slaves, and other settlers into the region from Virginia and the Carolinas intensified. These newcomers introduced a significant Protestant presence in the Gulf South and along the Mississippi that jarred culturally with the native Creole population. In New Orleans, Anglo-American migrants tended to regard the Creoles, both white and black, as exotic and decadent and to dismiss their Catholicism as illegitimate. They were sometimes fascinated, but more often repelled, by what they considered the barbarism of the large African population and its festive displays in Congo Square, and they moved quickly to impose stricter codes on the city's fluid social and racial order. Further upriver in former French colonial towns like St. Louis and Ste. Genevieve, Creole influence likewise began to ebb in the face of migration from Kentucky and Virginia. Slavery expanded along the river basin with the arrival of these newcomers, but only modestly. Slavery in Missouri was a lightning rod for the national political struggle over slavery, and African Americans, slave and free, composed just 2 percent of the population of St. Louis on the eve of the Civil War.[26]

Still, from the lower Mississippi valley to St. Louis, the river itself became a new cultural corridor for black Protestantism. Enslaved African American migrants from the upper South, many of them steeped in the emotional, heartfelt religion of the Methodists and Baptists, brought the language and practice of evangelicalism with them to the southwest territories and river towns like Natchez and Vicksburg. With an emphasis on conversion, continuing revelation, and visionary experience, the evangelical appeal was strong among African Americans seeking to rebuild families and communities displaced by the internal slave trade. Black Protestants in the river corridor often worshiped with white co-religionists in biracial churches; a black couple were among the eight people to establish the first Methodist church in the Mississippi Territory in 1799. But black worshippers also set up separate, semi-independent congregations for themselves under the leadership of black preachers and under white supervision that ranged from strict to nominal. Enslaved people often gathered in the woods as well to pray secretly away from the intrusive oversight of whites. Religious meetings, whether formal or informal, in church or in a plantation "praise house," became organizing nodes binding slave communities on adjoining plantations along the river.[27]

Religious knowledge must also have moved up and down the river from one community to the next, as other forms of black popular culture did, particularly by steamboat. Foreign travelers reported being mesmerized by the rhythmic chants and improvised lyrics of the "energetic black athletes" who constantly fed wood to boat furnaces. As the dividing line between sacred and secular songs, or work songs and spirituals, typically blurred in African American culture, such descriptions give intriguing glimpses into the possibility that religious songs, perhaps as well as prayers, exhortations, and biblical teachings, were an integral part of the river culture of the boatmen.[28]

For some, or many, the river itself served a kind of sacred function. Water had widespread spiritual associations in West African and African American cultures—of the intersection of spirit worlds, of birth and rebirth, initiation, cleansing, and sanctification. Think of the famous spiritual "Down by the Riverside," one version of which was recounted by Ellen King, a former slave in Mississippi:

> Down by the river side,
> Jesus will talk and walk,
> Ain't going to study the world no more,
> Ain't going to study the world no more,
> For down by the river side,
> Jesus will talk and walk.

Variations on this verse were sung in slave communities throughout the South, so King's version did not necessarily refer to the Mississippi. Still, her song distills the notion of the constant, intertwined presence of water and Jesus, and the Mississippi was the omnipresent water in the lives of thousands. Former slaves remembered being baptized in the river, signifying its sacred connotation, like all baptismal water, as a passageway to new life.[29]

Thus when Langston Hughes "heard the singing of the Mississippi," he heard, among other things, a soundtrack of religious enchantment along its banks recorded over generations by people of African descent. The Mississippi, however, defined not a unitary black Atlantic religious culture but rather the confluence of many—Bambara, Wolof, Kongolese; Francophone, Hispanophone, Anglophone; Caribbean Atlantic, upper South, lower South; Muslim, Catholic, Protestant. Down by the riverside they jarred, mingled, and created something new. And in the creating they forged a counterpoint to the theme of westward expansion by white Protestants that has dominated American religious history. Just as the Mississippi is the quintessential American river, the spiritual *bricolage* that emerged on its shores embodies the American religious narrative.[30]

NOTES

1. Sylviane A. Diouf, *Servants of Allah: African Muslims Enslaved in the Americas* (New York: New York University Press, 1998), 26.

2. Terry Alford, *Prince among Slaves: The True Story of an African Prince Sold into Slavery in the American South* (New York: Oxford University Press, 1972).

3. For other examples, see Randy J. Sparks, *The Two Princes of Calabar: An Eighteenth-Century Atlantic Odyssey* (Cambridge, MA: Harvard University Press, 2004), and Douglas Grant, *The Fortunate Slave: An Illustration of African Slavery in the Early Eighteenth Century* (New York: Oxford University Press, 1968).

4. Muyiwa Falaiye, "The Image of the Black Soul from the Hut near the Congo to the Banks of the Mississippi," in *Africa and Transatlantic Memories: Literary and Aesthetic Manifestations of Diaspora and History,* ed. Naana Opoku-Agyemang, Paul E. Lovejoy, and David V. Trotman (Trenton, NJ: Africa World Press, 2008), 395–404, quote at 401. See Joe William Trotter, *River Jordan: African American Urban Life in the Ohio Valley* (Lexington: University Press of Kentucky, 2008).

5. For guides to the literature on the French Atlantic imperial system, including Louisiana's place in it, see Laurent Dubois, "The French Atlantic," in *Atlantic History: A Critical Appraisal,* ed. Jack P. Greene and Philip D. Morgan (New York: Oxford University Press, 2009), 137–62; Kenneth J. Banks, *Chasing Empire across the Sea: Communications and the State in the French Atlantic, 1713–1763* (Montreal: McGill-Queens University Press, 2002); and Bradley G. Bond, ed., *French Colonial Louisiana and the Atlantic World* (Baton Rouge: Louisiana State University Press, 2005).

6. On Louisiana's connections to the Caribbean and the broader Atlantic, see Paul Christopher Johnson, "Vodou Purchase: The Louisiana Purchase in the Caribbean World," in *New Territories, New Perspectives: The Religious Impact of the Louisiana Purchase,* ed. Richard J. Callahan Jr. (Columbia: University of Missouri Press, 2008), 146–67, and the two-part special issue of *Atlantic Studies* 5, nos. 2–3 (2008), especially Kent Mathewson, "Greater Louisiana Connections and Conjunctions: Placing New Orleans in an Atlantic Time-Geographic Perspective," 223–36; Mark L. Thompson, "Locating the Isle of Orleans: Atlantic and American Historiographical Perspectives," 305–33; Douglas B. Chambers, "Slave Trade Merchants of Spanish New Orleans, 1763–1803: Clarifying the Colonial Slave Trade to Louisiana in Atlantic Perspective," 335–46; and Alexander B. Murphy, "Placing Louisiana in the Francophone World," 363–81. Other recent scholarship on New Orleans includes Peirce F. Lewis, *New Orleans; The Making of an Urban Landscape,* 3rd ed. (Charlottesville: University Press of Virginia, 2009); Shannon Lee Dawdy, *Building the Devil's Empire: French Colonial New Orleans* (Chicago: University of Chicago Press, 2008); Jennifer Spear, *Race, Sex, and Social Order in Early New Orleans* (Baltimore: Johns Hopkins University Press, 2009); Thomas Ingersoll, *Mammon and Manon in Early New Orleans: The First Slave Society in the Deep South, 1718–1819* (Knoxville: University of Tennessee Press, 1999); Emily Clark, *Masterless Mistresses: The New Orleans Ursulines and the Development of a New World Society, 1727–1834* (Chapel Hill: University of North Carolina Press, 2006); and Ned Sublette, *The World That Made New Orleans: From Spanish Silver to Congo Square* (New York: Lawrence Hill, 2008).

7. For a review of the literature on black Atlantic religions, see Sylvia R. Frey, "The Visible Church: Historiography of African American Religion since Raboteau," *Slavery and Abolition* (January 2008): 83–110. A sampling of recent work includes J. Lorand Matory, *Black Atlantic Religion: Tradition, Transnationalism, and Matriarchy in*

the Afro-Brazilian Candomblé (Princeton: Princeton University Press, 2005); Linda M. Heywood and John K. Thornton, *Central Africans, Atlantic Creoles, and the Foundation of the Americas, 1585–1660* (New York: Cambridge University Press, 2007); James H. Sweet, *Re-creating Africa: Culture, Kinship, and Religion in the African-Portuguese World, 1441–1770* (Chapel Hill: University of North Carolina Press, 2004); Sylvia R. Frey and Betty Wood, *Come Shouting to Zion: African American Protestantism in the American South and British Caribbean to 1830* (Chapel Hill: University of North Carolina Press, 1998); Jon F. Sensbach, *Rebecca's Revival: Creating Black Christianity in the Atlantic World* (Cambridge, MA: Harvard University Press, 2005); Patrick Bellegarde-Smith, ed., *Fragments of Bone: Neo-African Religions in a New World* (Urbana: University of Illinois Press, 2005); and Toyin Falola and Matt D. Childs, *The Yoruba Diaspora in the Atlantic World* (Bloomington: Indiana University Press, 2004).

8. Gwendolyn Midlo Hall, "The Formation of Afro-Creole Culture," in *Creole New Orleans: Race and Americanization,* ed. Arnold R. Hirsch and Joseph Logsdon (Baton Rouge: Louisiana State University Press, 1992), 68–71.

9. Gwendolyn Midlo Hall, *Africans in Colonial Louisiana: The Development of Afro-Creole Culture in the Eighteenth Century* (Baton Rouge: Louisiana State University Press, 1992), chap. 1; Michael A. Gomez, *Exchanging Our Country Marks: The Transformation of African Identities in the Colonial and Antebellum South* (Chapel Hill: University of North Carolina Press, 1998), chap. 3; Ibrahima Seck, "The Relationship between St. Louis of Senegal, Its Hinterlands, and Colonial Louisiana," in *French Colonial Louisiana and the Atlantic World,* ed. Bond, 265–90. For dissenting views on the difficulty of identifying a "Bambara" ethnic predominance among captives sent to Louisiana, see Peter Caron, "'Of a nation which the others do not Understand': Bambara Slaves and African Ethnicity in Colonial Louisiana, 1718–60," *Slavery and Abolition* 18 (1997): 98–121; and Philip D. Morgan, "The Cultural Implications of the Atlantic Slave Trade: African Regional Origins, American Destinations, and New World Developments," *Slavery and Abolition* 18 (1997): 122–45.

10. Paul LaChance, "The Growth of the Free and Slave Populations of French Colonial Louisiana," in *French Colonial Louisiana and the Atlantic World,* ed. Bond, 219–26; Hall, *Africans in Colonial Louisiana,* chap. 7; Daniel Usner, *Indians, Settlers, and Slaves in a Frontier Exchange Economy: The Lower Mississippi Valley before 1783* (Chapel Hill: University of North Carolina Press, 1992), 44; and Gomez, *Exchanging Our Country Marks,* 50–52.

11. Hall, *Africans in Colonial Louisiana,* 106–11, chap. 11.

12. Edward Kamau Brathwaite, "Gods of the Middle Passage: A Tennament," *Caribbean Review* 11, no. 4 (1982): 18–19. For powerfully imagined discussions of the experiences of Africans on board transatlantic slave ships, see Marcus Rediker, *The Slave Ship: A Human History* (New York: Penguin, 2007), chap. 9; and Stephanie Smallwood, *Saltwater Slavery: A Middle Passage from Africa to American Diaspora* (Cambridge, MA: Harvard University Press, 2007).

13. Hall, *Africans in Colonial Louisiana,* 45–52, which draws largely on a twentieth-century ethnography of Bambara religion, and Germaine Dieterlen, *Essai sur la Religion Bambara,* 2nd ed. (Brussels: Presses Universitaires de France, 1988).

14. Gomez, *Exchanging Our Country Marks,* 50–52; Diouf, *Servants of Allah,* 128–31, quote on 128–29.

15. Antoine Simon Le Page du Pratz, *History of Louisiana,* ed. Joseph G. Tregle Jr. (Baton Rouge: Louisiana State University Press, 1976, facsimile reproduction of 1774 edition), 377.

16. Ibid., 387.

17. Ingersoll, *Mammon and Manon;* and Sue Peabody, "'A Dangerous Zeal': Catholic Missions to Slaves in the French Antilles, 1635–1800," *French Historical Studies* 25 (2002): 53–90. The intermittent attempts of Jesuit and Capuchin priests to evangelize Africans in Louisiana, with mixed success, are discussed in Michael Pasquier, "'Without Knowledge of the True God': Capuchins, Jesuits, and African Slavery in French Colonial Louisiana," Colloquium on "Atlantic Catholicism: The French-American Connection," Cushwa Center for the Study of American Catholicism, University of Notre Dame, May 2010.

18. Clark, *Masterless Mistresses,* 177–81.

19. Carl Ekberg, *French Roots in the Illinois Country: The Mississippi Frontier in Colonial Times* (Urbana: University of Illinois Press, 1998), 145–57; Carl Ekberg, *Colonial Ste. Genevieve* (Gerald, MO: Patrice Press, 1985), 197–239; and Cécile Vidal, "Africains et Européens au pay des Illinois durant la période française (1699–1765)," *French Colonial History* 3 (2003): 51–68.

20. David Wheat, "My Friend Nicolas Mongoula: Africans, Indians, and Cultural Exchange in Eighteenth-Century Mobile," in *Coastal Encounters: The Transformation of the Gulf South in the Eighteenth Century,* ed. Richmond F. Brown (Lincoln: University of Nebraska Press, 2007), 117–31; Hall, "The Formation of Afro-Creole Culture."

21. Hall, *Africans in Colonial Louisiana,* chap. 9.

22. Nathalie Dessens, "From Saint Domingue to Louisiana: West Indian Refugees in the Lower Mississippi Valley," in *French Colonial Louisiana and the Atlantic World,* ed. Bond, 244–64; Hall, "The Formation of Afro-Creole Culture," 86–87; Johnson, "Vodou Purchase"; and John Stewart, "Spirituality and Resistance among African-Creoles," in *New Territories, New Perspectives,* ed. Callahan, 167, 184–88.

23. Benjamin Henry Latrobe, *Impressions Respecting New Orleans: Diary and Sketches, 1818–1820,* ed. Samuel Wilson Jr. (New York, 1951), quoted in Jerah Johnson, "New Orleans's Congo Square: An Urban Setting for Early Afro-American Culture Formation," *Louisiana History* 32 (1991): 117–18.

24. Johnson, "New Orleans' Congo Square," 118–19, 143.

25. Ibid.; Shane White and Graham White, *The Sounds of Slavery: Discovering African American History through Songs, Sermons, and Speech* (Boston: Beacon Press, 2005), xi–xii, 43–46; and Dena J. Epstein, *Sinful Tunes and Spirituals: Black Folk Music to the Civil War* (Chicago: University of Chicago Press, 1977), 184–85. On the ring shout, see Sterling Stuckey, *Slave Culture: Nationalist Theory and the Foundations of Black America* (New York: Oxford University Press, 1988).

26. On the evolution of slave society along one section of the river, see Christopher Morris, *Becoming Southern: The Evolution of a Way of Life, Warren County and Vicksburg, Mississippi, 1770–1860* (New York: Oxford University Press, 1995). On the waning Creole influence upriver, see Ekberg, *Colonial Ste. Genevieve,* chaps. 13–14, and Cyprian Clamorgan, *The Colored Aristocracy of St. Louis,* ed. Julie Winch (Columbia: University of Missouri Press, 1999), 4–5. On the jarring of Catholic and Protestant cultures following the Louisiana Purchase, see Callahan, ed., *New Territories, New Perspectives.*

27. Randy J. Sparks, *Religion in Mississippi* (Jackson: University Press of Mississippi, 2001), chap. 4; Anthony Kaye, *Joining Places: Slave Neighborhoods in the Old South* (Chapel Hill: University of North Carolina Press, 2007).

28. White and White, *Sounds of Slavery,* 41.

29. Ibid.; narrative of Laura Redham, in *The American Slave: A Composite Autobiography,* ed. George Rawick (Westport, CT: Greenwood Press, 1972), vol. 5, Texas narratives, parts 3 and 4, p. 238.

30. Johnson, "Vodou Purchase"; Michael Pasquier, "'Though Their Skin Remains Brown, I Hope Their Souls Will Soon Be White': Slavery, French Missionaries, and the Roman Catholic Priesthood in the American South, 1789–1865," *Church History* 77 (2008): 340–45; Jon F. Sensbach, "Before the Bible Belt: Indians, Africans, and the New Synthesis of Eighteenth-Century Southern Religious History," in *Religion in the American South: Protestants and Others in History and Culture,* ed. Beth Barton Schweiger and Donald Mathews (Chapel Hill: University of North Carolina Press, 2004), 6–7.

2

---◆---

Religion and American Empire in Mississippi

1790–1833

Sylvester Johnson

> Early in the autumn, the last party of the Choctaws departed for their new
> country at the West. The whole number removed was about 15,000. Many
> remained in the southern part of their old country, and a few in other
> parts; but the nation was gone, and they were mere individual Indians in a
> community of white men.
>
> —Cyrus Kingsbury, 1833

This essay explains how American Christian foreign missions functioned as
a "civilizing" religion of empire in strategic partnership with the War Department to transform the Mississippi Territory (which became the state of Mississippi in 1817) from a land of sovereign Indian nations to an Anglo-American region of white imperial dominion. Our story begins with the religious
and political conditions of the late 1700s. I focus on two nations among the
Mississippi Indians, the Choctaw and Chickasaw. The United States was a foreign country with respect to the Choctaw and Chickasaw, and the region organized in 1798 as the Mississippi Territory was a field ripe for harvest in the
eyes of Anglo-American missionaries. The Natchez, Choctaw, and Chickasaw
nations had established thriving trade networks throughout the region. For
centuries, Indians of the American South traveled hundreds of miles if necessary to reach the city of Natchez, where they participated in an international
exchange; this market network eventually incorporated Spanish, French, and
English commerce. Its proximity to the mouth of the Mississippi River was
not happenstance but the central reason that Natchez was one of the most
important urban centers among North Americans long before the European
invasions began. Hundreds of years before the South became defined as an

aberrant, diminutive expression of America in the wake of the cultural meanings of the Civil War, the Mississippi River valley—Natchez especially—was
renowned for its status as an international (in both Indian and European
terms) destination of exchange. Spanish and French colonizers in the American South were keenly aware of the strategic importance of Natchez and eventually pillaged and killed most of the Natchez nation to assume control of the
city in the 1700s. Other nations like the Chickasaw and Choctaw, however,
preserved their autonomy for decades longer by defending their lands from
violent white invasions and negotiating peace treaties with whites while easily
embracing and naturalizing white families or (far more typically) white bach-
elors seeking to marry into the Indian nations of Mississippi.[1]

The lands along the river were fertile and enriched by periodic flooding,
which deposited nutrient-rich silt. The warm, humid climate ensured lush
growth of vegetables, tobacco, and cotton. Equally valuable was the Mississippi
River's usefulness for transport; in an age when waterways were the highway
system of the Americas, the Mississippi, the continent's longest, was the "Route
66." This major artery of the transportation network, however, was also a border of an early American empire. For a few decades at least, it represented the
limits of Anglo-American military forays. The fledgling U.S. nation-state was
born an empire, inducing continual white invasions into the sovereign lands of
Native Americans like the Cherokee and the Creek. The thirteen colonies that
became the United States developed military institutions to wage a virtually
unending series of small-scale assaults and full-fledged wars against Indian
nations; gradual extermination and progressive displacement of Indians by the
nation-state merely continued and developed what had been happening since
the earliest invasions from Europe in the fifteenth century.[2]

In the decades following the American Revolution, another domain of
social power ran parallel to the U.S. nation-state's expansionist ambitions, one
no less important for understanding the relations between Anglo-America and
the Indian states. This was the Protestant missionary enterprise.[3] The earliest
intellectual strategies for conceiving of European colonialism in the Americas
were steeped in the tradition of Christian missionary conquest. Theologians
and political philosophers of Iberia, France, and England, though perched
in the metropole and separated from the Americas by the vast expanse of
the Atlantic Ocean, were no less lofty and impassioned when contemplating
how they might convert millions of "heathens" than those missionaries in the
Americas like Junipero Serra, John Eliot, and David Brainerd who abandoned
families and all familiar to live in Indian towns, devoting their lives to effect

a total erasure of Indian religion. They hoped to dispense, in its stead, the light of Christian civilization.[4] The "Awakenings," so familiar to the historical narratives that depict the religious revivalism of the American colonies, were viewed as part and parcel of a grand scheme of history's unfolding into a mighty act of divine agency that would culminate in a literally global dispensation of the Christian gospel.

It was the New World of the Americas, not the Old World of Europe, that was to be the stage of this divine drama. One need only consider the sentiment of New England's Puritan divine of great renown, Jonathan Edwards, to grasp the pivotal meaning of Indian missions to the Anglo-American imagination. As he penned his elaborate theology of world events, *History of the Work of Redemption,* Edwards opined that the Christian deity had meticulously timed the invention of the compass to promote European colonialism in the Americas and to coincide with the return of the Christian messiah and the subsequent inception of the millennial age. The American Indians were supposedly hidden by Satan from the light of Christian truth that first shined in biblical lands. They were the final frontier of that vast field of the unconverted, now ripe for harvest.[5]

Like many of his evangelical contemporaries, Edwards reconciled a Calvinist concern for the spiritual realm and the afterlife with a pragmatic interest in ameliorating temporal affairs, a synthesis of aims promoted by others who followed him, like Samuel Hopkins and Jedidiah Morse. This humanitarian and benevolent emphasis that burgeoned in Calvinist and evangelical theologies in the late 1700s and early 1800s was especially influenced by a growing orthodox resistance to liberalism (namely Unitarianism) in New England. The urgent task of the revivalists and missionary organizers was seemingly at its most critical moment ever.[6] These were not mere ideas bandied about by elite writers. The theology of missions, on the contrary, was a powerful principle that guided the interactions of whites and Indians, produced corporate institutions like Bible and tract societies, and forged rather unpredictable alliances between voluntary movements and the official state apparatuses of the American empire.[7] This latter development, indeed, became centrally important once the former colonies became an independent republic. The consequences of Anglo-American Christianity now having a nation-state were not lost on missionaries. American nationalism imbued them with a weightier sense of responsibility not only to Indians but to the entire non-Christian world. The foreign mission field, not merely domestic revivalism, was the new concern at hand. This only heightened the importance of the geopolitical space of the frontier, the interface of invasive white settlers and sovereign Indian nations. So the geographies of the Mississippi River valley that constituted the southwestern boundaries of the United States logically became central to the intellectual, religious, and political centers of Anglo-American power.

As one major consequence of this change, a group of clergy in Boston, Massachusetts, created the American Board of Commissioners for Foreign Missions (ABCFM hereafter) in 1810. A team of young divinity students studying at Andover Theological Seminary drafted an appeal for starting the foreign missionary society, and they delivered a signed copy to the General Association of Massachusetts Proper, a group of Congregational ministers who had recently organized on the basis of their shared conservative theology. Andover itself had been founded just three years earlier, in 1807, to train a vanguard of ministers to preserve Christian orthodoxy before the onslaught of Unitarianism and its liberal varieties, which were increasingly finding lively support among New England's elite. The Andover students were delighted to find their proposal uniformly embraced and speedily implemented. An executive committee was formed, and within another year it had raised $1,400; this flash of success lifted their hopes of supporting the students in the foreign field. By 1812, the students had embarked for India, and the ABCFM advanced its plans for sending more missionaries abroad.[8]

The resounding criticism from British missionaries and American churches, however, concerned the neglect of Indian nations who were not across the ocean but at the very door of the American churches. Why sail across the world when millions of American Indians were right at hand? Not that the mission society had not already aspired to develop Native American missions; from the start, they had identified the Iroquois nation to initiate their conversion of those they referred to as North America's "heathens." What ensued was a concerted effort by the ABCFM to alter completely the American Indian nations, making them "English in language, civilized in habits, and Christian in religion." By 1820, more than half of the ABCFM's resources were devoted to Indian missions, and several of these missions would operate in Mississippi until the 1830s.[9]

IMPERIAL EXPANSION AND EARLY CHRISTIAN MISSIONS
IN THE MISSISSIPPI RIVER VALLEY

The missions of the ABCFM were certainly not the first of Christian attempts to convert the Mississippi Indians. Spanish missionaries had pioneered this effort. By 1726, the first Christian missions had begun in the Choctaw nation in the Sixtown District.[10] A second mission was established in Yazoo the following year. These Jesuit missions produced few if any lasting Christian communities among the Choctaw. They did, however, create a complex of cultural meanings about Christian conversion that continued to circulate among the peoples of the Mississippi. One Choctaw convert inveighed against the Jesuit priest who had persuaded him to join Christianity; the recently proselytized man had experienced only failure in his hunting ever since he had allowed the priest to baptize him. Despite assurances that Christianity was superior to the Choctaw ways, which he had renounced as a condition of his conversion, he found Christianity to be a religion of worthless magic. It could not land game to provide food for hungry stomachs. So he demanded that the Jesuit "unbaptize" him and revoke the stultifying power of an "impotent" religion; the priest reluctantly complied.[11]

Both Protestants and Catholics would rely on the mission institution to convert Native Americans, although Protestants would do so to a lesser extent. Among the Mississippi Indians, however, the mission institution was absolutely central to creating Anglo-American Christian dominance among the otherwise sovereign nations of the Choctaw and Chickasaw. Protestant itinerants were active in the region by the end of the 1700s. Under Spanish rule, however, Protestant conversion was a punishable crime, as the Episcopal missionary Adam Cloud eventually discovered after being arrested in 1792 for proselytizing among the Choctaw. Cloud, who was from Delaware, had arrived in Natchez that same year and acquired 1,700 acres along St. Catherine's Creek, only two miles from the city.[12] Local Spanish administrators soon recognized the threat that his work represented to both Catholicism and to Spanish political aspirations in the region; they captured him and banished him from the region. Cloud would return to missionizing in the Choctaw nation and among white settlers almost twenty-five years later when the United States controlled the region, and he would establish Mississippi's first Episcopal church in 1820, just three years after the territory was granted statehood.[13]

In 1799, just a few years after Cloud's first appearance in Natchez, the Presbyterian Mission Board of New York decided to sponsor a graduate of Yale University to observe and report on the Chickasaw nation; the young minister was Joseph Bullen. His task was to assess the feasibility of creating a mission among the Chickasaw. Bullen was quite eager to promote Christian expansion in "Indian country," and he moved his family to live among the Chickasaw in the western part of present-day Georgia. He tried for three years to persuade the Chickasaw to convert to Christianity but saw little success. The disillusioned Bullen had decided to return to New England when two other missionaries, sent by the Carolina Synod, persuaded him to join their efforts to proselytize among white settlers farther south in the Mississippi Territory. After settling in Jefferson County, he taught school for the children of white settlers and, on weekends, preached as an itinerant to the white families throughout the area. In 1804, when the United States more firmly controlled the region after weakening Spanish claims, he established his denomination's first formal church in the territory, Bethel Presbyterian Church of Uniontown (in present-day Jefferson County). Bullen would eventually build more churches in Port Gibson, Bayou Pierre, and Union—all in the Mississippi Territory.[14]

THE CIVILIZING "MISSION"

But none of the missionaries, at that point, could boast of significant gains among the Chickasaw and Choctaw nations. The success of Bullen and other missionaries, rather, was to be had among white settlers who were already familiar with Christianity; these were readily coaxed into supporting a local church after hearing a few revivalist sermons. Christianizing Indian foreigners, however, was a task of a fundamentally different nature that required a radically different strategy. For what emerged within a decade of repeated failures by various white missionary organizations (e.g., the Presbyterian Mission Board of New York, the South Carolina Synod, the Missionary Society of the Synod of South Carolina and Georgia, and the Mississippi Baptist Association) was a model for producing numerous Indian converts by promoting Christianization as training in racial (white) civilization through apprenticeship in labor. In other words, white Christian missionaries decided to win Indian converts by creating a missionary plantation that promised, in return for intensive menial labor by Indian *youths* (apprentices/laborers), the education and religion that might equip Indians with literacy and technological advancement; this in turn would enable them to live as virtual whites, to be integrated into an Anglo-American civilization that was already changing the land of the Choctaw and Chickasaw nations (gradually being divided into private *latifundios* by whites who lived among the Indians). White Americans were remapping the political landscape as well by crafting and reshuffling land treaties between an expanding imperial U.S. state and the various Indian nations.

Throughout the Americas, the plantation synthesized within the same temporal period and compressed within a compact spatial context what had emerged in the western Mediterranean world over several centuries and usually in separate spheres—slavery, feudalism, and mercantilism—all in service to a global free-market capitalism that earned Europeans prosperity and that pauperized Africans and Indians.[15] On a regional scale, this meant that the plantation became a central means of developing the vigor of American capitalism as an enterprise of racial conquest in Mississippi. And it reflected the important linkage between racial capitalism and an imperial form of American religion.

By 1827, the ABCFM found it necessary to defend its public image in light of accusations that missionaries were fattening themselves at the expense of unrequited Indian labor and free money from the coffers of the U.S. Treasury that should have gone to Indians. The mission society printed riveting stories of frugal missionaries who sacrificed family and abandoned their comfortable New England homes out of unadulterated devotion to saving the "heathens" in the nation's hinterlands.[16]

Imperial Ambitions of the State

Undergirding the shift in missionary strategy were the fomenting ambitions of Anglo-American imperialism. The quest for expansion into Indian land was unrelenting. At the end of the eighteenth century, while Anglo-America formally recognized Spanish claims to the land of the Mississippi Indians, the United States was assiduously lobbying the political leaders of native nations to gain informal control of land. The principal means of doing so was to promote widening the roads and building postal stations. In 1799, U.S. Secretary of State Timothy Pickering suggested to Mississippi Territory Governor Winthrop Sargent that building more postal stations was an essential service to the growing number of whites who were living in the nations of the Choctaw and Chickasaw. Pickering complained that letters from Natchez required up to three months to reach federal government offices (in Philadelphia at the time); the passage was "as tedious as from Europe, when westerly winds prevail." But he was already hopeful that Congress would in its next session "ascertain the practicability of a regular mail through the *Indian Country*"; the means to this was to build numerous postal stations along the roads and in the lands belonging to Indians so that "forage and provisions can be laid up for the post-riders."[17] Even Pickering, however, realized that the Indians of Mississippi would be imprudent to go along with such a plan because it would require them to surrender even more land to an American empire that had already demonstrated its penchant for militarist and murderous methods of feeding its insatiable appetite for territory rightly belonging to sovereign Indian nations.

There was a promising strategy at hand, however. The Mississippi Indians maintained open societies and regularly naturalized non-Indians who lived among them, providing them with use of land and granting them the same rights and privileges enjoyed by Indian citizens (whites, for instance, could become chief executive leaders of Indian nations, but no Indian could ever be a U.S. senator or governor or president). More to the point, federal law, as early as 1790, stipulated that only "whites" could be naturalized, manifesting a philosophy of citizenship that could not have been more antithetical to the norms established by Indian nations. Pickering thus proposed to Sargent the possibility of getting white interpreters who already lived among the Indians to control larger amounts of land on which they could build privately owned stations. These whites could grow food on the additional land as provision for the stations as well.[18] Within two years, the postmaster general had appealed to the secretary of war, Henry Dearborn, to put U.S. Army troops to work (since it was peacetime) widening roads in Indian lands to improve postal service transportation. This industrious effort would not only boost troop morale but also improve the security of white American settlers against the Spanish and Indian nations. Of course the benefit to commerce was made explicit as well.

The War Department pursued just this strategy. The most important road was one created by the various native nations—the Natchez Trace. It ran from Nashville, Tennessee, to the city of Natchez, near the mouth of the Mississippi River, and had been in use for several centuries before the European invasions. The Natchez Trace was excellent for pedestrian travel, but the horse-and-wagon traffic of the Anglo-American military found it rough going. At some points, the road crossed creeks or streams that, depending upon the season and rainfall, often necessitated the use of canoes or ferry boats to traverse small but formidable portions. By 1806, Thomas Jefferson, then president, was pleased to inform the postmaster general that no less than $12,000 had been appropriated to widen roads throughout the American empire, half of which was specifically devoted to the Natchez Trace.[19] One month later, in August 1806, the government began soliciting bids for the road expansion project.[20] Jefferson had long been persuaded that the Indian lands of the Mississippi Territory (Spain still laid claim to some regions of Mississippi) would be central to the economic and military prosperity of the American empire; developing transportation routes through Indian country seemed a logical step forward.

Between 1799 and 1808, the United States busily negotiated multiple treaties with the Chickasaw, Choctaw, Cherokee, and Creek nations, each time seeking additional concessions for greater control over territory through which roads ran, particularly the Natchez Trace. By October 1801, the Chickasaw nation had agreed through a formal treaty to allow the U.S. government to fortify roads in their territory. Within two months, the Choctaw nation had made similar agreements. In 1804, the Creek nation finally agreed to this arrangement as well. The Treaty of Tellico (present-day Tennessee) of October 1805, for instance, warranted that "citizens of the U.S. shall have the free and unmolested use of" specific Indian roads, effectively nullifying the ability of putatively sovereign Indian nations to regulate, deny, or otherwise control the influx of white imperial capitalism, settler sprawl, and foreign (United States) military incursions. The United States was even negotiating with one Indian nation (like the Chickasaw) to alter their historic boundaries with another Indian nation (like the Cherokee).[21]

By 1808, the secretary of war was receiving correspondence reassuring him that the Cherokee and Chickasaw nations supported the commercial interests that might arise from the road expansion and, once the expansion had begun, would "immediately settle at convenient places for raising corn and other necessaries for travelers." Like convenience stores along contemporary interstate highways, these "stations" would make it possible for postal workers, the U.S. military, missionaries, or any other whites to travel from New England to the Gulf of Mexico with confidence that food, wares, and lodging would be available along the way. Thus, under the pretext of road-building, the American state was slowly controlling lands technically belonging to sovereign Indian nations. The seemingly innocuous project of improving transportation, joined to increasing settlement by American whites whom the Choctaw and Chickasaw continued to embrace as full-fledged Indian citizens, effectively crippled the ability of these Indian nations to exercise autonomous power over lands that, by rights of treaty, were under Native and not Anglo-American authority.

ALLIANCE OF RELIGION AND EMPIRE

The most important innovation in Anglo-American foreign missions was the strategy of employing the plantation (the Anglo-American *latifundio*) as an institution of Christian conversion in the Mississippi River valley. It was to be a civilizing mission. It was particularly the brainchild of the ABCFM. From 1816 to 1820, the mission society lobbied the political leadership of native nations and the U.S. secretary of war to accept the bold plan. As one missionary opined, no lasting success would result from "attempts to instruct the Indians, while they continue their wandering savage life." This alliance was encouraged by a convergence of interests and aims. Both the United States and the ABCFM wanted to eradicate the sustainable agricultural patterns of the native nations in Mississippi and replace these with industrial-scale plantation agriculture employing African slavery, an economic model that required "settled habitation."[22]

To achieve this earlier with the Cherokee, the ABCFM had already experimented with removing native children from their families, sending them far away to learn English Christianity in white missionary schools, then returning the Cherokee youths to their families as indigenous missionaries who had (hopefully) learned to regard Indian civilization as backward, a condition of cultural decadence to be replaced by their newly acquired Anglo-Christian civilization. In the wake of the War of 1812, a more ambitious model seemed a much better alternative—establishing schools right among the Indians.[23] These "schools" were to differ from those used earlier because they were actually *latifundio*-plantations, full-scale self-sufficient missions like those Spanish missionaries had employed for centuries throughout the Americas to transform Indian slave labor (sweat-and-blood tuition for Christianity's tutelage in civilization) into European economic prosperity.

The ABCFM's corresponding secretary, Samuel Worcester, authorized the minister-turned-missionary Elias Cornelius to serve as the society's agent to promote this new strategy for Christianizing and civilizing the Mississippi Indians. The ABCFM also commissioned Cyrus Kingsbury to promote the idea of a mission school in the Cherokee nation. Kingsbury had been working for a Connecticut foreign missions society, and he was to become one of the ABCFM's most valuable missionaries. In 1817, while traveling to the Tennessee-Georgia territory of the Cherokee nation, he made a pivotal stopover in Washington, DC, to pitch the idea of a partnership between the ABCFM and the federal government. President James Madison's administration was considerably impressed with the potential benefits of the ABCFM's missionary strategy, which if successful would all but guarantee that the Indian nations, by abandoning their own forms of subsistence farming and hunting in exchange for a sedentary plantation economy, could more easily be induced to surrender additional lands to white settlers. Civilizing the Indian nations, in other words, would be the most efficient, nonmilitary means of concentrating the habitation of Indians within a smaller region of land.

As a result, Secretary of War James Monroe promised Kingsbury direct funding from the federal coffers to support missionary schools.[24] Monroe would soon take office as the next president, and his relationship with Kingsbury and the ABCFM would only deepen the spirit of collaboration promoted by the Madison administration. With assurances of financial assistance and official backing from the nation's chief executive, Kingsbury arrived among the Cherokee officials with a high-powered proposal for advancing that nation's chances of surviving and even thriving amidst the expansion of Anglo-American civilization. In fact, Kingsbury made a point, as did other missionaries, of impressing upon his Indian audiences that Christianity was the secret to the material and economic success of the white race.[25] The Cherokee mission opened that same year. It was named Brainerd (in honor of the New England missionary David Brainerd), and it began with twenty-six students who were bequeathed, as a matter of policy, with Christian (i.e., English) names.[26] They worked from sunrise until nine in the evening, combining intense manual labor with instruction in English communication and Christian theology.

As if to confirm the quickening demise of Indian sovereignty, Mississippi became the twentieth state admitted to the Union that December. In 1818, the following year, Elias Cornelius was busily meeting with the Council members of the Choctaw, Creek, and Chickasaw nations to sell them on the idea of a similar project in their own nations. Like the Cherokee, the Mississippi Indians were quick to embrace a plan for mission schools. Kingsbury joined Cornelius in Mississippi that same year and, buoyed by the success of the Brainerd mission, helped to open a new mission among the Choctaw nation, the Elliot mission station (named for the New England missionary John Eliot). The Elliot mission followed the same structure of rigid, intensive labor developed for the Brainerd mission, and emphasized that Christian conversion was training in civilization and the racial technologies of industry and production. Kingsbury met with increasing support from Choctaw officials who recognized the utility of white industrial education for succoring their nation's survival. And they invited the ABCFM to establish more missions closer to the Indian towns. The Newell mission school opened among the Choctaw in 1821. In 1822, the ABCFM opened the Mayhew mission among the Choctaw, followed by the Martyn station in 1825 among the Chickasaw.

The Missionary Society of the Synod of South Carolina and Georgia opened a mission to the Chickasaw in 1821 following the same model of labor and instruction; this mission would later be transferred to control by the ABCFM.[27] Meanwhile, the ABCFM's lobbying efforts with the Madison and Monroe administrations were paying off handsomely; in 1819, Congress would pass the Civilization Act, which guaranteed federal funding to the missionary societies of Anglo-American churches. By the 1840s, the U.S. government would expend more than $214,000 to fund Christian missions among the Indians (the equivalent of over $4.5 billion in today's dollars).[28]

Why did the Indian nations so readily accept a plan to radically alter the economic and cultural foundations of their societies? The most important factor working in favor of the mission society was the sheer force of imperial, political, and demographic changes that, like an earthquake, rocked the foundations of the local and regional economies of American Indians. The Choctaw and Chickasaw had hunted and cultivated the Mississippi lands for centuries, and their methods of agriculture abundantly produced tobacco, corn, and vegetables. Their settlement patterns were thoroughly socialized, ensuring universal access to abundant land for all families. Yet they only mildly impacted the land, never depleted the soil, and avoided overhunting the abundant game. This is one reason that white travelers and settlers who continually invaded the lands of American Indians endlessly pontificated about the Edenic, virgin ambience of Indian country, as if no one had lived there before whites arrived. All of this was rapidly changing, however. By the early 1800s, it was not unusual for Choctaw and Chickasaw families to possess numerous African slaves to work industrial farms. The majority of these slaveholding Indian families consisted of white American men who joined Indian nations and married Indian women while still retaining the privileges of U.S. citizenship. In fact, the racial alliance between these white men and Anglo-American institutions of government and religion were of paramount importance for enabling the tentacles of American empire to reach into the lands of sovereign native nations. But even the families of Indian men and women were beginning to live as whites by creating the permanent settlements that slave-based industrial farming required. As a result, the plantation was becoming an increasingly common feature of Indian towns. And once Indians started down this slippery slope, it was virtually impossible to turn back because exchanging Indian ways for the civilization of white Christians literally meant that Indians had to depend on whites for physical survival.

Tisshamastubbe, who represented the Chickasaw nation in correspondence with the secretary of war around the time of the Louisiana Purchase, found himself in the awkward position of requesting assistance from the United States to obtain "spinners, weavers, and plows" to ensure that the Indian nation could feed and clothe themselves. Tisshamastubbe recalled how George Washington had initially "advised" the Chickasaw to "settle out, raise stock, and become farmers," in exchange for which they would receive assistance. This was a tragically diplomatic recollection of the early American empire's racist and genocidal ultimatum that held in abeyance the extermination of Indians on the condition that they prove they were fit for self-governance like the white race by living as whites instead of as beasts; Indian civilization, in other words, was taken as positive proof that Indians were animals. The Chickasaw, along with the other Indian nations, largely complied with this policy of Indian assimilation. As a result, nearly all the Chickasaw "left the old towns and settled over [their] country raising stock and working like white people." Of course, this really functioned, as Tisshamastubbe demonstrated in his appeal, to render Indians dependent on the American empire to provide basic necessities. And it ensured that Cornelius and Kingsbury would find a cooperative audience with Indians.[29]

When Elias Cornelius arrived in 1818 with his plan to open schools among the Mississippi Indians, less than two decades remained before every single Indian nation east of the Mississippi River would be eradicated. At the time, however, the ABCFM's proposal to arrange for children to learn English Christianity, to train children in European technologies of industry, and to open a blacksmith shop in Indian country to provide a local source of iron implements (vital for operating a plantation economy) seemed not merely logical but essential if Indians were to continue to survive. In a real sense, the mission school was a gift. It seemed perfectly sensible to the Indian councils, in this context, to expend thousands of dollars per year by foregoing their annuities and to allow the money to be used instead by missionaries to underwrite the expense of building mission stations. The irony is jolting, for this was to be an essential means of destroying the last foundations of Indians' national sovereignty.

The Mayhew mission (named for the famous New England missionary) was the earliest of these *latifundio*-plantations financed through Indian annuities. Each of the three districts of the Choctaw nation agreed to devote their $2,000 in annuity payments to provide schools so that their children could learn English and acquire the "arts of industry" necessary for thriving economically in a society rapidly changing to conform to industrial farming. As a result, the Mayhew mission was guaranteed an additional $6,000 of annual income, a figure that would have been difficult to match through additional fund-raising. In May and June 1820, the Mayhew mission built a wagon road sixty miles in length. By 1820, the lower district chiefs of the Choctaw council had agreed to divert $2,000 of their annuity payments to support the Elliot mission school and a blacksmith shop, including the purchase of steel and iron.[30] The Choctaw nation would eventually contribute $64,000 to support the ABCFM's missionary effort, more than the ABCFM itself spent on the Choctaw mission.[31] The Caney Creek mission station was established in 1826 and received $2,500 each year from the War Department's Indian annuity funds, which would have otherwise gone directly to the Chickasaw nation, in addition to the federal government's other Indian civilization funds.[32]

On October 6, 1821, the missionary Loring W. Williams arrived at French Camp, the white settlement that was to be the site of Bethel mission, on the Natchez road that ran from Nashville. His infant son, who was already ill before Williams arrived, would die two weeks later. By the month's end, Williams had organized a meeting of several white men with Indian families who resided within the Choctaw nation at French Camp. He proposed creating a school for their children, whom whites referred to as "half-breeds." The whites, who also owned a "considerable number" of African slaves, were fluent in both Choctaw and English after having lived among the Choctaw for years. Williams had already prepared a legal agreement that presented the terms to which prospective supporters of a mission school might commit themselves. The whites agreed that such a school would be a major asset, and they promised both their financial support and manual labor for construction. Around mid-November, as the mild Mississippi winter arrived, they began erecting the school, a five-room house with several decks. Within four weeks, the mission school officially began operation. The missionary board had invested $50 to produce a mission station whose asset value was now roughly $300.[33]

By January 1822, fifteen children were enrolled in the Bethel mission school, two of whom were supported through internal funding of the mission. Nine of the students had previously attended the Elliot mission and could read and write in English. The other six had never before attended school. The boys chopped firewood and performed other manual labor to afford their matriculation at the school. Within two years, Loring and his wife, who had taken over most of the teaching, could boast that several students had memorized the Christian catechism and scripture proofs in addition to several hymns. In

1824, twenty-four students were enrolled—seven girls and seventeen boys—including the two white Williams children; one-third of these had parents who were both Choctaw; the others were children of white men who had married Choctaw women. The Williamses were joined by another missionary couple who shared the load of teaching responsibilities.[34] And they eventually began to convene Sunday meetings that typically attracted about fifty people, a substantial number that promised to yield significant converts.

The Bethel mission, nevertheless, faced arduous and substantial challenges. The mission by its very nature produced strife among Choctaw families because the children, the majority of whom were boarding at the mission, were taught that progress demanded they repudiate Indian ways. A single family whose eight children all attended the school removed their children that same year. Furthermore, neither Williams nor his wife spoke Choctaw; instead, they depended on two students to serve as interpreters. Despite his own limited language skills, Williams was disappointed in the fact that "full-blooded Indians" usually required two years to become fluent in English. He complained that they were "uncivilized" and therefore naturally prone to idleness and play. The parents, furthermore, did not consistently return their children to the school after breaks and vacations. The end came in 1827, by which time most of the Choctaw families had abandoned French Camp.[35]

In January 1821, the Missionary Society of the Synod of South Carolina and Georgia opened the Monroe mission station to proselytize the Chickasaw nation. Located fifty miles from the Mayhew mission, it had enrolled thirty students by 1823. Encouraged by these numbers, the synod built a formal church that year and took in its first convert—an African woman named Dinah. Nine more converts were taken in over the next two years. The Africans living among the Chickasaw were typically fluent in both English and Chickasaw; the missionaries, with few exceptions, spoke only English and thus preached sermons in English. Because most Choctaw Indians were not fluent in English, most converts were either the Indian families of white men or Africans. Africans eventually accounted for more than two-thirds of the church's membership at the Monroe mission. The Presbyterian Synod operated four other missions among the Chickasaw: Tokshish, Martyn, Caney Creek, and Charity Hall.[36]

Despite early optimism and generous confidence among both the officials of the Mississippi Indians and the foreign mission societies, the mission to convert the Indian nations to a regionally concentrated habitation of quasi-white Christian agriculturalists was bound to crumble away. The reason was simple and, in hindsight, obvious. American citizens and the U.S. state were firmly committed to removing Indians by all means necessary, and as often as necessary, so that whites could possess the lands extending to the Mississippi River and beyond. Andrew Jackson's administration shattered any illusions that optimistic Indians and missionaries might have entertained about the continuing existence of Indian nations in the Mississippi River valley. Jacksonian democracy promised the opportunity for common white men of paltry means to enjoy a prosperous life of plenty, especially in terms of land. Although Anglo-America brandished civilization to Indians in hopes of whetting their appetite for prosperity, the sobering reality is that it was the Indians who had the prized possession that whites actually wanted, and that was land. As one writer has aptly quipped, "empires occupy space," and the expanding Anglo-American empire was steadily demanding more.[37] Under Jackson's administration, Congress passed the Indian Removal Act in 1830, which formalized and speedily implemented the violent removal of the Indians in the state of Mississippi and other native nations of the Southeast to lands west of the Mississippi River. The Choctaw nation's centuries-long abode in the Mississippi lands was to be forced to an abrupt and violent end.

By the end of that year, the ABCFM reported only 360 conversions among the Indians in the state of Mississippi.[38] Not only had the civilizing mission not saved the Indians but it had actually rendered their physical existence squarely dependent upon the very imperial nation that was unrelentingly devoted to removing and exterminating them. The white population would increase from 4.3 million in 1800 to 10.5 million in 1830. Within a decade, the white population would explosively increase by yet another one-third. In Mississippi, whites would remain a numerical minority vis-à-vis a powerless black majority from 1840 until 1940.[39] By the 1830s, however, they had already formulated a strategic advantage over the Choctaw and Chickasaw nations of the Mississippi region; Indian sovereignty had slowly succumbed to the dissipatory effects of an imperial Anglo-America.

ALLIES OF RACIAL EMPIRE

The alliance between the ABCFM and the War Department was not the result of any grand scheme to improve the colonial efficacy of Anglo-American Christianity; the foreign missionary society, after all, was conceived as a purely voluntary enterprise to achieve Christian dominion through religious conversion, not by removing and exterminating Indians. Nevertheless, it is clear from the ABCFM's records that the society embraced an understanding of Christianity rooted in the principle of racial civilization, to a degree that should give pause to any easy claims that Christianity is essentially a doctrinal, creedal religion. From the inception of the American empire, Anglo-American Christians widely agreed that their religion was truly a way of life, the substance of which was irreducibly white; it was a religion constituted through a structure of meanings defined in stark contrast to the economic and social institutions of Native American nations. Indians subsisted, but Christians (whites) produced through the means and on the commensurate scale of the plantation estate. Indians roamed, but Christians created sedentary institutions of massive settlements. Hence it becomes apparent that Anglo-American Christianity and the democratic American empire were symmetrical configurations. They both invested in a philosophy of vitality through expansion and absorption that was at once Manichean and monistic—the former as a strategy for asserting identity through radical otherness and the latter as the fruition of universalizing claims predicated on teleology. So, although the state and foreign mission institutions were unwitting bedfellows, following no scripted scheme of collaboration, theirs was nevertheless a match of seeming ineluctable attraction and dynamic reciprocity.

The Christian mission would emerge in the Mississippi River valley through a pragmatic arrangement with the secretary of war that won the missionaries robust funding from Congress, converted Indian reparations into missionary venture capital, and translated the American state's imperial power into a religion of racially exclusive civilization. These Mississippi missions were a pivotal institution of an Anglo-American religion that abetted a long process of destroying the sovereignty of Indian nations. The alliance of the ABCFM and the secretary of war, more specifically, meant the Christian mission in Mississippi was reshaped as a religion of empire that eventually enabled the expulsion of Indians from their Mississippi lands, despite the fact that most white Christian missionaries formally opposed Indian removal. What had been an international geography (Chickasaw, Choctaw, Creek) of multiracial Indian democracies (Indians, blacks, and whites) that increasingly employed African slavery was made to conform to the political and racial demands of a white American nation-state that relied on African slavery even more extensively; this white nation-state, furthermore, had no room for Indian citizens, instead tolerating them on an experimental basis to determine their ability to emulate white civilization.

Before the winter of 1833 had begun, the ABCFM missionary Cyrus Kingsbury, who had devoted his career to expanding the Christian mission institution throughout Mississippi, was coming to terms with the fact that the mission to convert Indians could not succeed if Indians were removed. He noted wistfully that more than 15,000 citizens of the Choctaw nation had been forced west of the Mississippi River. They were officially dispelled beyond the metropole's frontier of white settlement for the time being. Few cultural theorists could have more keenly articulated Cyrus Kingsbury's observation that "the [Choctaw] nation was gone" and in its place were "mere individual Indians in a community of white men."[40] Political rule had been seized by white citizens of an imperial, racial democracy who allowed Native Americans to live among them only as stateless Indians, severed from the protection of the Choctaw nation. They were to remain ambiguously tolerated but never incorporated by an American empire whose philosophy of democracy was an especially effective means of asserting white conquest from the Atlantic seaboard westward.

NOTES

1. James F. Barnett Jr., *The Natchez Indians: A History to 1735* (Jackson: University Press of Mississippi, 2007), 3–17, 63–80, 90–100.

2. John E. Worth, "The Lower Creeks: Origins and Early History," in *Indians of the Greater Southeast: Historical Archaeology and Ethnohistory*, ed. Bonnie G. McEwan (Gainesville: University Press of Florida, 2000), 265–98; and Charles M. Hudson, *The Southeastern Indians* (Knoxville: University of Tennessee Press, 1976), 77–82, 451–70.

3. Martin Marty, *Righteous Empire: The Protestant Experience in America* (New York: Dial Press, 1970), 5–14.

4. Louis Wright, *Religion and Empire: The Alliance between Piety and Commerce in English Expansion, 1558–1625* (Chapel Hill: University of North Carolina Press, 1943), 133.

5. Jonathan Edwards, *History of the Work of Redemption*, in *The Works of President Edwards* (New York: Burt Franklin, 1968 [1817]), 5:222–23.

6. Nathan O. Hatch, *The Democratization of American Christianity* (New Haven, CT: Yale University Press, 1989), 170; and Sydney Ahlstrom, *A Religious History of the American People*, 2nd ed. (New Haven, CT: Yale University Press, 2004), 393–96.

7. David Paul Nord, *Faith in Reading: Religious Publishing and the Birth of Mass Media in America* (New York: Oxford University Press, 2004), 89–103; Candy Gunther Brown, *The Word in the World: Evangelical Writing, Publishing, and Reading in America, 1789–1880* (Chapel Hill: University of North Carolina Press, 2004), 115–18; and Clifton Jackson Phillips, *Protestant America and the Pagan World: The First Half*

Century of the American Board of Commissioners for Foreign Missions, 1810–1860 (Cambridge, MA: Harvard University Press, 1969), 1–10.

8. William Ellsworth Strong, *The Story of the American Board* (New York: Arno Press/New York Times, 1969 [1910]), 3–9.

9. Strong, *Story of the American Board,* 35–36.

10. "Choctaw Nation," box 3, folder 1, Natchez Trace Research Collection (hereafter NTRC), McCain Library Archives, University of Southern Mississippi. This archival collection contains copies of missionary correspondence (largely that of the ABCFM) in addition to missives sent among federal, state, and local officials.

11. "Catholic Mission," box 3, folder 1, NTRC.

12. "Presbyterians," box 3, folder 2, NTRC.

13. "First Episcopal Church of Mississippi Located at Church Hill in 1820," *Jackson Clarion Ledger,* 31 December 1937.

14. "Bethel Church," box 2, folder 9, NTRC.

15. Eduardo Galeano, *Open Veins of Latin America: Five Centuries of the Pillage of a Continent,* 25th anniversary ed. (1973; reprint, New York: Monthly Review Press, 1997), 60. Galeano examines this synthesis within the context of the Caribbean sugar plantation and explains the layered economic structures that undergirded an explicitly racial imperial order.

16. "Missionary motives/Choctaw missions," box 2, folder 25, NTRC.

17. Secretary of State Timothy Pickering to Governor Winthrop Sargent, 20 May 1799, box 3, folder 28, NTRC.

18. Ibid.

19. "Th[omas] Jefferson to Mr. Granger," 18 July 1806, box 3, folder 28, NTRC.

20. "Improvements," box 3, folder 28, NTRC.

21. "Treaty of Tellico," box 3, folder 29, NTRC.

22. "Sketch of a Plan for Instructing the Indians," box 2, folder 26, NTRC.

23. "Origins (Choctaw Mission)," box 2, folder 26, NTRC.

24. Phillips, *Protestant America,* 61.

25. Clara Sue Kidwell, "Choctaws and Missionaries in Mississippi before 1830," *American Indian Culture and Research Journal* 11, no. 2 (1987): 61.

26. William Strong, *Story of the American Board,* 36–37.

27. "Mayhew," box 2, folder 24, NTRC; Kidwell, "Choctaws and Missionaries," 57–59.

28. Kidwell, "Choctaws and Missionaries," 201; W. B. Lewis, House Committee on Indian Affairs, *Civilization of the Indians,* Report to Secretary of War, 2 March 1843, 42, 27th Cong., 3rd sess., 1843.

29. "Chickasaw Nation," Tisshamastubbe to U.S. Secretary of War, n.d., box 2, folder 20, NTRC.

30. "Choctaw Missions," box 2, folder 23, NTRC.

31. ABCFM, "Memorial of the Prudential Committee of the American Board of Commissioners for Foreign Missions, Respecting the Property of the Board in the Choctaw Nation," 16, 22nd Cong., 1st sess., 1832.

32. "Chickasaw Missions," box 2, folder 19, NTRC.

33. "Bethel School (Choctaw Mission)," box 2, folder 8, NTRC.

34. "Bethel School (Choctaw Mission)," box 2, folder 8, NTRC.

35. "Bethel School (Choctaw Mission)," box 2, folder 8, NTRC.

36. "Monroe Mission/Tockshish," box 3, folder 39, NTRC.

37. Marty, *Righteous Empire,* 5.

38. Kidwell, "Choctaws and Missionaries," 69.

39. Campbell Gibson and Kay Jung, "Historical Census Statistics on Population Totals by Race, 1790 to 1990, and by Hispanic Origin, 1970 to 1990, for the United States, Regions, Divisions, and States," http://www.census.gov/population/www/documentation/twps0056/twps0056.html, accessed August 17, 2009.

40. Cyrus Kingsbury, report to ABCFM, 1833, box 2, folder 23, NTRC. Multiple removals of the Choctaw occurred over several years. The *Yazoo Banner* of 15 February 1845 reported that 1,100 Choctaw Indians were marched through Yazoo City to be expelled west of the Mississippi River.

3

Movement, Maps, and Wonder

CIVIL RELIGIOUS COMPETITION AT THE SOURCE
OF THE MISSISSIPPI RIVER, 1805–1832

Arthur Remillard

In his *Memoir of a Map of Hindoostan* (1788), British surveyor James Rennell noted that maps of India had placed the source of the Ganges either at the Lake of the Mind near the foot of Mount Kailasa or deep within the Himalayas at the Gangotri glacier. Mapmakers plotting the latter location relied on a local legend that the river originated in an ice cave, which itself resembled the appearance of a cow's mouth. Rennell agreed that the source was probably in the glacier, but then qualified, "The mind of superstition has given to the mouth of the cavern the form of the head of a cow, an animal held by the Hindoos in a degree of veneration."[1]

Equally dismissive of this bovine imagery were the first British explorers who led unsuccessful expeditions to the glacial source. In 1817, however, John Hodgson ventured deep into the Gangotri and came upon a curious sight. "I cannot think of any place to which they might more aptly give the name of a Cow's Mouth than this extraordinary [opening]," he confessed. Reasoning that he was at the source of the Ganges, his expedition "saluted her with a bugle march."[2]

The expedition was nothing if not dangerous, which begs the question: Why? After all, locating the river's origin served no practical purpose in the British colonial enterprise. But the Ganges is a sacred river, made such in part by voices from India and the West. As "the lifeblood of northern India," Hindu legend dictates that the Ganges is a goddess who trickled down to earth from Shiva's matted hair, settling first in the Himalayas. However, early Christians such as the so-called father of medieval geography, St. Isidore of Seville, repeated Josephus's claim that the Ganges was the Phison, one of the four rivers flowing first from the Garden of Eden.[3] Such symbolic competitions found new language in the nineteenth century as Great Britain extended its power throughout India. Only, while St. Isidore articulated Christian meaning for the source, Hodgson was a British agent who embodied a civil religious ideology anchored in what poet Rudyard Kipling would later call "the white man's burden." The implication was that Great Britain had a providential duty to extend their empire, not for material gain, but for the benevolent aim of "civilizing" primitive peoples. Coupled with this ideology was an assumption that "civilization" required Christianization. Thus a Christian missionary served similar ends as the explorer in that both aspired to actualize the empire's supposed destiny. Hodgson's salute, then, was both a commemoration of western "discovery" and a celebration of the presumed triumph of his homeland's "civilizing mission."[4]

At nearly the same time that Hodgson trekked into the Himalayas, army lieutenant Zebulon Pike, Italian adventurer Giacomo Beltrami, and Indian agent Henry Rowe Schoolcraft led separate expeditions into northwestern Minnesota to locate the source of the Mississippi River. As with Hodgson and the Ganges, finding the source served no pragmatic end. But this was no mere river. Later called "the body of the nation" by Mark Twain, the Mississippi had become a potent symbol of America in the early nineteenth century.[5] As such, the expeditions of Pike, Beltrami, and Schoolcraft had civil religious meaning. Of course, Pike and Schoolcraft translated the landscape through an American lens, while Beltrami referred more often to Italy and Europe. But the explorers held tight to the belief that their homeland was exceptional, assigned a special destiny from a providential source. In their minds, mapping the source was part of fulfilling this destiny.[6]

The expeditions were also exercises in civil religious competition. The explorers all made different claims to where the river began. To validate their discovery and elevate it beyond all others, they recounted their powerful feelings of wonder upon first seeing the source. This emotional response also did the work of discrediting the physical and social maps produced by Indians and traders living in the region. While instrumental in guiding each explorer, for Pike, Beltrami, and Schoolcraft, Indians and traders were part of a "wilderness" that required the "civilizing" force of western ideas and institutions. So in this era of exploration, the source of the Mississippi River—and the route to and from it—was an arena of competing civil religious discourses. Through movement, maps, and feelings of wonder, the explorers all sought to define, name, and claim this elusive and compelling sacred place.

"An Unknown Wilderness"

In 1805, Lieutenant Zebulon Montgomery Pike led the first official American expedition to the headwaters region. Pike was fifteen when he joined an infantry company led by his father, an accomplished officer of the Revolutionary War. The younger Pike began his career as a supply officer at forts throughout the Midwest, a position that did not suit his ambitions. In July 1805, General James Wilkinson, governor of the Louisiana Territory, ordered the twenty-six-year-old Pike to follow the Mississippi to its northernmost point, note the region's unique physical features, and "attach [the Indians] to the United States."[7] One month later, he assembled twenty soldiers and headed north from St. Louis.[8] For Pike, the source was both an opportunity to advance his military career and a chance to leave his mark on America's landscape. But to do this, he had to enter uncharted territory.

Pike set forth knowing only, as one historian phrased it, that the source was near "the geographical center of the North American continent."[9] Pike—as well as Beltrami and Schoolcraft—would repeat this geographic fact in their narratives. As such, we might consider the source an unidentified and imagined "center out there," to use anthropologist Victor Turner's wording, since this seemingly insignificant location developed a magnetic allure in the minds of the explorers.[10] Interest in the source of the Mississippi was a relatively new development in Pike's time. In the eighteenth century, the source was a point of curiosity, but not a "center out there." To locate it, mapmakers appealed to their imaginations, the accounts of fur traders, or the wildly fanciful writings of Father Louis Hennepin, who claimed, among other things, to have canoed the entire river from the source to the gulf and back—in a matter of days.[11] In 1798, English surveyor David Thompson speculated that the source was at Turtle Lake, near Bemidji. "All the other little sources are reckoned to be subordinate to this, as they are longer in forming so considerable a stream."[12] He wrote nothing more on the subject. But by the dawn of the nineteenth century, the Mississippi River had become an iconic symbol of an expanding nation. Well-to-do domestic and foreign travelers eagerly took steamboat trips along its waters, convinced that there they would have a definitive experience of America. And while the Louis and Clark expedition revealed new people and landscapes to the west, the project of mapping

America also moved northward. It was in this context that the idea of the Great River's diminutive source became a matter of interest.[13]

Pike's expedition embodied both a national curiosity and a civil religious ambition to domesticate new territories. Thus competing images of "wilderness" and "civilization" appeared throughout his journal. Upon departure, Pike expressed his anxiety over the "arduous undertaking" ahead, which would take him beyond the boundaries "of civilized man" and into "an unknown wilderness."[14] Among the perceived disordering forces of the wilderness were foreign traders. "It is astonishing that there are not more murders and affrays at this place," he fumed. Traders, drunk on "spiderous liquors," had little moral sense in Pike's eyes. Moreover, he claimed that they convinced Indians that Americans were "a very vindictive, ferocious, and warlike people." Overcoming this perception, Pike theorized, would necessitate persuading the Indians to understand that his motives—and the motives of America—were "guided by magnanimity." He idealized an Indian population that would both "respect" and "fear" Americans.[15]

Without a pacified Indian population, however, Pike worried that the region would never become sufficiently civilized. America was the explorer's ideal for stability, and symbols of his homeland gave Pike a sense of security. As he neared Lake Pepin, Pike described a winding river, a clear lake, glorious hills, and the open prairie. Within view was an encampment of soldiers and traders who flew three U.S. flags. Pike called the sight "a contrast to the still and lifeless wilderness around." The flags were a welcome disruption in the wilderness, but only American flags elicited this response. On his return journey, the explorer came upon an establishment of the Northwest Company. The precise location of the border separating the United States from Canada was vague, but Canadian trading posts were common in the region, as were the British flags flying above them. Bristling at the sight of the Union Jack, Pike ordered his crew to shoot down the foreign flag and replace it with the Stars and Stripes. This civil religious performance of destruction and appropriation imposed a new symbol on top of an existing one. In doing so, Pike made America's boundaries known to both Indians and foreign traders—some of whom had been extraordinarily hospitable to Pike along his journey.[16]

For Pike, the American flag was a valued symbol of his homeland, a contrast to foreign forces, and a statement of authority. It was also a symbol of peace. When Pike spoke with a Chippewa chief and encouraged him to meet with the Sioux the following summer, he assured the chief that the meeting location would be marked with a U.S. flag, "as a proof of [the Sioux chief's] pacific disposition." The tribes had a long-standing feud in the region. In his journal, Pike wrote that the British government had no success in quelling this war. Americans, he boasted, would succeed with "the concurrence of the Almighty" in subduing "the brooding spirit of revenge . . . and the echoes of savage barbarity [resounding] through the wilderness."[17]

The wilderness, in Pike's view, was the domain of warring Indians, foreign traders, and foreign governments. It also sheltered an undefined source. By October snow began falling, his crew became ill, and Pike became plagued with "the fantastics of the brain, called ennui." He quickly relinquished his languor, but came to recognize "why so many persons, who have been confined to remote places, have acquired the habit of drinking to excess." This made Pike even more skeptical of traders. "It appears to me that the wealth of nations would not induce me to remain secluded from the society of civilized mankind, surrounded by a savage and unproductive wilderness, without book or other sources of intellectual enjoyment, or being blessed with the cultivated and feeling mind of a civilized female companion."[18]

Committed to his mission, Pike forged ahead and eventually arrived at what he hoped was the headwaters region. On February 1, 1806, after trudging through the snow to Leech Lake, Pike briefly surveyed the scene and surmised that he was at the "lower source" of the Mississippi. He speculated that Red Cedar Lake, which was just north of Leech Lake, was the "upper source." Ambiguity notwithstanding, Pike exclaimed, "I will not attempt to describe my feelings on the accomplishment of my voyage, for this is the main source of the Mississippi."[19]

With anticipation, hopefulness, and danger characterizing the expedition, Pike finally came to where he believed the river originated. To mark the occasion, he used the language of wonder. According to historian Robert Fuller, wonder is an inherently spiritual emotion evoked through encounters with the physical world that offer pathways for experiencing transcendent realms. For Pike, his expression of wonder was both a response to the landscape and a means of colonizing it. Leech Lake was now part of his American map. More explorers would come, and the map would change as a result. But with each, the language of wonder would serve a similar function, making meaning and imposing authority.[20]

Standing at "the most elevated part of the north-east continent of America," Pike marveled at his accomplishment. His stay at this "center out there" was short, due in large part to the horrendous weather and his battered physical condition. Still, Pike took credit for discovering the source, even though

Indians occupied the region and a Northwest Company trading post sat on the shore opposite to where the explorer arrived at Leech Lake. Pike went on to lead another expedition to the southwest, achieve the rank of brigadier general, and die during the War of 1812. But his 1810 travel journal would leave an enduring mark. Published in the United States four years prior to Lewis and Clark's travel account, Pike's journal also appeared in England (1811) and was translated into French (1812), Dutch (1812–13), and German (1813). The source of the Mississippi had gained national and international audiences.[21]

Explorers who followed Pike read carefully from his journal and even praised him. Giacomo Constantino Beltrami called Pike a "bold and enterprising man" who first penetrated the "wild and repulsive" headwaters region. Had the conditions been more hospitable, Beltrami speculated, Pike would have found the "true source." As it stood, though, the Mississippi's point of origin remained a mystery.[22] For Beltrami, and later Schoolcraft, the source had been an imagined sacred landscape with a mistaken location. This sense of uncertainty would propel both into the "wilderness."

"THESE SOURCES ARE THE ACTUAL SOURCES OF THE MISSISSIPPI!"

Compared with Pike and Schoolcraft, Beltrami's translations of the headwaters region filtered through the political, social, and religious lens of Europe. The forty-two-year-old citizen of the Venetian republic had served as a jurist under Napoleon Bonaparte. But when the French Empire began to crumble, Beltrami retreated to Filottrano, which was soon annexed by the Papal States. By refusing to swear an oath of allegiance, Beltrami fed suspicions that he was part of a secret revolutionary organization dedicated to unifying Italy. In 1821, he was exiled from Italy, and he began to travel. In 1828, he published an account of his travels, *A Pilgrimage in Europe and America*.[23] As the title would suggest, in an even more forthright manner than Pike, Beltrami's narrative describes a purposeful journey to an imagined "center out there." This center was a contested location, and Beltrami sought to discredit Pike's discovery and validate his own.

When he arrived in America, Beltrami had no intention of searching for the Mississippi's source, planning only to see the major sites. He landed in Philadelphia and continued on to Baltimore and Washington, D.C., where he claimed to have met President Monroe simply by walking into the White House, "a grand structure—the earnest of a transatlantic Rome." When Beltrami departed for New Orleans from St. Louis on a steamboat, he met an army general who told him about the Indians of the northern territories. This image of "savage" Indians, Beltrami wrote, "re-awakened a curiosity which I had always intended to gratify." Since the time of Columbus, Indian iconography and literature had generated great interest among European audiences, a transatlantic exchange that no doubt shaped Beltrami's image of Indians. This moreover motivated the adventurer to redirect his travel northward in an effort to discover the "true source" of the Mississippi. He knew that danger waited. Before he left, Beltrami attended a ball in St. Louis, "where the ladies were so pretty, and so well dressed." The scene, he continued, "made me forget that I was on the threshold of savage life."[24]

When he reached Minnesota, Beltrami traveled with an expedition that was mapping the Canadian boundary. He stayed briefly with the group, but soon departed along with two Chippewa guides, who then abandoned Beltrami after being ambushed by a band of Sioux. Recalling the event, Beltrami wrote, "I really can scarcely help shuddering . . . whenever I think of it. Fortunately, I was not at the time overpowered and confounded. . . . I soon even changed tragedy for comedy. I began by smiling at my singular adventures."[25] To use Dutch cultural historian Johan Huizinga's phrasing, Beltrami was "playing on the borderline between jest and earnest."[26] The tourist-turned-explorer frequently noted his counterintuitive sense of confidence. Admittedly not talented with a canoe, Beltrami pushed and pulled his craft through the shallow water. When the weather took a turn for the worse, he covered his belongings with a red silk umbrella, a colorful display that confounded a passing party of Indians. Beltrami reported that he should have feared for his life, but instead he felt "no apprehension whatsoever." Moreover, it was at this point, immersed in "solitude," when the explorer expressed qualified admiration of the Indians, whose "genuine independence" had eluded Europeans. He understood "why the Indians consider themselves happier than cultivated nations."[27]

Here, Beltrami repeated a common trend in European travel literature, the use of Indians to critique European political distress.[28] The landscape, though, evoked positive images of acquaintances in his homeland. As he passed through the region, Beltrami recalled family and friends when renaming the lakes. "Alexander, Lavinius, Everard, Frederica, Adela, Magdalena, Virginia, and Eleonora. The purity of the waters of these lakes I considered a correct image of that of *their* minds; and their union reminded me of the affection by which members of this happy family are so tenderly connected." Then he "entered a noble lake" with "no other issue than the river's entrance and discharge." The "sublime" site "on the highest land of North America" filled Beltrami with an "almost heavenly ecstasy!" "THESE SOURCES ARE THE ACTUAL SOURCES OF THE MISSISSIPPI!" he exclaimed. "This is a work which belongs to the Creator of it alone to explain. . . . We can only adore in silence his omnipotent hand." If confronted with this sight, Beltrami continued, "the most determined infidel would be compelled to admit the existence of a Supreme Being." He then estimated that the "sublime temple" before him "dwarfed the monuments of antiquity. . . . [Even] the august temple of the Vatican" could not "excite . . . sentiments of faith and piety so perfect and profound as those inspired by the present enchanting, transcendant, and prodigious creations of divine omnipotence!" He named it Lake Julia, after the Countess of Albany, "the respectable lady whose life . . . *was one undeviating course of moral rectitude, and whose death was a calamity to all who had the happiness of knowing her;* and the recollection of whom is incessantly connected with veneration and grief by all who can properly appreciate beneficence and virtue." Beltrami then imagined Columbus, Vespucci, and Marco Polo standing together, marking this "high and solemn" moment and reveling that "one of their countrymen" had made this discovery.[29]

Instead of raising a flag, Beltrami's civil religious expression mapped the headwaters through a mix of wonder, European nationalism, and Christianity. He straddled different places and times, connecting his immediate location to his homeland, and relating his present discovery to discoveries from the past. Beltrami had no interest in colonizing the source on behalf of America. But he did write Christianity into his story of the headwaters. And Christianity was, in the minds of Americans and Europeans, a requirement of civilization. When returning on the Mississippi to New Orleans, Beltrami reflected, "nothing, in my opinion, resembles . . . the course of this great river as the career of that extraordinary *man* [Christ] who, originating in obscurity, exhibited a brilliant course of glory, and was at length entombed in the ocean of his own triumphs."[30]

Beltrami published his travel account in both New Orleans and London, no doubt hoping to attract the same fame that came to Pike. While garnering brief acclaim, the book nonetheless sold poorly. Academics and mapmakers picked apart Beltrami's claims, providing ammunition to one journalist who dismissed the "ridiculous Italian" who had left behind only "laughable stories . . . told on the frontier."[31] In 1826, Beltrami returned to Europe and wandered between London, Heidelberg, and Paris. He died in Italy in 1855, and his mark on America might have ended there. In 1866, however, the State

Historical Society of Minnesota established Beltrami County, which encompassed the area that he had explored.[32] The Italian's discovery, while ultimately discredited, became part of Itasca's history of mistaken discoveries.

Lifting the "Veil of Obscurity"

Unlike Pike and Beltrami, who stumbled into their expeditions to the source, Henry Rowe Schoolcraft had long been attracted to the Mississippi and its headwaters. His first encounter with the river was on July 1, 1818, while traveling the Ohio River. "The morning was calm and serene," he wrote, "scarcely a cloud obscured the atmosphere, and the sun rose majestically above the horizon, clothing in light the most sublime and beautiful scene."[33] Two years later, Schoolcraft accompanied the governor of the Michigan Territory, Leon Cass, on an expedition through the headwaters region. Schoolcraft recalled reaching what would become Cass Lake. While some of his companions believed that they were at the source, traders in the area informed them that it was sixty miles ahead at Elk Lake. This was unfamiliar territory, Schoolcraft explained, no doubt fraught with treacherous rapids, deep lakes, and thick swamps. "Anxious as all were to see the actual source of so celebrated a stream," Schoolcraft wrote, they chose not to continue, thus leaving a "veil of obscurity . . . cast about the actual source of the Mississippi."[34]

Schoolcraft would have another opportunity to lift this "veil of obscurity." In 1822, Cass appointed Schoolcraft an Indian agent in the Michigan Territory at Sault Sainte Marie, where he would meet and marry Jane Johnson. Her father was a prominent trader, and her mother was the daughter of a Chippewa chief. From his wife and in-laws, Schoolcraft learned about the region's culture, language, religion, and history.[35] When Cass became secretary of war and conflicts reignited between the Chippewa and Sioux, he commissioned Schoolcraft to quell the violence. "It is no less the dictate of humanity than of policy to repress this feeling [of hostility] and to establish permanent peace among these tribes," Cass wrote to Schoolcraft.

American efforts to pacify this Indian war had limited efficacy. Treaties had been signed, forts built, and boundaries established. The conflict continued.[36] Still, Schoolcraft was optimistic about his chances to dampen the violence. He also hoped to satisfy his curiosity about Elk Lake. As he departed on his journey, Schoolcraft decided that Elk Lake—if it was the source—required a name change. He settled on "Itasca," derived from the Latin words *veritas* and *caput* ("true head"). But discovering the headwaters was not an objective of the expedition. Schoolcraft made only passing reference to the source in his letters to the War Department. When he finally reached the source, he stayed for less than four hours. Yet this unauthorized and brief experience was central to Schoolcraft's 1834 account, *Narrative of an Expedition through the Upper Mississippi River to Itasca Lake.* "American geography may be said to have three important problems to solve, in modern times," he wrote in the introduction. Lewis and Clark had solved the first two, the source of the Missouri River and the termination of the Columbia. Left undetermined, however, was the source of the Mississippi. Similar to those who came before him, Schoolcraft discredited all previous discoveries and hoped that he would join the ranks of his nation's great explorers.[37]

Schoolcraft's expedition symbolized an extension of American power, images, and ideals into the headwaters region. Moreover, his civil religious discourse had a distinct evangelical Protestant edge. Prior to his marriage, Schoolcraft described himself as an Enlightenment rationalist, viewing the Bible as a moral guide rather than a revealed text. But while in Sault, he developed an interest in matters of faith, particularly after his son died in the winter of 1830. Schoolcraft soon converted and joined a Presbyterian church in Detroit. In a letter to his wife, he speculated that this conversion would influence "all of my future acts."[38] True to form, Schoolcraft went to great lengths to Christianize his 1832 expedition to the source. While preparing for departure, he wrote to the American Board of Commissioners for Foreign Missions, asserting that Indians in the area required "the introduction of Christianity." Political progress would not come without "moral" improvement, he averred, and any material advancements were "useless" unless the "Indian mind can be purified by gospel truth." Indians, Schoolcraft surmised, held close the corrosive "sin of a belief in magic, and from idolatry and spirit-worship." He concluded by requesting that Rev. William T. Boutwell accompany the expedition to this "very attractive field for evangelical observation."[39]

Boutwell joined the expedition, but his opinions of Indian life and culture were anything but favorable. In his journal, Boutwell described a Sunday evening when, while he was reading *Pilgrim's Progress,* a noisy ritual dance disrupted his quiet. He then complained that the "French half-breed voyagers" from the expedition participated in the Indian dance. In Boutwell's mind, the voyagers were "more hopeless than the Indians." One Sunday, he witnessed "[confusion] and profanity among the soldiers." Boutwell soon recognized that the voyagers were celebrating a Catholic holy day by, among other things, playing horseshoes. "Never was I before so sensible of the laxity of Catholic principles." The religion of the voyagers, he continued, "allows wicked men to live as they wish and trample upon one of the sacred institutions of God, the holy Sabbath."[40]

Unlike the rather dour observations of Boutwell, Schoolcraft scarcely mentioned the voyagers. His descriptions of church services focused on the Indians, who paid "strict attention" to Boutwell's sermons. Such religious instruction was greatly needed, the explorer believed, since Indians lived in "fragile" societies "ready to tumble on the application of the slightest power." In contrast to "the idolatrous nations of Asia and Africa," Indians "have no list of imaginary gods." Still, Schoolcraft admitted that "gross forms of idolatry" did exist. "They impute supernatural powers to certain material substances, which are preserved and guarded with religious care." He then claimed to have had conversations with Indians who admitted to the spiritual "insufficiency" of their practices. This indicated for Schoolcraft that the population was prepared to "embrace the doctrine of the Savior."[41]

Schoolcraft's treatment of Indians was both hopeful and paternalistic. Their "superstitions" made them part of a chaotic wilderness, but he believed that Christian instruction could better colonize this territory. Traders were another matter. At Leech Lake, the expedition came upon a trading post where a clerk informed Schoolcraft that posts just outside of American boundaries distributed British flags and "ardent spirits" to Indians. While British traders were not crossing the border, the clerk qualified, "I have heard that they took away an American flag given to an Indian on the United States' boarders . . . tore it, and burnt it, and gave him a British flag instead."[42] The rumor only fed Schoolcraft's outstanding contempt for the perceived foreign interlopers. Presenting himself as an expert on the history and culture of the region, Schoolcraft asserted that the fur industry was "intimately blended with the civil history of the country." What the French and English could never do, however, was enact a lasting peace between the Indians. Schoolcraft resolved that America would succeed because of the nation's superior moral posture. Traders used alcohol to conduct business with Indians, which in his view was an unqualified "evil." Schoolcraft lauded his government for banning the use of liquor for trading in Indian country and bemoaned the British for not following suit. "Posterity will probably regard this measure as reflecting more honor upon our national legislation, than if we had decreed a hundred monuments to fallen greatness."[43]

Along with traders and Indian superstition, alcohol was, for Schoolcraft, another profaning force in the headwaters region. But this was a relatively new position for the explorer. When serving as the territorial governor, Cass refused to enforce War Department orders banning the use of liquor for trading. Schoolcraft followed Cass's lead, choosing to look away when the American Fur Company openly used liquor as currency. In 1831, after Schoolcraft converted, he joined a temperance society. A rival accused him of breaking the society's pledge and distributing rum rations to his unchurched and Catholic voyagers. The event was disruptive enough that Schoolcraft imposed a ban on liquor for his expedition to the source.[44]

To examine Schoolcraft's expedition, one finds imprints of the era's most significant social forces, to include temperance, the growth of evangelical Protestantism, international tensions with America's neighbor to the north, and ongoing conflicts between Protestants and Catholics. But the quest to "discover" an undiscovered source dominated the narrative. As he neared the lake that he would call Itasca, Schoolcraft described laboring through forest and several thick swamps. While speculating that he was at the highest point in North America, he imagined himself joining other great explorers, most notably La Salle, who had reached the Mississippi's mouth nearly a century and a half prior. Then he saw it. "What had been long sought, at last appeared suddenly. On turning out of a thicket, into a small weedy opening, the cheering sight of a transparent body of water burst upon our view. It was Itasca Lake—the source of the Mississippi." Schoolcraft's words indicate that a feeling of wonder and the mere sight of Itasca certified the source's authenticity. His emotional response to the landscape would soon find an accompanying civil religious gesture. Schoolcraft quickly surveyed the area, collected plant and animal samples, and prepared to leave, "[but not] without leaving some memorial, however frail, of our visit." Members of the expedition erected a flag on an island in the middle of the lake. According to Schoolcraft, as they left, the entire party fixed its gaze on this national emblem.[45]

The expedition's mapmaker, Lieutenant James Allen, offered a less illustrative description of the discovery. The portage to the source "presented a picture of landscape more dismal and gloomy than any other part of this miserably poor country that we had seen." The animal life seemed nonexistent, and even flies were scarce. Then he saw "the *true source* of the great river" and noticed the entire expedition's "great satisfaction." Allen wrote very little more about Itasca. But he did note the contributions of their "intelligent" Indian guide, Oza Winib, or Yellow Head. To be sure, the Chippewa did draw praise from Schoolcraft. When they returned to Cass Lake, Schoolcraft presented Yellow Head with a flag and a presidential medal for his services. But the explorer more typically portrayed his Indian guide as a servant. When Yellow Head volunteered for the expedition, Schoolcraft quoted the Indian as saying, "My father, the country you are going to see, is my hunting ground. . . . I will myself furnish the maps you have requested, and will guide you onward."[46]

Using Indians as a means to an end would become a habit for Schoolcraft. After the expedition, he proceeded to portray himself as a leading authority on American Indians. Schoolcraft organized the Algic Society, which proposed to collect information on Indian life, language, culture, and religion for the benefit of missionaries. Similar to nearly all of Schoolcraft's ventures, the society barely functioned. By the mid-1840s, Schoolcraft's first wife had died and he had lost his position with the Agency of Indian Affairs after having been found guilty of misusing treaty monies for land speculations. Hoping to improve his finances, Schoolcraft republished his travel accounts with modified details. Among his most notorious revisions was a claim that Itasca was the name of a mythological Indian maiden who had lost her love and wept the tears that created the lake. As Schoolcraft's biographer has written, "[there] is not a word of truth in this version."[47] While Schoolcraft's 1832 account did not explain Itasca's Latin origin, newspaper articles published that year did.[48] And in 1880, Boutwell confessed that he had supplied Schoolcraft with the name.[49]

Schoolcraft died in 1864, but controversy over the source's physical location continued. In 1875, the United States Land Survey affirmed that Itasca was the source of the Mississippi.[50] Six years later, however, Willard Glazier suggested that a small lake just south of Itasca was the true source. His travel account drew brief national attention, but soon lost credibility when opponents determined that Glazier plagiarized from Schoolcraft. In 1889, Itasca State Park's first commissioner, Jacob V. Brower, published a definitive report validating Schoolcraft's map. Brower simply referred to Glazier as a "disreputable and insignificant plagiarist."[51]

CONCLUSION

"At what point in its course does the Mississippi become what the Mississippi *means*," asked T. S. Eliot.[52] A question with no definitive answer, the river and its source continue to mean new things. This essay has brought us to the smallest point of the Great River and, from here, we have seen how the source has both shaped, and been shaped by, American and European civil religious discourses. Through movement, maps, and feelings of wonder, explorers plotted physical and ideological boundaries around the source—boundaries that included some, excluded others, and continued to shift in the coming decades.

As lumber became a valued commodity in the late nineteenth century, sides formed over who owned the tall, stout pines of the headwaters region. "Itasca Lake and its preservation is sacred and dear to every American heart," proclaimed Minnesota governor Knute Nelson in 1895, speaking before state lawmakers. Four years prior, the governor recalled, the legislature had "acted wisely" when they voted to protect nearly 20,000 acres of land that became Itasca State Park. Private landowners nearby, however, had hinted that they would soon sell off their timber, "and thus the whole area will become a burnt, black and desert waste." Nelson demanded that "the lake and all its beautiful environment should . . . be kept intact in its primitive and normal condition" and that the legislature should buy up these lands. The governor's plea went unheard. In 1905, Itasca's first commissioner, Jacob V. Brower, reminded Governor Samuel R. Van Sant that the park had been "in an admirable condition of perfect preservation" when his term began. The "glistening picturesque lake," however, was under siege. Nearby logging had caused fires and floods and damaged the western shoreline. The lake, Brower explained, was "an emblem and promise of continuity in the sacred preservation to the whole body of a vast rapidly increasing nation." As such, it was the governor's duty to protect it. It was not until 1921 that the state purchased the remaining segments of cutover timberlands and, as historian Steve Hall summarized, "the age of conservation had become entrenched in the park."[53]

While explorers sought to stabilize the wilderness, conservationists wanted to protect it. But this was a different time. Explorers, animated by a national impulse to expand and domesticate, replaced and redefined the maps of Indians and traders. Now conservationists were taking their turn.

The conservationists of the early twentieth century helped make Itasca a state park. At this time, state and national parks appeared elsewhere in America, but Itasca was unique.[54] Yellowstone, the Grand Canyon, Niagara Falls, and the Adirondacks protrude from the American map and draw visitors who expect to experience a sublime vision of magnitude and grandeur.[55] In contrast, Itasca State Park enshrines a small trickle of water. Like the source of the Ganges, though, this little stream is a big attraction. Despite its remote location, more than 500,000 people arrive at the park each summer. A noted landmark at Itasca is a rock bridge that straddles the channel where the Mississippi's first waters spill forth. Scarce is the visitor who does not shed his or her shoes and walk across it. "I grew up thinking of it as a rite of passage, somewhere between baptism and confirmation," quipped one Minnesotan. Constructed in the 1930s, the Civilian Conservation Corps built the rock bridge after redirecting the channel to its present location, away from a marshy and inaccessible area.[56] As we have seen, relocation is nothing new for the source. Much as the waters of the Mississippi defiantly create new pathways through Minnesota and the nation, so too does the meaning of this unstable sacred landscape.

Notes

1. James Rennell, *Memoir of a Map of Hindoostan* (London: M. Brown, 1788), 233.

2. J. A. Hodgson, "Journal of a Survey to the Heads of the Rivers, Ganges and Jumna," *Asiatick Researches* 14 (1822): 118.

3. Steven G. Darian, *The Ganges in Myth and History* (New Delhi: Motilal Banarsidass, [1978] 2001), xiii; Flavius Josephus, *The New Complete Works of Josephus,* trans. William Whiston (Grand Rapids, MI: Kregel Publications), 51. See also Stephen A. Barney et al., eds., *The Etymologies of Isidore of Seville* (New York: Cambridge University Press, 2006), 280.

4. Brian K. Pennington, *Was Hinduism Invented? Britons, Indians, and the Colonial Construction of Religion* (New York: Oxford University Press, 2005); Michael Mann, "'Torchbearers upon the Path of Progress': Britain's Ideology of a 'Moral and Material Progress' in India," in *Colonialism as Civilizing Mission: Cultural Ideology in British India,* ed. Harald Fischer-Tiné and Michael Mann (New York: Anthem Press, 2004).

5. Mark Twain, *Life on the Mississippi* (New York: Penguin, [1875] 1980), preface.

6. On definitional debates surrounding civil religion, see James A. Mathisen, "Twenty Years after Bellah: Whatever Happened to American Civil Religion," *Sociological Analysis* 50, no. 2 (1989). For an updated assessment of the civil religion discussion, see Marcella Cristi, *From Civil Religion to Political Religion: The Intersection of Culture, Religion, and Politics* (Waterloo, Canada: Wilfrid Laurier University Press, 2001). This article reflects more of Cristi's definition of civil religion. "Civil religion," she writes, "tends to sacralize certain aspects of civil life by means of public rituals and collective ceremonies. In so doing, beliefs and behaviors, acquire a 'religious' dimension. As such, civil religion may be considered a belief system or a surrogate religion that expresses the self-identity of a collectivity. Yet, like secular ideologies of different kinds, civil religion may also attempt to force group identity and to legitimize an existing political order, by injecting a transcendental dimension or a religious gloss on the justification." Unlike definitions of civil religion that assume widespread consensus, then, Cristi recognizes that a civil religion represents one point of view, and sometimes suppresses opposition.

7. Letter from James Wilkinson to Pike, July 30, 1805, quoted in Zebulon M. Pike, *Exploratory Travels through the Western Territories of North America* (Denver: W. H. Lawrence, [1811] 1889), xvii.

8. W. Eugene Hollon, *The Lost Pathfinder: Zebulon Montgomery Pike* (Norman: University of Oklahoma Press, 1949), 3–20, 54–72.

9. Walter Havighurst, *Upper Mississippi: A Wilderness Saga* (New York: Farrar and Rinehart, 1937), 4.

10. Victor Turner, "The Center Out There: Pilgrim's Goal," *History of Religions* 12, no. 3 (1973).

11. John O. Anfinson, *The River We Have Wrought: A History of the Upper Mississippi* (Minneapolis: University of Minnesota Press, 2003); and Timothy Severin, *Explorers of the Mississippi* (Minneapolis: University of Minnesota Press, [1967] 2002).

12. Joseph B. Tyrrell, ed., *David Thompson's Narrative of His Explorations in Western America, 1784–1812* (Toronto: Champlain Society, 1916), 269.

13. Thomas Ruys Smith, *River of Dreams: Imagining the Mississippi before Mark Twain* (Baton Rouge: Louisiana State University Press, 2007), 79–110.

14. Pike, *Exploratory Travels through the Western Territories of North America*, 114.

15. Ibid., 42, 37.

16. Ibid., 52, 95; Severin, *Explorers of the Mississippi*, 254–56.

17. Pike, *Exploratory Travels through the Western Territories of North America*, 109, 132. I have chosen to identify these tribes as Chippewa and Sioux rather than Ojibway and Dakota because the narratives each do.

18. Ibid., 67, 91.

19. Ibid., 92.

20. Robert C. Fuller, *Wonder: From Emotion to Spirituality* (Chapel Hill: University of North Carolina Press, 2006). Shaping my thinking on the amalgam of meaning, power, and colonial expansion as they relate to travel is Thomas A. Tweed, *Crossing and Dwelling: A Theory of Religion* (Cambridge, MA: Harvard University Press, 2006), 37, 111, 132.

21. Pike, *Exploratory Travels through the Western Territories of North America*, 94; Mark L. Gardner, "Introduction," in *The Southwestern Journals of Zebulon Pike, 1806–1807*, ed. Stephen Harding Hart, Archer Butler Hulbert, and Mark L. Gardner (Albuquerque: University of New Mexico Press, 2006), 46.

22. Giacomo Constantino Beltrami, *A Pilgrimage in Europe and America* (London: Hunt and Clarke, 1828), 445.

23. Severin, *Explorers of the Mississippi*, 258–77; Augusto P. Miceli, *The Man with the Red Umbrella: Giacomo Constantino Beltrami in America* (Baton Rouge: Claitor's Publishing, 1974).

24. Beltrami, *A Pilgrimage*, 53, 101, 124; Dagmar Wernitznig, *Europe's Indians, Indians in Europe: European Perceptions and Appropriations of Native American Cultures from Pocahontas to the Present* (Lanham, MD: University Press of America, 2007).

25. Beltrami, *A Pilgrimage*, 369, 380–81.

26. Johan Huizinga, *Homo Ludens: A Study of the Play-Element in Culture* (Boston: Beacon Press, 1955), 5.

27. Beltrami, *A Pilgrimage*, 387, 389.

28. Richard Slotkin, *Regeneration through Violence: The Mythology of the American Frontier, 1600–1860* (Middletown, CT: Wesleyan University Press, 1973), 371.

29. Beltrami, *A Pilgrimage*, 402, 408, 413, 410, 414.

30. Ibid., 543.

31. *New York American,* July 19, 1834, quoted in *Schoolcraft's Expedition to Lake Itasca: The Discovery of the Source of the Mississippi,* ed. Philip P. Mason (East Lansing: Michigan State University Press, [1958] 1993), 360.

32. Miceli, *The Man with the Red Umbrella: Giacomo Constantino Beltrami in America,* 141–44.

33. Henry Rowe Schoolcraft, *A View of the Lead Mines of Missouri* (New York: Charles Wiley, 1819), 221.

34. Mason, ed., *Schoolcraft's Expedition,* 5.

35. Richard G. Bremer, *Indian Agent and Wilderness Scholar: The Life of Henry Rowe Schoolcraft* (Mount Pleasant: Clarke Historical Library, Central Michigan University, 1987), 91–104.

36. Mason, ed., *Schoolcraft's Expedition,* xix; Bremer, *Indian Agent,* 121–23.

37. Mason, ed., *Schoolcraft's Expedition,* 3.

38. Quoted in Bremer, *Indian Agent,* 113.

39. Letter from Henry Rowe Schoolcraft to Rev. David Greene, Corresponding Secretary, American Board of Foreign Missions, Sault St. Marie, February 25, 1832, in *Schoolcraft's Expedition,* ed. Mason, 136.

40. Ibid., 332, 317, 326, 311.

41. Ibid., 43.

42. Ibid., 19.

43. Ibid., 21, 28. Congress passed the law mentioned in 1832. See Francis Paul Prucha, ed., *Documents of United States Indian Policy,* 3rd ed. (Lincoln: University of Nebraska Press, 2000), 62.

44. Bremer, *Indian Agent,* 127–29.

45. Ibid., 35, 38.

46. Ibid., 202, 203, 25, 45.

47. Richard G. Bremer, "Henry Rowe Schoolcraft: Explorer in the Mississippi Valley, 1818–1832," *Wisconsin Magazine of History* 66, no. 1 (1982): 56.

48. *Detroit Journal and Michigan Advertiser,* September 26, 1832; *Detroit Free Press and Michigan Intelligencer,* October 25, 1832.

49. Letter from W. T. Boutwell to Julius Chambers, Stillwater, MN, July 27, 1880, in *Schoolcraft's Expedition,* ed. Mason, 351.

50. N. H. Winchell, "The Source of the Mississippi," *Minnesota Historical Society* 8 (1898).

51. Jacob V. Brower, *Itasca State Park: An Illustrated History* (St. Paul: Minnesota Historical Society, 1904).

52. T. S. Eliot, "Introduction to *The Adventures of Huckleberry Finn,*" in *Huckleberry Finn: Text, Sources, and Criticism,* ed. Kenneth S. Lynn (New York: Harcourt, Brace, and World, [1950] 1961), 202.

53. Quoted in Brower, *Itasca State Park,* xvi, xxii. On Nelson's time as governor and his ordeals with the timber industry, see Millard L. Gieske and Steven J. Keillor, *Norwegian Yankee: Knute Nelson and the Failure of American Politics, 1860–1923* (Northfield, MN: Norwegian-American Historical Association, 1995), 173–98. On the conflicts surrounding logging near the headwaters, see Steve Hall, *Itasca: Source of America's Greatest River* (St. Paul: Minnesota Historical Society, 1982), 24.

54. Richard West Sellars, *Preserving Nature in the National Parks: A History* (New Haven, CT: Yale University Press, 1999), 7–27.

55. See John F. Sears, *Sacred Places: American Tourist Attractions in the Nineteenth Century* (Amherst: University of Massachusetts Press, [1989] 1998); John Gatta,

Making Nature Sacred: Literature, Religion, and Environment in America from the Puritans to the Present (New York: Oxford University Press, 2004); Anne Farrar Hyde, *An American Vision: Far Western Landscape and National Culture, 1820–1920* (New York: New York University Press, 1990); and Marguerite S. Shaffer, *See America First: Tourism and National Identity, 1880–1940* (Washington, D.C.: Smithsonian Institution Press, 2001).

56. Beth Gauper, "For Generations Itasca Has Been a Sacred Spot," *Saint Paul Pioneer Press*, September 26, 2005; Hall, *Itasca: Source of America's Greatest River.*

4

Looking for the New Jerusalem

ANTEBELLUM NEW RELIGIOUS MOVEMENTS
AND THE MISSISSIPPI RIVER

Thomas Ruys Smith

> You wouldn't like to be concerned in the New Jerusalem, would you? . . . It
> stands on the Mississippi
>   —Herman Melville, *The Confidence Man,* 1857

In 1830, in common with many of his contemporaries, Lyman Beecher was looking to the West. As he described in a letter to his daughter Catherine, what he saw in that direction was of the utmost importance: "The moral destiny of the nation, and all our institutions and hopes, and the world's hopes, turn on the character of the West." Beecher himself was about to transplant his family to Cincinnati in order "to spend the remnant of my days in that great conflict, and in consecrating all my children to God in that region who are willing to go." The stakes were high, and Beecher was resolute about the potential significance of the struggle that waited for him there: "If we gain the West, all is safe; if we lose it, all is lost . . . this is not with me a transient flash of feeling, but a feeling as if the great battle is to be fought in the Valley of the Mississippi."[1]

In many ways, Beecher was right: throughout the antebellum years the Mississippi valley was a spiritual battlefield. Given the role that the Mississippi River played in popular thought, this is perhaps unsurprising. On the one hand, it was commonplace to think and write about the Mississippi River in theological terms. As Alexis de Tocqueville marveled in 1835, "The valley watered by the Mississippi seems to have been created for it alone; it dispenses good and evil at will, and it is like the valley's god." "The Mississippi Valley," he continued, "is all in all, the most magnificent dwelling that God has ever prepared for the habitation of man."[2] It was also commonplace to think of the river in biblical terms. In particular, the Mississippi was often asserted to be, in Zadok Cramer's words in 1814, "this Nile of North America"—a description that brought with it a variety of associations.[3]

For all the typology, it was also common to think of the river frontier as a location in dire need of spiritual reformation. As missionary Timothy Flint admitted in the early nineteenth century, "This whole region . . . wears an aspect of irreligion."[4] The spiritual vacuum did not last for long: the western rivers were subject to a flood of preachers and circuit riders in the antebellum years. Presbyterians, Methodists, Baptists, and an assortment of Protestant evangelists all made their presence felt in the area. In his autobiography, pioneering Methodist circuit rider Peter Cartwright wondered at "the insurmountable disadvantages and difficulties that the early pioneer Methodist preachers labored under in spreading the Gospel in these Western wilds in the great valley of the Mississippi."[5] As William Henry Milburn noted in 1860, the separate denominations generally coexisted in a "sort of pugnacious rivalry or 'free fight'" that was characteristic of the frontier: "There is an active, rough, resolute courage, independence, and pluck about the western people, which inclines them to close scuffling and grappling . . . and their clergy are not free from the same peculiarities."[6] But their influence was profound. The frontier sermonizing of popular figures like Peter Cartwright, Lorenzo Dow, and Barton Stone helped to drive what David S. Reynolds has described as "a widespread shift of popular religious discourse from the doctrinal to the imaginative." In their wake, "popular sermon style . . . came to be dominated by diverting narrative, extensive illustrations, and even colloquial humor."[7]

As influential as these pioneering preachers undoubtedly were, they only tell part of the story of religion along the western rivers in the antebellum years. For alongside the evangelizing of the major denominations, the river frontier was also a very fertile environment for new religious movements. Despite their numerous doctrinal differences, they were united by a common trajectory—one that was entirely characteristic of the age and in keeping with the movement of the nation. They tended to ferment in the "Burned-Over District" of New York State, an area, in Whitney Cross's words, "extraordinarily given to unusual religious beliefs, peculiarly devoted to crusades aimed at the perfection of mankind and the attainment of millennial happiness."[8] They then followed the line of emigration, traveling down the Ohio until reaching the Mississippi—and, sometimes, stepping across into the Far West, moving into new territories offering the freedom of isolation. In the early antebellum years, the river retained enough of a frontier quality—and enough mystery—to call strongly to such groups. As Timothy Flint explained when he traveled to the river in 1816: "The Mississippi . . . at that time was to the great proportion of the American people, as it was to us, the 'ultima Thule'—a limit almost to the range of thought."[9]

While the beliefs and practices of these new religious groups often seemed far removed from the mainstream, it is important to remember that the first half of the nineteenth century was an era marked by utopian dreams. While the various pilgrims who were drawn to the river added a visionary—if not fanatical—spice to such schemes, they also crystalized ideas about the Mississippi valley that were nascent in antebellum culture—in particular, the idea that the New Jerusalem which would stand at the heart of the American Millennium would be found on the Mississippi itself. This notion, though apparently the province of extremists, was in many ways an inevitable extension of secular hopes for the Mississippi valley. As early as 1792, for example, Gilbert Imlay was giving a millennial flavor to his economic hopes for the territory of the western rivers—a vision which, in the end, proved to be no less chimerical than the hope for a New Jerusalem: "while we are likely to live in the regions of perpetual peace, our felicity will receive a zest from the activity and variety of our trade. . . . Thus in the centre of the earth, governing by the laws of reason and humanity, we seem calculated to become at once the emporium and protectors of the world."[10] New religious movements were therefore more expressive of national conceptions of the Mississippi valley than may be immediately apparent.

It was the quest for a New Jerusalem, with very different results, which drove Isaac Bullard's Vermont Pilgrims on their journey to the river in 1817 and Joseph Smith's Mormons to their temporary home on the Mississippi in Nauvoo in 1839. The river also witnessed the millennial expectations of the Millerites in the 1840s, when the idea of apocalypse on the Mississippi—that potent symbol of nationhood—seems to have carried particular significance. In turn, the conceptions of the river found in the beliefs and actions of these new religious movements were disseminated throughout popular culture in a variety of forms and reached audiences throughout the nation. Their distinctive stories can tell us a great deal about both the nature of the Mississippi's religious meaning in the antebellum imagination and the role of the river in the formation of antebellum new religious movements. As Timothy Flint concluded in 1825, "Let none think that the age of fanaticism has gone by."[11]

"Southwest to find the New Jerusalem":
Isaac Bullard and the Pilgrims

Even in the early years of the nineteenth century, prophets were nothing new along the western rivers. In his autobiography, pioneering Methodist circuit rider Rev. James B. Finley recorded that a variety of "new isms"—characterized by him as a "train of evils"—entered the Ohio valley at this time, particularly in the wake of the Cane Ridge revival in Kentucky in 1801. Notable amongst these new prophets, for example, was Abel Sargent, a former Universalist who appeared along the Ohio early in the new century "with twelve disciples—all women." Finley remembered, "It was spread over the country that he was inspired and conversed with angels daily, from whom he received revelations."[12] Rev. Peter Cartwright encountered him at Marietta on the Ohio River in 1807 and debunked one of his miracles: "Sargent got some powder, and lit a cigar, and then walked down to the bank of the river, one hundred yards, where stood a large stump. He put his powder on the stump, and touched it with his cigar. The flash of the powder was seen by many at the camp. . . . He said God had come down to him in a flash of light, and he fell under the power of God, and thus received his vision. . . . I walked up to the stump, and called on the people to come and see for themselves. The people rushed up, and soon saw through the trick, and began to abuse Sargent for a vile imposter."[13] Still, both circuit riders recorded that the devotion of one of Sargent's followers was so profound that he attempted to "fast as long as the Savior did—forty days and forty nights . . . and persisted in abstaining from food for sixteen days, when he died. The halcyon declared that he would resuscitate himself after three days, and they kept his body till decomposition had progressed so far that they were compelled to bury it out of their sight."[14]

While the early river frontier proved to be a fertile location for a variety of similar new religious movements, one group in particular—described by F. Gerald Ham as "the most bizarre and primitive sect in American religious history"—and their journey to and along the Mississippi in 1817 serves as a microcosm for larger religious developments along the antebellum western rivers.[15] Indeed, as Stephen J. Stein has argued, "The Vermont Pilgrims are only a footnote in the pages of religious history, but they embody patterns typical of alternative religious communities in the United States." The Pilgrims were led by Isaac Bullard (sometimes given as Buller), a man more commonly referred to simply as the Prophet. In essence, they were animated by many of the same desires as more conventional religious groups of this period. In Stein's description, "The Prophet denounced the established churches of the day as corrupt and sinful. He hoped to restore a pure and simple Christianity, free of creeds, rituals, and sacraments."[16] It was the manner of their devotion that most shocked onlookers. As Flint describes, "it was a maxim with them to wear the clothes as long as they would last on the body, without washing or changing. . . . They made it a point, in short, to be as ragged and dirty as might be." They also rejected a conventional diet: "Their food was mush and milk, prepared in a trough, and they sucked it up, standing erect, through a perforated stalk of cane."[17] Apparently originating in Canada, the Pilgrims spent some time in the vicinity of Woodstock, Vermont, before embarking on their voyage to the Promised Land of the Mississippi valley in the summer of 1817. Josiah Morrow records, "In all, about one hundred persons started, under his leadership, for the Promised Land. The Prophet stood his cane upright and let it fall. Thus was indicated the direction they should go. The cane always fell toward the Southwest."[18]

While traveling through New York, the Pilgrims came in contact with another significant group of religious outsiders. They stayed with the Shakers of New Lebanon for a brief period, during which time the two groups argued about their separate modes of belief. The Pilgrims were obdurate that they would "cleave to their dirt, rags, laziness and wives, and that they ought to go due southwest to find the New Jerusalem."[19] When the Pilgrims left the Shakers, their pilgrimage to the Mississippi began in earnest. Finally reaching the Ohio River at Cincinnati, Zadock Thompson recorded that "they sold their wagon, took boats, and proceeded down the river, and a more filthy, lousy, squalid and miserable set of beings the world never saw." When the party eventually reached the Mississippi, their fortunes swiftly took a turn for the worse. "From this time," Thompson explained, "their number rapidly diminished. Many died by sickness produced by hardship and privation, and others abandoned the company to avoid the same catastrophe."[20] But their search for a New Jerusalem was still very much in evidence.

They made landfall at New Madrid, Missouri, on the Mississippi, making an extraordinary impression on its inhabitants: "they walked ashore in Indian file, the old men in front, then the women, and the children in the rear. They chanted a kind of tune, as they walked, the burden of which was 'Praise God! Praise God!'" As Flint described, their extraordinary appearance and behavior "had in it something imposing to a people, like those of the West, strongly governed by feelings and impressions." But New Madrid was not to serve as a New Jerusalem. They headed downriver, and disease and starvation traveled with them. Numerous Pilgrims died; others deserted. They stayed for some time on Pilgrim Island, approximately thirty miles below New Madrid, but their fortunes did not improve. Flint recorded that "a great number of boatmen . . . robbed them of all their money, differently stated to be between five and ten thousand dollars."[21] And so their pilgrimage continued, finally terminating somewhere near the mouth of the Arkansas River when their flatboat ran aground.

When Flint visited the Pilgrims in their Promised Land in 1819, there were approximately "six persons of them left,—the 'prophet,' so called, and his wife, and another woman, and perhaps three children." Their condition was deteriorating: "They were sick and poor; and the rags with which they were originally habited to excite attention, and to be *in keeping* with their name and assumption, were now retained from necessity. The 'prophet' was too sick to impart much information."[22] Traveling to New Orleans in January 1820, Thomas Nuttall also encountered "the miserable remnant of what are called the Pilgrims." At the time of Nuttall's visit, "If I am correctly informed, there now exists of them only one man, three women, and two children. Two other children were taken from them in compassion for their miserable situation, and the man was but the other day seized by a boat's crew descending the river, and forcibly shaved, washed, and dressed."[23] What became of the Prophet—presumably the figure who was taken in hand by the boatmen—is unknown. There are suggestions that he finally died on the Mississippi. In his autobiography, for example, Finley makes mention of an "Elder Holmes" who sounds suspiciously like Bullard: "Elder Holmes rose up with his pilgrims, and started out in quest of the Holy Land. He had many followers, and, after wandering about for some time, died on an island in the Mississippi river."[24] Whether or not that figure was Bullard, after Nuttall's visit no further mention was made of him or his quest for the New Jerusalem.

"A NEW RELIGIOUS EMPIRE ON THE MISSISSIPPI": JOSEPH SMITH AND THE MORMONS

The nascent search for the Mississippi Promised Land found in the expressive story of the Prophet and the Pilgrims was replayed in the fortunes of numerous other new religious groups. In the wake of the Pilgrims' descent down the river, Timothy Flint noted that "an aged man, with a long beard . . . as wild and visionary as they were" claimed that he too "was descending the Mississippi, as he said, to the *real* Jerusalem in Asia. He appeared deeply impressed, that by going on in that direction he should finally reach that city."[25] The disgraced Prophet Matthias, who achieved much notoriety in New York City, also followed the seemingly inexorable path to the Mississippi. In one account of his fate, he crossed the river and attempted to convert the Sac and Fox Indians that he found there to his cause. Matthias declared to a Chief Keokuk that he was "Jesus Christ the only true God, and that he was come to gather the Indians, who were of the seed of Israel." Keokuk was unimpressed with his pronouncement and decided to put his divinity to the test: "If you are Jesus Christ, you cannot be killed. If you are not Jesus Christ, you are a rascal and deserve to be shot."[26] Matthias declined the challenge.

Of all those groups that hoped to find their Promised Land along the western rivers, none came as close to fulfilling their hopes—or garnered as much attention in the process—as the Mormons. By 1839, when they began the process of establishing a city named Nauvoo on the Upper Mississippi, they had already suffered a series of failed attempts to establish a New Jerusalem elsewhere in the Mississippi valley. Nauvoo, as Launias and Hallwas have described, was to be "the fulfillment of the shattered dreams of previous church-dominated communities in Kirtland, Ohio, and Independence and Far West, Missouri. They believed that God had finally enabled them to begin the establishment of his kingdom on earth, a utopia called Zion."[27] However, it is clear from Joseph Smith's own account of the selection of the site of Nauvoo (the existing settlement of Commerce) that its location was as pragmatic as it was spiritual. Certainly, it was a more calculated decision than the apparent randomness of Bullard's pilgrimage:

> When I made the purchase of White and Galland, there were one stone house, three frame houses, and two block houses, which constituted the whole city of Commerce . . . the place was literally a wilderness. The land was mostly covered with trees and bushes, and much of it so wet that it was with the utmost difficulty a footman could get through, and totally impossible for teams. Commerce was so unhealthy, very few could live there; but believing that it might become a healthy place by the blessing of heaven to the saints, and no more eligible place presenting itself, I considered it wisdom to make an attempt to build up a city.[28]

Just as the Pilgrims' chaotic journey to their Promised Land chimed with secular expectations for the Mississippi valley, so the Mormons' development of Nauvoo was deeply connected to the frenzy of land speculation that was characteristic of life on the river in the 1830s and 1840s. Indeed, in an account of "Mormonism in Illinois" in the *American Whig Review* in 1852, R. W.

Mac made it clear that prior to Smith's arrival, Commerce had been subject to the kind of boosterism common to most river towns: "Splendid lithographed plots of the flourishing city . . . had been exhibited by the most industrious and enterprising agents, in all the principal Eastern cities; on which were pointed out spacious and elegant churches, hotels, banks, and other public buildings." Such visions had failed to drum up much interest: "Eastern capitalists had been already too sorely bitten by the adroit cunning of Western sharpers. . . . It was not strange," Mac concluded, "that Smith should be received with the utmost kindness by these speculators, who would no doubt have extended the same welcome to Lucifer."[29] In turn, Smith himself was not shy about talking up his New Jerusalem, describing Nauvoo to a prospective convert as "the best & most beautiful site for a city on the River" with "every prospect of its becoming one of the largest cities on the river if not in the western world."[30]

It was this very secular dimension of Nauvoo's role as the New Jerusalem that Herman Melville reworked for its ironic potential in his enigmatic novel *The Confidence Man* (1857). An agent for the Black Rapids Coal Company inquires of a fellow steamboat passenger, "You wouldn't like to be concerned in the New Jerusalem, would you? . . . It was originally founded by certain fugitive Mormons. Hence the name. It stands on the Mississippi." Producing a map, the agent points out, in typical booster fashion, "the public buildings . . . the park . . . the botanical gardens . . . a perpetual fountain." Although he can't interest his prospective customer in a sale, he concludes optimistically, "Still, considering that the first settlement was by two fugitives, who had swum over naked from the opposite shore it's a surprising place. It is, *bona fide*."[31]

For a brief time, Nauvoo was indeed *bona fide*, particularly in comparison to many other river towns founded in this period. As Launias and Hallwas elucidate, "Nauvoo's population doubled every year between 1839 and 1842. . . . The city eventually became the second largest in Illinois, rivaling Chicago."[32] During Nauvoo's heyday, the Mississippi became a popular route of pilgrimage for would-be Saints. As one commentator noted in the pages of the *Southern Quarterly Review* in 1842, at the arrival of some recently converted English Mormons: "One hundred and thirty of these misguided men passed through New Orleans and St. Louis last summer, on a single steam-boat, on their way to Nauvoo, the 'Holy City.'"[33] Smith also went some way toward realizing the kind of public building program that river town boosters often fabricated in their promotional material. In January 1841, he published a revelation from God which declared that the Mormons of Nauvoo should "build a house in the land of promise . . . for the beginning of the revelations and foundation of Zion"—in short, a place of worship.[34] Even after its destruction in 1848, the Mormon Temple became one of the most notable antebellum sights on the Upper Mississippi.

The significance—both secular and spiritual—of these civic developments was not lost on some contemporary commentators. Writing in the *New York Herald* in 1842, James Gordon Bennett proclaimed, "Here is a new prophet . . . establishing a holy city and a new religious empire on the Mississippi, that numbers 10,000 persons in the city and 30,000 beyond its limits—with a splendid temple for public worship—and a military organization of 1500 'pretty well' disciplined troops." But this increase in earthly power and prestige brought Nauvoo increasing problems—both internal and external. Their neighbors, as Fawn Brodie describes, "were desparately afraid of being crushed" by the Mormons' growing power.[35] Illinois governor Thomas Ford noted in his 1854 *History of Illinois*: "The Mormon press at Nauvoo, and the anti-Mormon papers at Warsaw, Quincy, Springfield, Alton and St. Louis, kept up a continual fire at each other."[36] At the same time, schisms split the Mormons internally. As John Hallwas described, "Nauvoo's symbolic identity as Zion was shattered by the very notion that the Mormon community was apparently not the divinely inspired ensign of peace and freedom but a place of discord."[37] These forces reached a head in 1844, when Joseph Smith and his brother Hiram were lynched by an armed mob. Harried by their neighbors even after the death of their leader, most Mormons readied themselves for another exodus, leaving behind their hopes for a New Jerusalem on the Mississippi River. Ford related, "All the houses in Nauvoo, and even the temple, were converted into work-shops; and before spring, more than twelve thousand wagons were in readiness. . . . By the middle of May [1846] it was estimated that sixteen thousand Mormons had crossed the Mississippi and taken up their line of march with their personal property, their wives and little ones, westward across the continent."[38]

The antagonism that marked the Mormons' time on the river and the eventual destruction of their Promised Land belies the fact that both before and after its desertion the city of Nauvoo was a constant source of fascination to antebellum audiences and became one of the river's most storied locations. On the one hand, and in stark contrast to its role as the Mormon New Jerusalem, it featured in a wealth of anti-Mormon literature as a veritable Mississippi Sodom. In the early 1840s, for example, having "heard much of this famous city, and the character of its inhabitants," Joseph Jackson determined to visit Nauvoo for himself in order to "find out whether Joe Smith was in reality as bad a man as he was represented." He soon found his answer and warned his readers accordingly: "I am aware that such is the nature of the disclosures made in the following pages—such the blackness of the record—that it will be difficult to induce men to believe that such depravity could possibly exist."[39] Rev. Samuel Pickard agreed, asserting that "Nauvoo was a congenial place" for "the thieves, gamblers and counterfeiters who infested that region" and noting that Mormons themselves were "consummate scoundrels."[40] Indeed, in his autobiography, the "arch-fiend" Green H. Long related that to hide out from a recent murder he decided to "proceed up the river to Nauvoo [. . .] I stayed a few months there, too."[41]

But the reaction of antebellum audiences to Nauvoo was not just one of suspicion. The city, before and after its depopulation, became one of the most notable locations for travelers on the Upper Mississippi. As Robert Flanders asserts, "Nauvoo . . . was a prime attraction to the Mississippi River tourist traffic."[42] It supplied the river's early tourists with an ideal combination of sensational (and, indeed, sentimental) history and picturesque views. As such, Nauvoo was given special mention in a variety of antebellum travel guides. In 1852, for example, Daniel Curtiss rhapsodized: "For picturesque scenery and extent of prospect . . . there are few, if any, positions on that long river, from St. Louis to St. Anthony's, that surpass this."[43] Travelers produced their own appreciations of the city and its location, particularly the Temple. In 1846, Charles Lanman "tarried a few hours at the far-famed city of Nauvoo." The "gloomy streets" of the vacated city inspired "a most melancholy disappointment": "Where lately resided no less than twenty-five thousand people, there are not to be seen more than about five hundred; and these, in mind, body and purse, seem to be perfectly wretched." To add to the pathos, there was much about the city that impressed him: "I had an opportunity to muse upon superb panorama which met my gaze upon every side. I was in a truly splendid temple,—that temple in the centre of a desolate city,—and that city in the centre of an apparently boundless wilderness." Little wonder, then, that upon leaving Nauvoo, "I felt like one awakened from a dream."[44]

In turn, Nauvoo's picturesque appeal meant that it became a favorite location for artists. In particular, it was a vital location for the numerous showmen who created vast moving panoramas of the Mississippi enjoyed by audiences throughout the nation. The moving panorama was a compelling mixture of artistry and showmanship: an enormous canvas fastened between two rollers, slowly wound at a steady pace from one roller to the other in front of a paying audience. It simulated physical movement and presented the viewer with a succession of landscapes and views. The Mississippi River was one of the most popular subjects for a moving panorama, and Nauvoo was often a featured location. As John Francis McDermott noted, "Nauvoo . . . was excellent copy, and they made the most of it."[45] In the journal of his sketching trip along the Mississippi in 1848, panoramist Henry Lewis demonstrated the importance of this "celebrated city" to his project. Upon arrival in Nauvoo he marveled, "The scene was beautiful in the extreme, as the history of this unfortunate city is a melancholy one." He then "hurried up to take a look at the temple and see it by sun set." He was impressed with what he found: "Taking into consideration the circumstances under which it was built it is a wonderful building."[46] Lewis stayed in Nauvoo long enough to interview Joseph Smith's widow and make a variety of sketches. But other panoramists were less sympathetic, at least in the lectures with which they entertained their audiences. When his panorama reached Nauvoo, John Rowson Smith noted that it was situated on "one of the finest locations for a town upon the river"—but he also informed his audience that the Mormons themselves had been "living representatives of the 'Forty Thieves.'"[47] It is clear, however, that a trip to Nauvoo via the medium of a Mississippi panorama could be a moving experience. At some point in the early 1850s, Henry David Thoreau "went to see a panorama of the Mississippi" and came to a profound realization: "as I worked my way up the river in the light of to-day, and . . . gazed on the fresh ruins of Nauvoo . . . I felt that *this was the heroic age itself,* though we know it not."[48] In such ways, Nauvoo became a vital part of the mythology of the Mississippi.

And yet the Mormon exodus was not quite the end of Nauvoo's role in antebellum utopianism on the Mississippi. In 1849, Temple Square was sold to a new group looking to create their own New Jerusalem. The Icarians were a utopian group that originated in France, dedicated to the ideas of Etienne Cabet. Nauvoo was to be the place where the Icarians founded, in Cabet's words, "a second promised land, an Eden, an Elysium, a new earthly paradise."[49] For a time it seemed that they might have done just that. As Steve Wiegenstein notes, "In 1855, the peak year for the community, nearly 500 Icarians were living at Nauvoo."[50] Unlike the city's previous inhabitants, they were apparently accepted by their neighbors; in 1852, Daniel Curtiss remarked that they were "said to be a peaceful, intelligent and industrious people."[51] Along the banks of the Mississippi, the Icarians hosted elaborate festivals and feasts. "After having picked a grove of trees in the woods situated along the river," related Icarian Pierre Bourg in his journal, "our orchestra played some quadrilles and waltzes in order to make us sing and pirouette like the mythological hosts of the ancient forest."[52] But their time in paradise was fleeting, too. By 1860, riven by schisms, the Icarians also vacated Nauvoo and headed west for Iowa, still in search of their Promised Land.

"A burning flood of lard oil": Millerites on the Mississippi

While the quest to establish a New Jerusalem was the most important trope for new religious groups that sought the antebellum Mississippi, the river had other roles to play in the popular expectation of the millennium. Millenarianism was present to a lesser or greater degree in most of the new religious movements of the day. But the idea that the end of the world was on its way sooner rather than later was given a particular urgency by the work of William Miller. Although a Deist in his youth, Miller was part of the religious awakening of the early nineteenth century. He became a Baptist after the War of 1812. Then, through an intensive program of scriptural examination and interpretation, Miller became convinced that the Second Coming of Christ would occur between March 1843 and April 1844.[53] As David L. Rowe points out, one of the events that encouraged him in his work was "the dramatic New Madrid earthquakes that struck the Mississippi valley from 1808 to 1812" and "aroused popular apocalyptic fears." Rowe also notes that at the moment that "Miller was engaged in his bible study" in 1817, Bullard and his Pilgrims were beginning their fateful journey in Vermont, very close to Miller's home.[54] Although Miller began to preach his millennial message in 1831, it was not until the late 1830s that he gained a popular following. Judging the scale of his support is difficult, since Millerism was never a formal denomination, but Whitney Cross estimates that "Probably well over fifty thousand people in the United States became convinced that time would run out in 1844, while a million or more of their fellows were skeptically expectant."[55] Though Miller was never keen to set a precise date for the coming apocalypse, after April 1844 passed without event he accepted the revised suggestion of October 22 from one of his followers. Outlandish tales of Millerite preparations for the end were swiftly followed by reports of their so-called Great Disappointment.

Millerism, as Cross notes, "was at no time a peculiarly localized phenomenon."[56] It gained adherents throughout the nation and across the world. But the idea of apocalypse on the Mississippi seems to have contained a particular fascination. Perhaps the efforts of groups like the Pilgrims and the Mormons had conditioned antebellum audiences to associate the river with the coming of the new Millennium; perhaps secular conceptions of the Mississippi valley's role in America's future helped to forge a potent image of end times on the western rivers. As Ernest Sandeen has described, there were other reasons why life on the Mississippi chimed with antebellum apocalyptic concerns: "Many millenarian newspapers in that day carried a column entitled 'Signs of the Times,' which contained news of ominous events and portents of the end of the world. One of the most common items in these columns was the notice of the explosion of a steamboat. The steamboat harnessed new power and moved with unprecedented rapidity. . . . The passengers knew that their voyage might possibly end by their being blown to smithereens. In such a world, millenarianism was not out of place."[57] Whatever the cause, numerous writers toyed with the idea of the end of the world as it played out on the Mississippi.

Intrepid correspondent Matt Field was on the Mississippi itself, in a steamboat en route to St. Louis, on one of the fateful days allotted by Millerites to mark the end of the world. The "last day" began much like any other on the river, marked by "the clattering of machinery and the blowing off of steam." The passengers waited patiently "to see the Mississippi turned into a roaring cataract of lurid flame. . . . Many waited in great fear and trembling until noon day, expecting to hear the grand 'crack of doom' as the clock struck twelve." Some expected the apocalypse to come as "a burning flood of lard oil . . . pouring down the Ohio from Cincinnati." But all were disappointed: "Parson Miller has not set the river on fire at all," Field reported, "*La Belle Riviere* came bounding into the bosom of the Father of Waters with the same chrystal purity that has been her characteristic of old."[58]

Humorist John S. Robb was happy to play the same scenario for laughs. His short sketch "The Second Advent!" told of the misadventures of steamboat engineer Tom Bangall on the expected day of destruction. Robb notes that the predictions of the "general blowing up of the world" had been of particular concern to "some of the engineers upon our western waters, who had been used to blowing up its inhabitants" and "became a little frightened at the prospect of having to encounter, in another world, the victims of steamboat disaster." At first, Tom Bangall is not one of them, proclaiming all such prophecies to be "moonshine—humbug—smoke." Tom declares: "'I'd like to see old Miller set fire to the Mississippi!'" But his colleagues set out to convince him otherwise. A friend of the captain "passed himself off as a preacher of the doctrine, and talked learnedly on the prophecies whenever the engineer was nigh." Slowly, Tom becomes "savage with excitement." When a steam-pipe bursts and scalds him, Tom is certain that the apocalypse has arrived and he has been sent to hell: "Jest as I thought—the d——l's got me, *s-l-i-c-k* enough, and I'm burnt already to a cinder!"[59] In 1850, Henry Clay Lewis also found brutal humor in those who were "on the lookout for the end of the world" along the Mississippi. In "The Day of Judgement," the narrator describes the time that he and his friends interrupted a Millerite camp-meeting in Louisiana, in the Loosa Chitta swamp, by setting fire to a mule: "The meeting, awakened from their slumbers by his turmoil, rushed out, and when they too saw the approaching fire-breathing mass, they believed . . . that the day of judgment had passed, and Pandemonium—hot at that—was coming with its awful torments."[60]

The idea of apocalypse on the Mississippi did not end with the disappointment of the Millerites. In 1854, Samuel Baldwin published *Armageddon,* a work that articulated his vision of America's role in the end times. As Baldwin's exhaustive interpretation of biblical prophecy revealed, "The United States will, in the Millennium, be the great ruling power of the world, and it will never apostatize." Whilst this Millennium would begin with an alliance between America and Europe, "the Europeans will, after a thousand years, apostatize, and gather the world against America." The ramifications of the ensuing conflict would be extraordinary: "in the midst of their war, the spiritual judgment will come, and the earth will be burnt up, and changed into the paradise of God." As for the location of the battle of Armageddon itself, Baldwin had an answer: "Our policy will be to let them enter the country, and reach the Mississippi, or Ohio valley, and then pour hail and brimstone into them. We shall fight with the certainty of success."[61]

Baldwin might have had faith in the coming of the Mississippi millennium, but others were less certain about the river's divinity. If God, in a variety of guises, was felt to walk the waters of the western rivers in the antebellum years, the devil wasn't far behind. After all, according to Timothy Flint, the boatmen called the Mississippi the "wicked river."[62] In 1839, Frederick Marryat asserted: "It is a river of desolation; and instead of reminding you, like other beautiful rivers, of an angel which has descended for the benefit of man, you imagine it a devil, whose energies have been only overcome by the wonderful power of steam."[63] In 1854, Emil Klauprecht felt that there was a palpable "evil spirit of the Mississippi" that originated with the "old divinities" who demanded a "harvest of corpses" in recompense "for the vanished sacrifice of their red worshippers."[64]

Joseph Holt Ingraham took these conceits further in "The Spectre Steamer," a short story first published in 1841. Determined to make the fastest trip from St. Louis to New Orleans, Hugh Northup commissions the construction of a new steamer that he names the *Lucifer.* Before the boat's inaugural voyage, Northup makes a fateful oath: "There have been boasts of brag trips between

Saint Louis and Orleans! Such boasters shall be for ever silenced by the *Lucifer*! I am her captain, and I've got the devil for my chief-engineer. I sail this day for New Orleans, and if she is one hour over three days on her trip, I'll up steam and drive her to the devil." Unfortunately for Northup, his boast proves empty. After a year of spectral wandering, the *Lucifer* heads toward its final destination in an extraordinary image of damnation on the antebellum Mississippi:

> Immediately the forecastle was thronged with a demon crew, who began to 'fire-up' with appalling activity. The boilers and chimneys grew red hot with the intense fires, on which, with hellish cries, they never ceased piling wood. . . . Onward and *downward* went the doomed vessel. The forest yawned—the earth opened, and she entered a vast inclining cavern on a river of molten fire. Downward and onward she descended beneath the forests—beneath the water, and gradually disappeared in darkness and gloom.[65]

Though less sensational, Herman Melville's *Confidence Man* itself displayed apocalyptic overtones clearly influenced by the tenor of antebellum new religious movements, combined with the distinct whiff of brimstone. As R. B. F. Lewis has asserted, "this often disconcertingly realistic fable is . . . the pivotal text in the history of apocalyptic literature in America." Although Melville's allegorical steamboat *Fidele,* traveling on April Fool's Day, is supposedly heading for New Orleans, there is a sense that its passengers, an antebellum version of Chaucer's Canterbury pilgrims, are actually on course for a less auspicious destination—one not far removed from that of the *Lucifer*.[66] "What's that about the Apocalypse?" mumbles a sleeping passenger, just before the titular Confidence Man extinguishes "the waning light," leaving the steamboat (and the reader) in "the darkness which ensued."[67]

"The tint of the prevailing gloom": Postbellum Influence

These startling antebellum visions of salvation, apocalypse, and damnation on the western rivers left deep impressions in the popular imagination. They had a particular effect on a number of midwestern writers who would play a major role in the postwar reinvention of American literature. In *A Boy's Town* (1890), his memoir of his early years in Ohio, William Dean Howells remembered that his childhood was a time when many believed that the "world was going to be burned up": "the believers had their ascension robes ready, and some gave away their earthly goods so as not to be cumbered with anything in their heavenward flight."[68] As Susan Goodman and Carl Dawson describe,

Howells's grandfather was at their vanguard: "Neighbors joked that whenever Joseph saw an ominous cloud in the sky, he donned his ascension robes in readiness for eternity."[69] Even though his father assured him that this was a "crazy notion," Howells himself was still affected by "the tint of the prevailing gloom."[70] And this fascination remained with him. In 1916, in one of his last published works, Howells reached back into his childhood to tell the story of *The Leatherwood God.* The novel was based on the documented activities of Joseph H. Dylks, another prophet who had flourished in Ohio in the early years of the nineteenth century. As Richard Taneyhill described in 1870, in Howells's major source for the novel, Dylks's modus operandi was a familiar one. He told the inhabitants of Salesville "that he could disappear and reappear at pleasure, perform miracles, and finally that he was the true Messiah come to set up the millennium, and establish a kingdom that should never end."[71] "You see," one of Howells's characters describes after Dylks's death, "life is hard in a new country, and anybody that promises salvation on easy terms has got a strong hold at the very start."[72]

Another early midwestern realist, Edward Eggleston, framed his entire 1872 novel *The End of the World* around the Millerite excitement of the 1840s as it played out along the Ohio River. In Eggleston's view, "The people liked the prospect of the end of the world because it would be a spectacle, something to relieve the fearful monotony of their lives. . . . Here was an excitement, something worth living for." The novel reaches its climax on the night of the expected apocalypse, on a hill overlooking the Ohio as a powerful storm builds. While Eggleston notes that the prospect of the millennium and the "deepening gloom gave all objects in the river valley a weird, distorted look . . . something seen in a dream or a delirium," heroine Julia Anderson was able to discern something more inspirational in the Ohio below her—a vision of the New Jerusalem: "'But how beautiful the new earth will be,' said Julia, still looking at the sleeping river, 'the river of life will be clear as crystal!'. . . . 'I think,' said Julia, 'that it must be something like this river.'"[73]

But perhaps the most important expression of the influence of the new religious movements of the Mississippi can be found in the life and work of Mark Twain. Growing up in antebellum Hannibal, Missouri, on the Mississippi River, in William Phipps's words, Twain's "religious associations . . . were mainly with Presbyterians."[74] But he was also surrounded by a rich and influential series of alternative theologies that clearly formed an important part of his cultural education. His close friend Will Bowen's grandfather, for example, was Barton Stone, a renowned Campbellite preacher. For a significant portion of his childhood, the Mormons at Nauvoo were practically neighbors—even though they weren't always welcomed as such by the residents of Hannibal. As Dixon Wecter relates, "At the time of the Nauvoo troubles . . . when a boatload of the harried Saints was reported ascending the River, some local citizens rigged up a shotted cannon to salute them with a hot reception."[75] The Millerites also made their presence felt. In October 1844, they gathered on Hannibal landmark Lover's Leap to wait for the millennium. As Gary Scharnhorst has noted, this small band "made a lasting impression on Mark Twain, though he had been but nine years old."[76] In Ernest Tuveson's words, Hannibal was a place where the "millennium . . . was one of the liveliest issues in the popular mind."[77] Indeed, even during Twain's years as a steamboat pilot, the idea of apocalypse on the Mississippi was still a pressing one. In 1861, at the beginning of the Civil War, which would see the river play host to some very real battles, Twain was taking interest in a particular book. He demanded of his brother, en route to St. Louis: "Orion bring down 'Armageddon' with you if you have it. If not, *buy* it."[78]

The impress of these youthful influences on his later work is easily discernible, from his treatment of the Mormons in *Roughing It* (1872) to his references to Millerism in *Innocents Abroad* (1869), *Adventures of Huckleberry Finn* (1884), and, as Gary Scharnhorst and Ernest Tuveson have outlined, *A Connecticut Yankee in King Arthur's Court* (1889). At other moments, too, the flavor of the religious life of the antebellum Mississippi is readily discernible in Twain's work. In a telling scene in *The Gilded Age* (1873), Twain's first published novel written with Charles Dudley Warner, slave Uncle Dan'l mistakes the arrival of a steamboat for the coming of a vengeful God: "The coughing grew louder and louder, the glaring eye grew larger and still larger, glared wilder and still wilder. A huge shape developed itself out of the gloom, and from its tall duplicate horns dense volumes of smoke, starred and spangled with sparks, poured out and went tumbling away into the farther darkness. . . . 'It's de Almighty! Git down on yo' knees!'"[79] In *The Adventures of Tom Sawyer* (1876), too, Aunt Polly declares, "'Tom! The sperrit was upon you! You was a prophecying—that's what you was doing! Land alive, go on, Tom!'"[80] Alongside a continual engagement with these childhood influences in his written work, Twain evinced a fascination with new religious movements throughout his life, right through to his complicated relationships in older age with spiritualism, Mary Baker Eddy and Christian Science, and the prophetic works of George Woodward Warder.[81] The memories of a millennial childhood on the Mississippi never left him. In 1902, Twain returned to his boyhood home for the last time. Having climbed Holliday Hill with childhood friend John Briggs, gazing out across the river, he began to reminisce about antebellum life in Hannibal. One particular location stood out: "There is where the Millerites put on their robes one night to go up to heaven," Twain remembered. "None of them went that night, John, but no doubt many of them have gone since."[82]

The new religious movements that incorporated the Mississippi River into their theological worldviews may appear, at first glance, to have been on the margins of the nation and the fringes of conventional thought. Their efforts—to found a New Jerusalem, to welcome in the millennium on the western rivers—may appear to have been in vain. And yet the visions of the Mississippi valley generated by the vibrant religious movements of the antebellum river frontier were, in essence, deeply characteristic of their times. At one and the same time they reflected and influenced popular conceptions of the Mississippi valley in the antebellum years—an influence, in ways that have not been fully recognized, that still persists. On an individual level, too, they may have come closer to finding a New Jerusalem on the Mississippi than is at first apparent. In 1824, John Hunt traveled down the river by flatboat and visited with two remaining members of Isaac Bullard's Pilgrims, both women, near the mouth of the Arkansas. As Josiah Morrow related in his history of Warren County, Ohio, Hunt and his party "found the Promised Land a most forbidden place, situated on a narrow ridge of dry land, almost surrounded by a swamp." The women, however, Hunt found to be "Neat and clean in their persons and dress and intelligent in their conversation." Even after Hunt offered to pay for them to return to their homes, they were insistent that they were content just where they were: "They thanked him very kindly for his offer, but said they had started out for the Promised Land, they had found it, and nothing on earth would induce them to leave it."[83]

NOTES

1. Lyman Beecher, *Autobiography, Correspondence, Etc.,* ed. Charles Beecher (New York: Harper and Brothers, 1865), 224.

2. Alexis de Tocqueville, *Democracy in America,* eds. and trans. Harvey C. Mansfield and Delba Winthrop (London: Folio Society, 2002), 21.

3. Zadok Cramer, *The Navigator* (Pittsburgh: Cramer, Spear, and Eichbaum, 1814), 145.

4. Timothy Flint, *Recollection of the Last Ten Years* (Boston: Cummings, Hilliard, 1826), 275.

5. Peter Cartwright, *Autobiography of Peter Cartwright* (London: Arthur Hall, Virtue, 1862), vii.

6. William Henry Milburn, *The Pioneers, Preachers, and People of the Mississippi Valley* (New York: Darby & Jackson, 1860), 355.

7. David S. Reynolds, *Beneath the American Renaissance* (New York: Alfred A. Knopf, 1988), 15, 18.

8. Whitney Cross, *The Burned-Over District: The Social and Intellectual History of Enthusiastic Religion in Western New York, 1800–1850* (New York: Harper & Row, 1965), 3.

9. Flint, *Recollection of the Last Ten Years*, 88.

10. Gilbert Imlay, *A Topographical Description of the Western Territories of North America* (London: J. Debrett, 1792), 108.

11. Flint, *Recollection of the Last Ten Years*, 280.

12. James B. Finley, *Autobiography of Rev. James B. Finley* (Cincinnati: R. P. Thompson, 1853), 373.

13. Cartwright, *Autobiography of Peter Cartwright,* 38

14. Finley, *Autobiography of Rev. James B. Finley,* 258.

15. F. Gerald Ham, "The Prophet and the Mummyjums: Isaac Bullard and the Vermont Pilgrims of 1817," *Wisconsin Magazine of History* 56, no. 4 (Summer 1973): 290.

16. Stephen J. Stein, *Communities of Dissent: A History of Alternative Religions in America* (New York: Oxford University Press, 2003), 4, 3.

17. Flint, *Recollection of the Last Ten Years,* 276, 277.

18. Josiah Morrow, "The History of Warren County," in *The History of Warren County, Ohio* (Chicago: W. H. Beers, 1882), 413.

19. Flint, *Recollection of the Last Ten Years,* 276.

20. Zadock Thompson, *History of Vermont* (Burlington: Chauncey Goodrich, 1842), 204.

21. Flint, *Recollection of the Last Ten Years,* 277, 278–79.

22. Ibid., 275.

23. Thomas Nuttall, *A Journal of Travels into the Arkansas Territory* (Philadelphia: Thos. H. Palmer, 1821), 226–27.

24. Finley, *Autobiography of Rev. James B. Finley,* 373.

25. Flint, *Recollection of the Last Ten Years,* 280.

26. Henry Caswall, *Three Days at Nauvoo in 1842* (London: J. G. F. & J. Rivington, 1842), 31.

27. Roger D. Launius and John E. Hallwas, introduction to *Kingdom on the Mississippi Revisited: Nauvoo in Mormon History* (Urbana: University of Illinois Press, 1996), 2.

28. Joseph Smith, *History of the Church of Jesus Christ of Latter Day Saints,* ed. Heman C. Smith, 4 vols. (Lamoni, IA: Board of Publication of the Reorganized Church of Jesus Christ of Latter Day Saints, 1912), 2:367–68.

29. R. W. Mac, "Mormonism in Illinois," *American Whig Review* 15, no. 87 (March 1852): 223.

30. Richard Lyman Bushman, *Joseph Smith: Rough Stone Rolling* (New York: Vintage, 2007), 405.

31. Herman Melville, *The Confidence Man* (New York: Dix, Edwards, 1857), 76, 77.

32. Launius and Hallwas, introduction to *Kingdom on the Mississippi Revisited,* 2.

33. "History of Mormonism," *Southern Quarterly Review* 1, no. 2 (April 1842): 411.

34. Smith, *History of the Church of Jesus Christ of Latter Day Saints*, 2:507.

35. Fawn Brodie, *No Man Knows My History: The Life of Joseph Smith* (New York: Vintage, 1995), 270, 380.

36. Thomas Ford, *A History of Illinois* (Chicago: S. C. Griggs, 1854), 404.

37. John E. Hallwas, "Mormon Nauvoo from a Non-Mormon Perspective," in *Kingdom on the Mississippi Revisited: Nauvoo in Mormon History* (Urbana: University of Illinois Press, 1996), 170.

38. Ford, *A History of Illinois*, 412.

39. Joseph H. Jackson, *The Adventures and Experience of Joseph H. Jackson Disclosing the Depths of Mormon Villainy Practiced in Nauvoo* (Warsaw: Printed for the publisher, 1846), 5–6, 3.

40. Samuel Pickard, *Autobiography of a Pioneer* (Chicago: Church and Goodman, 1866), 45–46, 24.

41. Green H. Long, *The Arch Fiend; or, The Life, Confession, and Execution of Green H. Long* (Little Rock: A. R. Orton, 1852), 24.

42. Robert Bruce Flanders, *Nauvoo: Kingdom on the Mississippi* (Urbana: University of Illinois Press, 1975), 6.

43. Daniel S. Curtiss, *Western Portraiture and Emigrants' Guide* (New York: J. H. Colton, 1852), 80.

44. Charles Lanman, *A Summer in the Wilderness* (New York: D. Appleton, 1847), 31, 33.

45. John Francis McDermott, *The Lost Panoramas of the Mississippi* (Chicago: University of Chicago Press, 1958), 59.

46. Bertha L. Heilbron, ed., *Making a Motion Picture in 1848: Henry Lewis' Journal of a Canoe Voyage from the Falls of St. Anthony to St. Louis* (Saint Paul: Minnesota Historical Society, 1936), 20, 51.

47. McDermott, *The Lost Panoramas of the Mississippi*, 60.

48. Henry David Thoreau, "Walking," *Atlantic Monthly* 9, no. 56 (June 1862): 664–65.

49. Etienne Cabet, *Travels in Icaria*, trans. Leslie J. Roberts (Syracuse: Syracuse University Press, 2003), 4.

50. Steve Wiegenstein, "The Icarians and Their Neighbors," *International Journal of Historical Archaeology* 10, no. 3 (September 2006): 291.

51. Curtiss, *Western Portraiture and Emigrants' Guide*, 80.

52. Robert P. Sutton, *Les Icariens: The Utopian Dream in Europe and America* (Urbana: University of Illinois Press, 1994), 79.

53. Daniel Walker Howe, *What Hath God Wrought: The Transformation of America, 1815–1848* (New York: Oxford University Press, 2007), 290.

54. David L. Rowe, *God's Strange Work: William Miller and the End of the World* (Grand Rapids: Wm. B. Eerdmans, 2008), 77, 78.

55. Cross, *The Burned-Over District*, 287.

56. Ibid.

57. Ernest Sandeen, "Millennialism," in *The Rise of Adventism: Religion and Society in Mid-Nineteenth-Century America*, ed. Edwin S. Gaustad (New York: Harper & Row, 1974), 117.

58. John Francis McDermott, *Before Mark Twain: A Sampler of Old, Old Times on the Mississippi* (Carbondale: Southern Illinois University Press, 1998), xxiv.

59. John S. Robb, *Streaks of Squatter Life, and Far-West Scenes* (Philadelphia: Carey and Hart, 1847), 148, 150, 151, 152, 155.

60. Madison Tensas [Henry Clay Lewis], "Taking Good Advice," in *Odd Leaves from the Life of a Louisiana "Swamp Doctor"* (Philadelphia: A. Hart, 1850), 61, 64.

61. Sanuel Baldwin, *Armageddon; or, The Overthrow of Romanism and Monarchy* (Cincinnati: Applegate, 1854), 405, 398.

62. Flint, *Recollection of the Last Ten Years*, 93.

63. Frederick Marryat, *A Diary in America, with Remarks on Its Institutions: Part Second*, 3 vols. (London: Longman, Orme, Brown, Green, and Longmans, 1839), 1:249.

64. Emil Klauprecht, *Cincinnati, or The Mysteries of the West*, ed. Don Heinrich Tolzman and trans. Steven Rowan (New York: Peter Lang, 1996), 299, 80.

65. Joseph Holt Ingraham, *The Spectre Steamer, and Other Tales* (Boston: United States Publishing Company, 1846), 14, 17.

66. R. W. B. Lewis, *Trials of the World* (New Haven, CT: Yale University Press, 1965), 210, 10.

67. Herman Melville, *The Confidence Man* (New York: Dix, Edwards, 1857), 380, 394.

68. William Dean Howells, *A Boy's Town* (New York: Harper & Brothers, 1890), 203.

69. Susan Goodman and Carl Dawson, *William Dean Howells: A Writer's Life* (Berkeley: University of California Press, 2005).

70. Howells, *A Boy's Town*, 203.

71. Richard H. Taneyhill, *The Leatherwood God: An Account of the Appearance and Pretensions of Joseph C. Dylks in Eastern Ohio in 1828* (Cincinnati: Robert Clarke, 1870).

72. William Dean Howells, *The Leatherwood God* (New York: Century, 1916), 232.

73. Edward Eggleston, *The End of the World* (New York: Orange Judd, 1872), 59, 273, 269.

74. William E. Phipps, *Mark Twain's Religion* (Macon: Mercer University Press, 2003), 31.

75. Dixon Wecter, *Sam Clemens of Hannibal* (Boston: Houghton Mifflin, 1961), 90.

76. Gary Scharnhorst, "Mark Twain and the Millerites: Notes on Millenarianism and *A Connecticut Yankee*," *American Transcendental Quarterly* 3, no. 3 (September 1989): 297.

77. Ernest Lee Tuveson, *Redeemer Nation: The Idea of America's Millennial Role* (Chicago: University of Chicago Press, 1968), 216.

78. Mark Twain, *Mark Twain's Letters Volume 1: 1853–1866*, eds. Edgar Marquess Branch, Michael B. Frank, and Kenneth M. Sanderson (Berkeley: University of California Press, 1988), 120.

79. Mark Twain, *The Gilded Age: A Tale of To-day* (Hartford: American Publishing Co., 1874), 36–37.

80. Mark Twain, *The Adventures of Tom Sawyer* (Hartford: American Publishing Co., 1876), 151.

81. Joe B. Fulton, "Mark Twain's New Jerusalem: Prophecy in the Unpublished Essay 'About Cities in the Sun,'" *Christianity and Literature* 55, no. 2 (Winter 2006): 173–94.

82. Gary Scharnhorst, *Mark Twain: The Complete Interviews* (Tuscaloosa: University of Alabama Press, 2006), 457.

83. Morrow, "The History of Warren County," in *The History of Warren County, Ohio*, 414.

5

---◆---

"Go Down into Jordan: No, Mississippi"

MORMON NAUVOO AND THE RHETORIC OF LANDSCAPE

Seth Perry

About 490 miles from Minneapolis, there is a small bend in the Mississippi River. On a typical map of the United States, the bend and the space of land it defines are not uniquely prominent—the upper Mississippi makes innumerable curves and cuts. To a person on the ground at this spot, however, the scene defined by the little river bend is quite striking. On the spur of land jutting out into the river, the bluffs that characterize this stretch of the Mississippi's banks are set back from the water, creating both an arresting view from the river and, from atop the bluffs, *of* the river. It has inspired poetry.

> [T]here was one object which was far more noble to behold, and far more majestic than any other yet presented to my sight—and that was the wide-spread and unrivalled father of waters, the Mississippi river, whose mirror-bedded waters lay in majestic extension before the city, and in one general curve seemed to sweep gallantly by the devoted place. . . . [T]he romantic swell of the river soon brought my mind back to days of yore, and to the bright emerald isles of the far-famed fairy land. The bold and prominent rise of the hill, fitting to the plain with an exact regularity, and the plain pushing itself into the river, forcing it to bend around its obstacle with becoming grandeur, and fondly to cling around it add to the heightened and refined lustre to this sequestered land.[1]

The first Euro-American settlement at the place was christened *Venus*, of all things. The city described above is Nauvoo, Illinois, a successor to Venus founded by Joseph Smith and the Church of Jesus Christ of Latter-day Saints on the "plain pushing itself into the river" in 1839. Today Nauvoo is a tiny village of just under 1,200, but that figure was closer to 12,000 in 1843, when the site inspired a visiting Methodist minister to send these lines to the Church's newspaper.[2] As indicated by the poetic stylings of Rev. Samuel Prior—a nonbeliever in Mormonism, the form of devotion regnant in this "devoted place"—the river-dominated landscape of Nauvoo could have significant influence on the way the city and its inhabitants were regarded. Further, the fact that the letter was published in the Mormon press demonstrates the Church leadership's encouragement of those aesthetic impressions. The symbolic significance of the river played out in these two interrelated ways during the Nauvoo period of Mormon history: the river bend directly impressed visitors and residents, while written versions of such impressions were printed and reprinted to perpetuate an idealized vision of Nauvoo among its residents, the Saints abroad, and potential critics. In short, the river site was used to sell Mormons on Nauvoo and to sell outsiders on Mormons.

The potential rhetorical power of sites like Nauvoo's river bend was well established by the time of Reverend Prior's visit. Scholars view the aesthetic appreciation of American landforms as a construction developed by Euro-Americans through various discourses beginning in the sixteenth century, but by the 1830s Hudson River School painter Thomas Cole could assert with little fear of protest that anyone who could "see and feel" could appreciate "the loveliness of verdant fields, the sublimity of lofty mountains, or the varied magnificence of the sky." Moreover, like others of his day, Cole found moral meaning objectively attached to such beauty: "There is in the human mind an almost inseparable connexion between the beautiful and the good, so that if we contemplate the one the other seems present."[3]

Applying the work of theorist Kenneth Burke, such associations indicate the rhetorical power of landscape, because the viewer is moved to identify with the trait suggested: the viewer "surrounds himself with a scene which, he is assured, attests to his moral quality. For he can feel that he participates in the quality which the scene itself is thought to possess."[4] For Burke, this type of promotion of identification is the essential characteristic of rhetoric.[5] The beauty of Nauvoo's river-dominated landscape featured prominently in the rhetorical construction of Mormon identity in the early 1840s: to use Cole's terms, the contemplation of the river bend's beauty was to make present the goodness of Mormonism. As will be shown, the rhetoric of Nauvoo's boosters gave various forms to this goodness—through the symbolism of the river, Nauvoo was associated with industry, civility, and ethical morality, attributes intended to promote the settlement of Nauvoo and which were deeply important to Mormon identity in the early 1840s as rumors of polygamy began to swirl around the city. The river bend was also figured into a sense of religious awe attached to Nauvoo. Joseph Smith claimed the role of a prophet of God and led his people to view themselves as God's chosen. Simply put, the dramatic river bend *fit* these bold self-identities in a way that more mundane tableaus could not have.

Burke's theories have taken the name "dramatism," as they extend terms from theater to the wider realm of experience. In his terms, landscape serves as a "scene": it "contains" human actions and actors, shaping them and being shaped by them. "It is a principle of drama that the nature of acts and agents should be consistent with the nature of the scene."[6] To Mormons, the stirring view of the river from the high bluffs of Nauvoo and the view of the city's temple from the river endorsed a providential view of themselves and of their leader. At the same time, the fact that outsiders could view the same scene with a sharp sense of dissonance—lamenting that a scurrilous religion had profaned a beautiful river setting—points to the importance of deliberate rhetorical efforts in making the river bend into a Mormon symbol. Gregory Clark, who synthesizes and expands Burke's ideas about scene in his *Rhetorical Landscapes in America* (2004), identifies such efforts as the difference between "land" and "landscape": "*Land* is material, a particular object, while *landscape* is conceptual. . . . *Land* becomes *landscape* when it is assigned the role of symbol."[7] The beauty of the river bend as land was apparently a constant for those who visited Nauvoo, but the effect of that beauty was conditioned by the Mormon rhetoric which turned that land into landscape. Perceptions of Nauvoo's "propitious" location were informed by both published descriptions and the Church leadership's use of the landscape to its best advantage, notably in the selection of the site for the city's monumental temple. The river was made to bear symbolic weight that had important consequences for the development of Mormonism at Nauvoo and beyond.

The doctrine of the "gathering of the Saints" underscored the geographical component of nineteenth-century Mormonism. Smith issued a revelation in late 1830 in which God commanded the Church "to bring to pass the gathering of mine elect." The theological underpinnings of the gathering stemmed from Smith's early millennialism—the gathered would "be prepared in all things, against the day when tribulation and desolation are sent forth upon the wicked."[8] In practice it had obvious social, economic, and political advantages.

It also had the disadvantage of drawing focused opposition from neighbors nervous about followers of the Prophet buying up land and influencing elections. The Church arrived in what would become Nauvoo after fleeing previous gathering sites in Ohio and Missouri. Kirtland, Ohio, remained an active Mormon settlement into the Nauvoo period, but Smith personally abandoned the town for Missouri in January 1838, in the face of a web of growing pressures from inside and outside his Church. Throughout the 1830s, in and around Jackson County, Missouri, the Saints had endured relentless pressure and violent assault, culminating in the infamous extermination order issued by Missouri governor Lilburn Boggs in 1838. Giving up on Missouri, the main body of Saints fled across the Mississippi to Quincy, Illinois, and began searching for a new home.

That the area of the little river bend became this home is an accident of history—a Mormon official made the acquaintance of one Isaac Galland, who had large land holdings in the area which he was willing to let go "for no money down and long years to pay." The easy terms were dictated by the fact that Galland, a typical land speculator of the day, had nothing resembling a clear claim on the land he wanted to sell.[9] The Prophet was in jail in Missouri when Church officials began considering Galland's lands, which included the spur on which Nauvoo would be built along with several tracts further east in Illinois and west across the river in Iowa. Smith set out to evaluate the area a few days after escaping from his jailors and arriving in Quincy, and the first contracts with Galland were made soon after.

Numerous studies have noted Smith's obvious preoccupation with the "geographic component of religion," encapsulated in the doctrine of the gathering.[10] Nauvoo, though, tends to get short shrift in discussions of Mormon ideologies of landscape and place, despite being the most successful gathering site established during Smith's lifetime. Such studies generally cover Smith's fascination with the mysterious Indian mounds of upstate New York, the Hill Cumorah from which he said he dug the Book of Mormon, his various pronouncements about the religious significance of Missouri, and then pass glancingly over "sick, swampy, malarial" Nauvoo on the way to extended discussion of Brigham Young's Zion in the intermountain West.[11] Nauvoo was the setting for the most important years of Joseph Smith's prophetic career, however, and the founding prophet never saw the Rocky Mountains.

Smith's earliest impressions of the river bend smack of a certain disappointment. "The place was literally a wilderness. The land was mostly covered with trees and bushes, and much of it so wet that it was with the utmost difficulty a footman could get through, and totally impossible for teams." Smith alludes in this passage to the landscape feature of Nauvoo that would have the greatest impact on actual daily life there: its swampland. Numerous springs ran down the bluffs above the city and pooled on the flat stretch of land below without finding an outlet to the river, producing acres of swampland on the western edge of the city. Additionally, water from the rising and falling river saturated two islands adjacent to Nauvoo, now vanished due to the damming of the river in the twentieth century.[12] Swampland is the inverse of desert (a geographic feature that later Mormons would have to counter), but to early nineteenth-century farmers of New England extraction, they shared a characteristic uselessness. Perpetual standing water renders land as unusable as the opposite extreme—brackish, fetid muck cannot be plowed or planted. More significantly, standing water begets mosquitoes, which in the nineteenth century meant "the ague" (what we would now call malaria). Although attempts were made to drain the swamps, outbreaks of malaria and probably typhus continued to be an annual part of life at Nauvoo throughout the Mormons' time there.[13] A scholar writing about the history of Mormons and medicine has called the place "the Beautiful Pesthole."[14]

Whatever his first impressions, the Prophet fixated on the spur of land, its bluffs, and the river flowing on three sides. Despite the fact that the large majority of the Church's land purchases at this time were on the dry, fertile Iowa side of the river, the Prophet selected a home site on the southern side of the swampy spur of land, just below the bluff he chose for building a temple for the Lord. Robert Flanders, author of the best-known study of Nauvoo, writes that Smith gave no reason for choosing to settle on the Illinois side of the river, but it seems plain that as in upstate New York and Missouri, he had an eye for landscape—the Iowa land may have lacked malaria, but it also lacked the commanding height and the sweeping river.[15] The flat prairie did not look like a place where God's prophet would set up shop. Joseph Smith moved to Nauvoo on May 10, 1839.[16]

Aware of the practical difficulties of the swamp, in describing the new site to his flock, Smith appealed to its aesthetic advantages, describing the little river bend as "probably the best and most beautiful site for a city on the river."[17] By the time of his arrival, Venus had been given the less descriptive, more aspirational name of Commerce and had been joined by a second tiny settlement, Commerce City. Smith determined to return to the descriptive in naming his own town: "The name of our city is of Hebrew origin, and signifies a beautiful situation, or place, carrying with it, also, the idea of rest; and is truly descriptive of the most delightful location."[18] The name Nauvoo was in use at least as early as September 1839. By April 1840, the other towns had been more or less swallowed up by the first burst of Mormon settlers, and a request to change the name of the post office from Commerce to Nauvoo was honored by the office of the postmaster general.[19]

Despite this growth, the status of Nauvoo as a new primary gathering site was unclear until the winter of 1840–41. Missouri had been, and would always be, Zion—the land in which the Saints' scriptures told them they should dwell, which made focusing on a new site problematic. Malaria and typhus took a terrible toll in the first summer. Moreover, having developed holdings in other places only to be driven from them, leaders were wary of concentrating the Mormon population yet again—in a letter, Smith qualified his enthusiasm for Nauvoo's prospects by saying that it would become a great city, "if we are suffered to remain."[20]

The eventual call for all Saints to settle in the area of Nauvoo grew out of religious, economic, and political considerations. In early December 1840, the Illinois legislature approved a generous charter for Nauvoo, granting the city's government sweeping powers, including the authority to raise and maintain a militia.[21] Feeling sufficiently secure, aware of the religious importance of the gathering, and desperately in need of land buyers in order to turn the Church's large land holdings in the area into cash, a full-scale campaign was on to encourage settlement.[22] Smith issued a proclamation in January 1841 encouraging orderly immigration—the wealthy should come first, to develop industry that would provide jobs for the poor when they arrived. In May, he upped the ante by declaring all settlement sites outside of Hancock County, Illinois, and Lee County, Iowa, "discontinued."[23]

The campaign to recruit immigrants was carried out most prominently in the Church's newspapers. *Times and Seasons* was published twice monthly at Nauvoo and circulated widely to Mormon converts throughout the United States through subscriptions sold by traveling missionaries. Material from *Times and Seasons,* along with a variety of original content, also appeared in *The Latter-day Saints' Millennial Star,* the Church's monthly paper published in Manchester, England, for the Church's rapidly growing number of British converts. From early 1841, the editors of both publications—*Times and Seasons* was, at least officially, edited by Smith himself for some time—took every opportunity to promote Nauvoo's settlement.

The city's river-dominated aesthetic was central to the campaign to recruit immigrants, because despite political improvements Nauvoo still had
little going for it as a city site. Both the industry and "healthfulness" described
in Church publications were much more potential than realized—the summer malaria season of 1841 was "calamitous," and real wealth was still difficult to come by.[24] Early rhetoric aimed at encouraging settlement focused on
developing Nauvoo as a scene, in Burke's terms, for industrial development.
Calls for the Saints to gather at Nauvoo highlighted its "most delightful location" and singled out the river as a setting for a virtually infinite number of
factories: "The waters of the Mississippi can be successfully used for manufacturing purposes to an almost unlimited extent."[25] In August 1841 the *Millennial Star* published a lengthy excerpt from the serial encyclopedia *Chambers's Information for the People* (Edinburgh) on immigration to the United
States which reported that "the capabilities of the Mississippi for purposes
of trade are almost beyond calculation, and are hardly yet developed." It also
represented swampland as a scene for seasoned, mindful settlers rather than
widespread sickness and death, noting that while "agues and fevers" were
common, "with due caution [they] are seldom fatal and are looked on by the
inhabitants with little apprehension."[26]

The industrialization of the river was not presented as a merely economic
boon: it was also given a moral valence attached to its perceived "civilizing"
effects, a persistent Mormon concern during these years. "For thousands of
years this magnificent American river rolled its placed [placid] and undis-
turbed waters . . . unnoticed save by the wandering savage of the west or the
animals which browse upon its banks. At length it came under the observation of civilised men and now has begun to contribute to their wants and
wishes."[27] Here, natural landscape becomes a scene of human civilization, and
attention to landscape is presented as an essential part of being civilized—the
"savage" may notice the river on an animal level, but "civilized" men evaluate
and use, uniquely human capacities. The published reflections of an English
immigrant to Nauvoo similarly connected the civilizing effect of settlement
to the natural beauty of the river and its economic potential: "tongue cannot express the beauty of its windings and prospects on each side; no man of
understanding can come up the Mississippi without being filled with wonder
and astonishment at the vast extent of country, enough to sustain the world
if cultivated."[28]

The manufacturing theme was carried through the years of promoting
Nauvoo for settlement.[29] In addition to water power, the river was of course a

symbol of trade—the names of erstwhile towns of Commerce and Commerce City indicate that the Mormons were not the first to recognize this potential. The recessed bluffs at Nauvoo allowed space for a steamboat landing, which alone was said to render "it equal to any town on the Mississippi river for commercial improvements."[30] In this way, the agricultural prospects of the area were also tied to the river, as it was promised to provide a ready outlet to markets. One important element in this rhetoric no longer exists. Nauvoo sat at the head of Des Moines Rapids, an eleven-mile stretch of the Mississippi where the water had worn its bed down to bedrock.[31] The Rapids were bypassed by a canal in 1877 and finally erased from the Mississippi's topography when the water level was raised by the Keokuk Dam in 1913.[32] During the 1840s, the Rapids closed the river to steamboat traffic for several months a year and often required heavy ships to employ "lighters," smaller boats to which they could shift cargo in order to ride higher in the water until past the shallows. The Des Moines Rapids were used in publications aimed at potential emigrants to Nauvoo as evidence of the site's unique potential. At high water, the "rapidity of the current" engendered by the rapids presented a powerful source of power for "all kinds of machinery," according to an 1840 editorial, a claim repeated frequently in the Church's publications.[33] Church leaders proclaimed that the combination of the Rapids and the landing constituted a major advantage. "It is the only good Steam Boat landing on the Rapids, and during a considerable part of the year the Boats on the upper trade receive their freight and passengers at this place, which is brought from the foot of the Rapids, in Lighters."[34]

The industrial power which the river was made to symbolize remained largely a figure of rhetoric—many of the effects of the Rapids touted as advantages to Nauvoo also made them a hindrance to trade and industry in the twentieth century. Without improvements, the river's potential advantages could not be efficiently exploited. Repeated plans to dam the river and improve the steamboat landing came to nothing.[35] Although Nauvoo certainly saw some steamboat traffic, when English traveler Henry Caswall came upriver to Nauvoo in April 1842, the steamboat he was on could not land on the Nauvoo side of the river precisely due to "the rapidity of the current."[36] Moreover, the realities of development of this sort, along with the distraction of outside pressures, meant that very little industry had developed in Nauvoo by the time the Saints began abandoning the city in 1846.[37] At least as important as actual industrialization in Nauvoo's brief history, though, was the rhetoric of civilization which the promise of development furthered, and within that rhetoric the river played a second role as the anchoring feature of the pastoral beauty of Nauvoo's situation.

Time and again Church publications emphasized the beauty of the river bend. "On approaching this place in sailing up the mighty Mississippi and while ascending the lower rapids[,] on the east bank of the river appears the city of Nauvoo and at the very first sight they will be ready to exclaim what a beautiful place for a city."[38] In 1840 Robert B. Thompson, the Prophet's personal secretary, drew (somewhat haphazardly) on a bit of verse written originally about his English homeland to describe the little spur of land: "ne'er sun, view'd in its wide career, a lovlier spot." A more complete and corrected version of the same quotation, from Joseph Cottle's *Alfred,* appeared the following year in both *Times and Seasons* and the *Millennial Star.* Over the course of Nauvoo's settlement, the leaders of the Church reached ever higher in extolling the beauty of the place and linking that beauty to the piety and success of its inhabitants: "[W]e have peace without, and love within the borders of our beautiful city; beautiful, indeed, for situation, is Nauvoo; the crown of the great valley of the Mississippi, the joy of every honest heart."[39]

The rhetorical flourishes printed and reprinted in the Mormon press were intended both to excite immigrants to make the trek and to prepare them to receive the landscape in a certain way when they arrived—to turn beautiful land into faith-confirming landscape. The beauty of the place was a given, acknowledged even by critics of Mormonism. An 1845 editorial in Boston's *Christian Reflector* called Joseph Smith a "wicked imposter" and "a miserable bar-room fiddler" but credited him with having "founded a city in one of the most beautiful situations in the world,—in a beautiful curve of the 'father of waters.'"[40] The meaning of that beauty, however, could be directed and formed by the leaders' rhetoric. What the rhetoric of Nauvoo's boosters added to the experience was the sense that the landscape was not just beautiful but also, as one of *Times and Seasons*'s most vociferous editorials pointed out, "propitious."[41] The landscape was not simply striking, but fitting for the holy settlement established there, an essential part of the religious awe Nauvoo inspired. "[T]he sight of the beautifully sloping heath—situated near half a mile from the Mississippi—on whose delightful summit the Temple of God was being erected, filled my mind with emotions still more pleasing and delightfully intense; emotions to which the corrupt and profane world is a stranger, and which the acknowledged pen of sublimest eloquence and profound erudition, would prove infinitely inadequate to describe."[42] Immigrants traveling up the river often reported the efforts of non-Mormon fellow passengers to dissuade them from settling at Nauvoo by deriding the "'villainy and roguery' of its inhabitants" and "the 'awful delusion of Mormonism.'" One convert described the mere view of the city as a "striking contrast" to such descriptions—"The whole site and aspect of the city, presenting a most cheering picture of enterprise and industry of its inhabitants, exhibiting a remarkable difference to many of the western towns which we passed in coming up the Mississippi, of far longer standing and origin."[43]

Nauvoo's river site, moreover, easily invited explicitly religious resonances that were encouraged by the town's boosters. The river had a direct religious role as the site of baptisms, and baptism by immersion was an essential Mormon doctrine. Smith instituted the practice of baptism for the dead during the Nauvoo years, and these were held in a specially constructed font in the completed temple basement, but the living were baptized into the Church in the Mississippi.[44] Smith appears to have favored a point on the south side of Nauvoo near his home, which would have afforded those present a dramatic view of the city as the Prophet of God brought new souls into the covenant, a scene resonant in published descriptions. "[A]t the appointed hour the bank of the Mississippi was lined with a multitude of people, and President Joseph Smith went forth into the river and baptized with his own hands 80 persons, for the remission of their sins. . . . At the close of this interesting scene the administrator lifted up his hands towards heaven, and implored the blessing of God to rest upon the people; and truly the spirit of God did rest upon the multitude, to the joy and consolation of our hearts."[45]

Nauvoo was also routinely associated with its biblical antecedents. Apostle Orson Hyde reported the success of his missionary efforts in Illinois in the spring of 1840 by extolling the numbers who had been led to baptism, going "down into Jordan: no, Mississippi."[46] John C. Bennett, the city's mayor and greatest booster until his break with the Church, described the biblical Zion of Psalm 48:2 as merely the "great prototype of Nauvoo."[47] The comment is even more striking in light of Hyde's published impressions of the "original" holy land. Smith dispatched Hyde as a missionary to Palestine in 1840, and the latter related that he found the land there sorely lacking in a way that he believed only enhanced the religious awe of the American landscape.

> What were anciently called Mount Zion and Mount Calvary, are both within the present walls of the city. We should not call them mountains in America, or hardly hills; but gentle elevations or rises of land. . . . [A]s I stood upon

it and contemplated what the prophets had said of Zion in the last days, and what should be done in her, I could no more bring my mind to believe that the magnet of truth in them which guided their words, pointed to this place, any more than I could believe that a camel can go through the eye of a needle, or a rich man enter into the kingdom of God.

The landscape of Palestine, Hyde thought, was inadequate to serve as a scene for the events of the last days. Judging by the landscape, Hyde found it evident that biblical prophecy must refer to "the land of Joseph [and here he means Smith], far in the west, where the spread eagle of America floats in the breeze and shadows the land; where those broad rivers and streams roll the waters of the western world to the fathomless abyss of the ocean."[48]

Joseph Smith's most important contribution to the widespread impression of the appropriateness of Nauvoo's landscape was his selection of the temple site. Temples were an essential focus of earlier town plans designed by Smith in Ohio and Missouri. His original 1839 plat of Nauvoo, however, designated no temple site, due to the fact (as Flanders surmised) that the site he knew he wanted had not yet been purchased by the Church and was still in private hands.[49] Smith knew that the landscape could only be used to its best effect with the temple planted on the high bluff overlooking the river. Unique among the temple sites Smith selected, the Nauvoo site was dictated by natural landforms, rather than by the ideal plat of the town. Unlike previous temple sites, Nauvoo's was not at the center of Smith's town plan until the plat was essentially redrawn around it sometime later. Also in striking contrast to Smith's previous temple plans, this one faced west rather than east, taking full advantage of the dramatic view of the river and presenting the best possible view of the temple from the river.[50]

The Prophet intended for the thing to be noticed. The temple's prospect featured prominently in an 1840 letter to the Church's leadership, then serving as missionaries in England, regarding initial plans for promoting immigration. "We have secured one of the most lovely situations for it in this region of the country. It is expected to be considerably larger than the one in Kirtland, and on a more magnificent scale, and which will undoubtedly attract the attention of the great men of the earth."[51]

The temple was unfinished at Smith's death in 1844. Throughout his time at Nauvoo, though, the building temple overlooking the river had the desired effect on Mormons and non-Mormons alike. "Every thing about it is on a magnificent scale, and when finished and seen from the opposite side of the river, it will present one, if not the most beautiful, chaste, and noble specimens of architecture to be found in the world."[52] One non-Mormon visitor called the unfinished temple "the wonder of the world."[53]

No travelers seem to have rhapsodized about plain, humble Kirtland, Ohio, and the broad landscape of Missouri, which had so inspired Smith, was never so easily appreciated in a focal, defining view. Missouri was the "land" of Zion—a dispersed group of settlements in an area promised to God's people. Prevented from beginning temples there beyond laying cornerstones, and without the Prophet in regular residence, it never presented the focal point that Nauvoo's river prospect provided. Sailing up the wide river, with the temple of God visible on the highest hill under the instruction of the Prophet, Nauvoo told beleaguered immigrants that they were the people of God come home.

Just as Mormon rhetoric presented the landscape of Nauvoo as a fitting backdrop for some events, it also described it as unfit for others. In 1842, the pastoral, civilized, and civilizing scene of the little river bend became a favorite rhetorical device in denials and denunciations of plural marriage. Although rumors of sexual transgression had followed Joseph Smith since his time in Kirtland, talk of polygamy reached a fever pitch in 1842 when John C. Bennett, a member of the Prophet's inner circle, turned against him and began bellowing his knowledge of the practice to anyone who would listen. Smith had, in fact, been a practicing polygamist at least since 1841—he married at least eight and as many as thirteen women in 1842 alone.[54] By the time of his death in 1844, Nauvoo was home to dozens of secretly polygamous families, but the Prophet publicly denied such accusations for as long as he lived.[55]

The denials that appeared in the Church's publications had a rhetorical intent aimed not just at outside critics but at the majority of Mormons who had not yet been introduced to the doctrine of plural marriage. Denials relied heavily on a cultivated image of Nauvoo's civility and a parallel public agreement with the common assumption that polygamy was a backward, barbaric practice. The October 1, 1842, issue of *Times and Seasons* drove those dual strategies home in dramatic fashion. In that issue, the paper published an account of the archaeological travels of Frederick Catherwood and John Lloyd Stephens, explorers whose findings Smith referenced on a few occasions as proof of the prehistoric American civilization described in the Book of Mormon. While often discussed in terms of Smith's desire to demonstrate empirical support for his scriptural productions, the timing and content of this particular reference to Catherwood and Stephens suggests that it may have been prompted by a different concern. In addition to descriptions of ruins, the excerpt happens to feature a town on the bank of a river and a man with interesting marriage practices.

> On a fine morning, after a heavy rain, they set off for the ruins. After a ride of about half an hour, over an execrable road, they again reached the Am-ates. The village was pleasantly situated on the bank of the river, and elevated about thirty feet. The river was here about two hundred feet wide, and ford-able in every part except a few deep holes. Generally it did not exceed three feet in depth, and in many places was not so deep; but below it was said to be navigable to the sea for boats not drawing more than three feet [of] water. They embarked in two canoes dug out of cedar-trees, and proceeded down the river for a couple of miles, where they took on board a negro man named Juan Lima, and his two wives. This black scoundrel, as Mr. C. marks him down in his notebook, was to be their guide.[56]

The appearance of the "pleasantly situated" river village and the polyga-mous Juan Lima in a publication edited by Joseph Smith in the fall of 1842 might be dismissed as coincidence if this same issue did not also feature both an extended description of the "industry" of Nauvoo and a direct rebuttal of the charges of polygamy. In an editorial called simply "Nauvoo," the genteel character of the city is extolled yet again in the pages of *Times and Seasons:* "For three or four miles upon the river and about the same distance back in the country, Nauvoo presents a city of gardens, ornamented with the dwell-ings of those who have made a covenant by sacrifice, and are guided by rev-elation, an exception to all other societies upon the earth." A section later in the same issue gives a detailed exposition of the Church's official views on marriage, which dictate "according to the custom of all civilized nations" that they be monogamous. Below that are carefully worded affidavits from male leaders of the Church and members of the women's organization denying a polygynous "secret wife system." In short, this is a special anti-polygamy issue of *Times and Seasons,* and we can see here how the rhetoric of landscape was used to counter such scandalous charges. Unlike the little village known to the "black scoundrel" Juan Lima—elevated slightly, on a shallow river traversed with dug-out canoes, bordered by "execrable" roads—the neat, tidy, industri-ous Nauvoo—with a beautiful temple on a high point, on the deep and power-ful Mississippi traversed by commerce-bearing steamboats—could not be the scene for a vice such as polygamy.

Nauvoo's landscape could help convince even non-Mormons that polyg-amy was a myth. A letter published in *Times and Seasons* with the signature "Hospes" repeatedly emphasizes the visual element of visiting Nauvoo—"I am not about to relate any thing wonderful in itself . . . or any thing but what every individual may see, would he but take the trouble to come here and open his eyes." Hospes finds the site to be "indeed one of surpassing beauty; probably the most beautiful of any on the river" and connects that beauty to the impossibility of "iniquitous" polygamy taking place there. He ends with a visual challenge: "Gentlemen come and see for yourselves."[57]

On the other hand, outsiders predisposed to suspicion of Mormonism experienced the beauty of Nauvoo's scene as a dissonance. English traveler William Aitken lamented the desecration of such natural beauty by the activities of Joseph Smith: "Alas! That the beauties of nature should be sullied by superstition, and the choicest gifts of nature stained by the avarice, cupidity, and petty ambition of man."[58] Caswall considered the "beautiful situation" of Nauvoo at odds with the "most astonishing and unaccountable delusion" of Mormonism.[59] In their writings, both Aitken and Caswall evince a starkly negative view of Mormonism prior to their visits. Both English, they were concerned about the number of their countrymen "disposed to follow the miserable phantom which Joseph Smith has set up."[60] Their reflections on Nauvoo further illustrate the rhetorical capacity of landscape—the scene of Nauvoo conjured certain expectations for action which critics of Mormonism found frustrated by the presence of what they were already convinced was a false religion. Just as converts were prepared by their leaders' rhetoric to find the beauty of the river bend fitting, visitors to Nauvoo sympathetic to anti-Mormon rhetoric found it "sullied" by its Mormon inhabitants.

The sort of challenge to Nauvoo's neighbors to which the bold temple contributed—sending, in the words of one historian, "an ominous signal to other residents of Hancock County about what the Mormons could accomplish"— helped precipitate Smith's murder by a mob in June 1844.[61] Mormon leaders regrouped and attempted to hold onto Nauvoo, making plans to dam the river and continuing to encourage settlement with the promise of "water power to any amount; and after all our troubles, a prospect of peace and protection."[62] The pressure from the Illinois government to leave was overwhelming, however, and eventually rivers farther west replaced the Mississippi in Mormon rhetoric. *Times and Seasons* reported that in California, considered for settlement before the eventual selection of Utah, "the rivers are full of fish; the woods of game." In February 1846, Brigham Young began the Church's exit from Nauvoo in dramatic fashion, leading the first group of emigrants across the frozen Mississippi.

A little over three years later, a French newspaper reported on an abandoned Nauvoo that "Située sur le fleuve du Mississipi . . . la position de cette ville est vraiment magnifique." Etienne Cabet, founder of a group of utopian socialists known as Icariens, had determined that his group should buy up the abandoned Mormon buildings and settle on the little river bend, and the landscape once again became a rhetorical tool to promote its settlement. Cabet recognized the value of Nauvoo's situation. "The Mormons had very practical men as their head: the wise choice of this locality is an obvious proof of their understanding and their wisdom."[63]

After the Church was driven from Nauvoo, the arid Great Basin became the defining feature of Mormon landscape, and the Mississippi became a symbol of past depredations and persecution. It appeared in Mormon rhetoric overwhelmingly as a barrier, most often associated with forms of the verb cross: a border long and happily left behind. "The very moment the Saints began to cross the Mississippi River the cloud began to disperse," a leader declared in 1853.[64]

Currently, however, the river view is being revisited as a symbol in invocations of Mormon historical identity. The original temple was destroyed in the years after the town was abandoned, but was rebuilt by a much-changed LDS Church in 2002. The first words of *Sacred Stone,* a Mormon-produced film about the rebuilt temple, conjure the river view: "On a bluff overlooking a horseshoe bend in the Mississippi River stands a dramatic stone edifice facing the setting sun."[65] The river is the first image featured in the promotional video produced by Nauvoo's tourism office.[66] Like the new temple itself, the aesthetic invocation of the river is a reconstruction, Mormon rhetoric returning to a focal image of its formative years. Thousands of converts in the United States and Britain made the trek to Nauvoo with an image in their minds of their new religion defined by a bend in the Mississippi River—a fitting scene for God's chosen to flourish. By drawing and affirming members of the young faith, the power of that scene helped make later scenes possible.

NOTES

I am indebted to Michael Pasquier for providing the prompt for this essay, to the American Religious History Workshop at the University of Chicago Divinity School for reading an early draft, and especially to Nenette Luarca-Shoaf for reading a late draft and helping me to refine my discussion of nineteenth-century American landscape appreciation.

1. Samuel A. Prior, "A Visit to Nauvoo," *Times and Seasons,* 15 May 1843, 198–99; *Latter-day Saints' Millennial Star,* November 1843, 107.

2. U.S. Census Bureau, 2008 Population Estimates.

3. Thomas Cole, "Essay on American Scenery," *American Monthly Magazine,* January 1836, 7. For a fuller discussion of the construction of "objective" landscape appreciation in America, see Kenneth John Myers, "On the Cultural Construction of Landscape Experience: Contact to 1830," in David C. Miller, ed., *American Iconology: New Approaches to Nineteenth-Century Art and Literature* (New Haven, CT: Yale University Press, 1993), 58–79. Myers points to the period under discussion here as the moment when Americans had begun "to forget the role of the self in the production of environmental meaning," making it possible for them to imagine landscapes embodying inherent rather than consciously constructed meanings. This "forgetting," he says, is what permitted the beauty of "found" landscapes such as Nauvoo to become contested symbols. "As increasing numbers of Americans learned to forget the mental labor involved in the work of landscape appreciation," he writes, "the national landscape became increasingly important as a repository of cosmological, moral, and social truths. Because arguments from landscape could claim to be disinterested, they carried ideological heft" (77–78).

4. Kenneth Burke, "The American Way," *Touchstone,* December 1947, 5; quoted in Gregory Clark, *Rhetorical Landscapes in America: Variations on a Theme from Kenneth Burke* (Columbia: University of South Carolina Press, 2004), 3. I am indebted throughout to Clark's organization and synthesis of Burke's many musings. See also Jared Farmer, *On Zion's Mount: Mormons, Indians, and the American Landscape* (Cambridge, MA: Harvard University Press, 2008), a less theoretically preoccupied, elegant look at similar themes, tracing the rhetorical "discovery" and use of elements of landscape in an area of north-central Utah.

5. Clark, *Rhetorical Landscapes,* 5.

6. Burke, *A Grammar of Motives* (New York: Prentice-Hall, 1945), 3.

7. Clark, *Rhetorical Landscapes,* 9.

8. H. Michael Marquardt, *The Joseph Smith Revelations: Text and Commentary* (Salt Lake City: Signature Books, 1999), 80; *Doctrine and Covenants of the Church of Jesus Christ of Latter-day Saints* (Salt Lake City: Church of Jesus Christ of Latter-day Saints, 1981), 29:7–8.

9. Robert Bruce Flanders, *Nauvoo: Kingdom on the Mississippi* (Urbana: University of Illinois Press, 1965), 34, 29–30.

10. Farmer, *On Zion's Mount,* 36.

11. Ibid., 44.

12. B. H. Roberts, *History of the Church of Jesus Christ of Latter-day Saints* (Salt Lake City: Deseret News, 1908), 4:268.

13. See Erwin H. Ackerknecht, *Malaria in the Upper Mississippi Valley, 1760–1900* (Baltimore: Johns Hopkins University Press), 1945.

14. Robert T. Divett, *Medicine and the Mormons* (Bountiful, UT: Horizon, 1981), 64; quoted in George Givens, *In Old Nauvoo: Everyday Life in the City of Joseph* (Salt Lake City: Deseret Book, 1990), 112.

15. Flanders, *Nauvoo,* 38.

16. Dean C. Jessee, Ronald K. Esplin, and Richard Lyman Bushman, eds., *The Joseph Smith Papers* (Salt Lake City: Church Historian's Press, 2008), 1:338.

17. Roberts, *History of the Church,* 4:177.

18. Ibid., 268.

19. Ibid., 8, 121.

20. Ibid., 178.

21. Ibid., 239.

22. See Flanders, *Nauvoo,* 115–43.

23. Roberts, *History of the Church,* 4:362.

24. Flanders, *Nauvoo,* 54.

25. Joseph Smith, Sydney Rigdon, and Hyrum Smith, "A Proclamation to the Saints Scattered Abroad," *Times and Seasons,* 15 January 1841, 274. See also Roberts, *History of the Church,* 4:268.

26. "Information to Emigrants," *Millennial Star,* August 1841, 56–57.

27. Ibid.

28. John Needham, "Letter from Nauvoo," *Millennial Star,* October 1843, 87.

29. See *Times and Seasons,* September 1840, 174; 15 November 1841, 602; 1 October 1844, 669.

30. Ibid., June 1840, 123.

31. John O. Anfinson, *The River We Have Wrought: A History of the Upper Mississippi* (Minneapolis: University of Minnesota Press, 2003), 15.

32. Calvin R. Fremling, *Immortal River: The Upper Mississippi in Ancient and Modern Times* (Madison: University of Wisconsin Press, 2005), 207.

33. *Times and Seasons,* June 1840, 122.

34. John Smith, "To the Saints Scattered Abroad," *Times and Seasons,* September 1840, 174.

35. See Donald L. Enders, "A Dam for Nauvoo: An Attempt to Industrialize the City," *BYU Studies* 18, no. 2 (Winter 1978): 246–54.

36. Henry Caswall, *The City of the Mormons; or, Three Days at Nauvoo in 1842* (London: J.G.F. and J. Rivington, 1842), 7.

37. Flanders, *Nauvoo,* 154

38. "War! War!! and Rumors of War!!!" *Times and Seasons,* 2 August 1841, 496; *Millennial Star,* October 1841, 84.

39. Brigham Young et al., "Epistle of the Twelve," *Times and Seasons,* 2 May 1842, 767.

40. "The Mormon Prophet," *Christian Reflector,* 2 January 1845, 8; *Times and Seasons* 1 April 1845, 855.

41. "War! War!! and Rumors of War!!!"; *Millennial Star,* October 1841, 84.

42. L. O. Littlefield, "Sights from the Lone Tree," *Times and Seasons,* 15 November 1841, 587.

43. W. Rowley, *Times and Seasons,* 1 February 1844, 429.

44. "Conference Minutes," *Times and Seasons,* 15 April 1842, 763.

45. W. Woodruff, "Sabbath Scene in Nauvoo," 15 April 1842, 752.

46. *Times and Seasons,* June 1840, 116.

47. JOAB, General in Israel [John C. Bennett], *Times and Seasons,* 1 January 1842, 650; "Extract from a Letter," *Millennial Star,* July 1842, 48.

48. Orson Hyde, "A Sketch of the Travels and Ministry of Elder Orson Hyde," *Times and Seasons,* 15 July 1842, 851.

49. Flanders, *Nauvoo,* 43.

50. Steven L. Olsen, "The Mormon Ideology of Place: Cosmic Symbolism of the City of Zion, 1830–1846" (PhD diss., University of Chicago, 1985), 222–23.

51. Roberts, *History of the Church,* 4:229.

52. "Extract from the Salem (Mass.) *Advertizer and Argus,* [from] a lecture delivered in Salem, by Mr. J. B. Newhall," *Times and Seasons,* 15 June 1843, 234.

53. "An Englishman," *Times and Seasons,* 15 October 1843, 357.

54. See George D. Smith, *Nauvoo Polygamy* (Salt Lake City: Signature Books, 2008), 36; and Todd M. Compton, "Fawn Brodie on Joseph Smith's Plural Wives and Polygamy: A Critical View," in *Reconsidering* No Man Knows My History: *Fawn M. Brodie and Joseph Smith in Retrospect* (Logan: Utah State University Press, 1996), 173–94.

55. Smith, *Nauvoo Polygamy,* xv.

56. "Extract from Stephens' 'Incidents of Travel in Central America,'" *Times and Seasons,* 1 October 1842, 927.

57. *Times and Seasons,* 1 June 1844, 547–48.

58. W. Aitken, *A Journey up the Mississippi River, from its Mouth to Nauvoo, the City of the Latter-day Saints,* 2nd ed. (Ashton-under Lyne [Eng.]: W. B. Micklethwaite, 1845), 36.

59. Caswall, *The City of the Mormons,* 25.

60. Aitken, *A Journey up the Mississippi River,* 3.

61. Roger D. Launius and John E. Hallwas, eds., *Kingdom on the Mississippi Revisited: Nauvoo in Mormon History* (Urbana: University of Illinois Press, 1996), 3.

62. *Times and Seasons,* 1 October 1844, 669.

63. "Renseignemens sur la contrée de Nauvoo," *Le Populaire,* 15 April 1849, 3.

64. Ezra T. Benson, "'Necessity of Opposition,' a Discourse by Elder Ezra T. Benson, Delivered at the Seventies' Conference in the Tabernacle, Great Salt Lake City, February 16, 1853," *Journal of Discourses,* 2:350.

65. R. Scott Lloyd, "'Sacred Stone': Nauvoo Temple Documentary Premieres," *Church News,* 28 September 2002. [Online] Available at http://www.ldschurchnews.com/articles/55328/Sacred-Stone.html.

66. "Beautiful Nauvoo," Nauvoo Tourism Office, Nauvoo, Illinois. [Online] Available at http://www.beautifulnauvoo.com/videos.html.

6

The Mississippi River and the Transformation of Black Religion in the Delta

1877–1915

John M. Giggie

Recently I jumped into my rusty Honda Accord and drove due west from Oxford, Mississippi, toward the River. In this part of the South, you don't have to explain which river you mean; everyone knows it's the Mississippi. My goal was to return to the Delta and revisit sleepy towns whose fortunes historically rose and fell with the River. I wanted to see if the region's dismal economy had improved since my last trip several years ago. It hadn't.

My short, two-hour drive bridged two very different worlds. Leaving behind a favorite haunt whose boutiques, upscale restaurants, and colorful coffee houses symbolized the recent economic successes of the central part of the state, I soon entered its opposite. Riding the ashen heat-baked asphalt of Highway 6 and watching the landscape change along my route, I couldn't help but think that nature itself was signaling a transition from a place of abundance to one of rural decline. Tall pine and spruce trees slowly gave way to a wide flat landscape blanketed by acres of cotton and soybean plants and, every now and then, a massive catfish farm. I saw only a few workers. The sun shone straight and hard, unfiltered by any cloud. The air hung heavy and moist. Communities along the highway were small and scattered, often no more than a stoplight, gas station, and convenience store. Arriving in Clarksdale, a birthplace of the blues, I immediately noted a new eatery and a blues bar but just as quickly spotted shuttered storefronts, pawn shops, and check-cashing businesses with winking neon signs. The scene was much the same in nearby Shelby, Mound Bayou, Cleveland, and Greenville: a few bright emblems of economic rebirth struggling to shine among older and darker symbols of economic decay.

One of the hidden casualties wrought by the long-running depression gripping the Delta is history itself, especially African American religious history. It is hard to look beyond the Delta's current plight and see it as anything other than a forlorn and forgotten place. Yet no region in the country was more important in remaking black spiritual life during the first generations of freedom. Indeed, it birthed a series of revolutions in black Christian worship and liturgy whose effects rippled deep into the twentieth century.

A reconsideration of the Delta's role in the African American sacred past begins with a simple reminder of the region's blackness. Blacks, first as slaves and then freed people, provided the agricultural muscle that transformed the thick, loamy soil of the Delta into a national center for cotton production during the nineteenth century. The black population peaked shortly after the Civil War. From 1870 to 1910, when 90 percent of all black Americans lived in the South, the Delta had an overall population that was about 75 percent black.[1] It ranked first nationally in the total number of black-majority counties, some of which possessed a ratio of blacks to whites that ran as high as 15:1.[2] Although many Delta blacks moved north during the Great Migration in the 1910s and 1920s, the region has always remained densely settled by blacks.

This essay will take up the question of the Delta's black religious history and focus on the post-Reconstruction era, from 1875 to 1915. Although scholars have traditionally derided this period as the lowest point of African American cultural advancement after bondage, believing that blacks widely acceded to the rising power of white supremacy, the achievements of Delta blacks suggest otherwise.[3] This essay will argue that African Americans from the Delta reformed their sacred lives as they came into contact with modern racial strictures and new technologies and markets. As they integrated fresh experiences with train travel, fraternal orders, and commercial markets into their religion, they minimized the pressures of segregation and at times even overcame them, if only temporarily.

Religion and Train Travel

At the base of the major changes to black religion in the Delta after slavery lay the development of the railroad. Prior to the late nineteenth century, it was not a major part of the South's economy or politics, and consequently it played little role in black spiritual life. That changed quickly in the 1880s, when northern investors propped up flagging southern railroads, southern politicians declared the railroad to be the key to the economic rebirth of the region, and jurists legalized the racial segregation of train passengers. Also important was the taming of the Mississippi River. A new system of levees and drainage basins put in place along the River in the 1880s greatly limited its destructiveness and allowed for the railroad's rapid growth.[4]

As the railroad became central to southern society, it emerged as a setting for the unfolding of religious drama for blacks. By the late 1890s, Delta blacks frequently hosted prayer meetings and revivals at depots. Reverend E. M. Collet, a conference revivalist with the Colored Methodist Episcopal [CME] Church in the southeastern states, often ended his work by hosting his last prayer meeting at the railroad station just before the train pulled away.[5] Blacks also began to evangelize and construct new churches near railroad stations. In the early 1890s, black agricultural workers scattered throughout Saline County, Arkansas, heard about the construction of a line connecting the area to Little Rock. As small towns sprang up around the new route, blacks steadily moved toward them, seeking employment. Those who were African Methodist Episcopalian pooled their resources in 1893 and organized a denominational church in Alexander, a town just south of the capital close to a new railroad depot. Local historians of this church explained the move as an effort "to centralize the location after the RR was built, thus causing more of the members to move there."[6]

At more subtle levels, blacks incorporated the experience of train travel into spiritual narratives of institutional growth. In his 1904 report detailing the early growth of the CME Church, Reverend J. W. Spearman extolled the dynamic labors of early preachers by comparing it to the building of a new railroad. He referred to the older church leaders singularly, as "the old man who has tunneled the mountain . . . [and] laid the rails on which [run] the rumbling wheels, the swinging cars and screaming engine of Christianity which is making her schedule."[7] In the second half of his letter, Spearman inserted his forefathers into the Christian story of salvation, which he represented as a train ride. He told his audience the development of their denomination depended on the labors of men who, just like "conductors" on a special train heading for heaven, took "passengers who have purchased their tickets at the Calvary's union station stamped with the blood of Christ and the insignia of God to meet Christ the Lord."

Similarly, Delta blacks experienced private moments of religious conversion while taking the train or imagining doing so. In 1904, an unnamed man with the CME Church described his participation in a revival and his subsequent conversion by evoking the physical dimension of train travel. In a letter to his denomination's weekly newspaper, the *Christian Index,* he labeled the revivalist as the engineer who had "booked the gospel train" for all to board and "thundered [it] along the rail of time." The revivalist worked swiftly. He "didn't carry us very far, before seemingly all the 'blood bought' souls began dashing fuel at the place that makes the steam rise. Then the old train traveled at a rapid rate and soon we were standing at the 'Judgment' seat. After allowing us to hear sentences, some that made us tremble, cry and shout, he landed us back."[8] In this story, the author evoked the fear, excitement, and ecstasy that accompanied his conversion by evoking the speed, steam, and bodily stress of traveling on a fast-moving train.

These new practices collectively challenged the popular wish among white southerners that the railroad represented an instrument of modernity that would reinscribe racial hierarchy onto black-white interactions in the post-Reconstruction South. They also helped blacks expand the social meaning of the railroad from a vehicle of racial segregation to one of liberation. By the early twentieth century, Delta blacks commonly embedded the train into the biblical narrative of the Exodus, viewing it as the modern means of transportation that would carry them to the Promised Land of racial and religious deliverance. Early bluesman Blind Lemon Jefferson sang of this form of travel in his song "All I Want Is That Pure Religion."

> When you're journeyin' over Jordan don't have no fear, Hallelu
> When you're journeyin' over Jordan don't have no fear, Hallelu, Hallelu.
> Journeyin' over Jordan don't have no fear,
> Jesus gonna be my engineer.[9]

Tens of thousands of Delta blacks would take this literary and religious use of the railroad a step further during the Great Migration and board trains bound for cities like Chicago and St. Louis in what they prayed was a journey to greater opportunity and freedom.

Religion and Fraternal Orders

The rise of the railroad also helped make possible the explosive growth of African American fraternal orders in the Delta. Also called "lodges" and "secret societies," they were private clubs reserved for men, although most formed women's auxiliaries, and divided into local, state, and regional chapters. They typically required successful applicants to secure letters of reference from leading citizens in the local community and upstanding lodge brethren, pass a character and physical exam, and swear to respect the Bible and lead abstemious lives. Famous for their elaborate rituals, Christian beliefs, parades, military-themed uniforms, and rare social benefits that included life insurance and small loans, they provided black men with new pathways to financial stability, social authority, and racial pride. Indeed, at a time when disfranchisement effectively eliminated black involvement in electoral politics, fraternal orders were an alternative black civil space in which African American men organized themselves. Besides the Odd Fellows, the most popular black orders, many of which claimed tens of thousands of members, included the Knights of Pythias, the Mosaic Templars, the United Brotherhood of Friendship, the Grand Compact Masons, and the Prince Hall Masons. Black men regularly joined more than one order and, if they were churchgoers, usually maintained their status as a congregant.

The historical relationship between fraternal orders and African American spiritual life in the Delta was rocky. It contained three distinct stages—cooperation (1865–early 1880s), conflict (early 1880s–early 1900s), and reform (early 1900s–1910s)—that each shaped, in incremental ways, the evolution of black religion. In the first stage, fraternal orders expanded quickly. They worked closely and, for the most part, easily with churches, providing black men with new cultural opportunities that promoted economic enterprise and racial self-help in an environment filled with familiar elements of southern African American Protestantism.[10] Many lodge leaders doubled as preachers. Reverend Thomas Stringer, pastor of Bethel African Methodist Episcopal [AME] Church in Vicksburg from 1865 to 1893, devoted much of his professional life to building black fraternal orders. Stringer, born a free man in Maryland in 1815, came to the Mississippi Delta after the Civil War and simultaneously spearheaded the local development of the AME Church, the Prince Hall Masons, and the Negro Knights of Pythias. Stringer established the Most Worshipful Stringer Grand Lodge of the Prince Hall Masons in 1867 and the AME Annual Conference for the state a year later.[11]

Yet by the early 1880s, as the membership rolls of fraternal orders swelled, many religious leaders started to worry over the possibility that lodges might displace churches as the dominant voluntary institution in black life. Even more alarming was the frightening possibility raised by one black member of the Methodist Episcopal [ME] Church that "our people are rapidly being led into the idea that the doctrines and teachings of secret societies are equal and as beneficial as the doctrines and teachings of the church of Christ."[12] This was the start of the second phase, which was marked by nearly twenty years of bitter disagreements and public feuds between the two organizations. At the height of the conflict, editors of the *Christian Index* summarized matters for their readers by bluntly stating that "[t]here are two institutions existing among the people, that to some extent are trying to rival one another." Unsure how the competition would conclude and affect the quality of black life, they despaired over whether "the church or the society [would] dominate."[13] Ultimately the winner was the church, but only after it and fraternal orders underwent substantial changes.

In the third stage, fraternal orders publicly emphasized their subservience to churches in spiritual matters and banned some of their more objectionable public practices, such as parading on Sundays. These changes made it easier for church leaders to conclude that fraternal doctrines were not heretical but instead supportive of basic Christian theology and precepts. As a result, Baptists and Methodists previously unnerved by the growth of secret societies now pledged, though still with some degree of hesitancy, to work closely with fraternal orders to improve black society. By extending this olive branch, they signaled their realization that most blacks viewed fraternal orders and churches as partners in the new emerging structural ecology of their religion. In this popular consensus, they generally saw churches as their primary spiritual institution but relied on fraternal orders to reinforce many of their Christian beliefs and to provide new resources—particularly insurances, vocational training in mechanical arts, and celebrations of black accomplishment—critical to their progress and survival during Jim Crow.

RELIGION AND MARKETS

At the same time that Delta blacks investigated fraternal orders as a source of inspiration for their spiritual life they also explored the expanding consumer market for new ways to build their religious communities. As with fraternal orders, the key to the new relationship between the market and black religion was the growth of the railroad. The manufacturing revolution in the North during the late nineteenth century produced domestic commodities in greater number and at cheaper cost than ever before. New train lines speeded their flow into the Delta, where rising numbers of commercial salesmen and general stores sold them.

The enlarging scope and size of the consumer market quickly became an important if restricted resource for black Baptists and Methodists eager to grow their new religious organizations, such as churches, presses, schools, unions, and district associations. Black religious leaders, especially college presidents and newspaper editors, increasingly raised money by treating their constituents as consumers. They began rewarding financial supporters and active workers with small, mass-produced items often stamped with recognizable emblems of African American history. In 1896, editors of the *Southwestern Christian Advocate,* the newspaper for blacks in the ME Church, presented new subscribers with a free set of communion implements.[14] During subscription drives, editors offered the most industrious agents with a "fine $75 Mead Bicycle."[15] That same year black Baptists in the Delta learned that a new, leather-bound Bible could be theirs for free if they subscribed to the *Baptist Vanguard.*[16] Or they could select an "Emancipation Chart," a two-feet high reproduction of the Emancipation Proclamation framed by winged angels and a series of elaborate sketches of blacks progressing from slavery to freedom.[17]

Whether it was a calendar, bike, or wall hanging, blacks began to discover and gain access to a narrow range of consumer goods by patronizing their ministers and denominational newspapers. Even more important, they saw how an act of consumption performed through a black religious institution carried distinctive meaning. In these examples, Delta black men and women witnessed how their financial support for a beloved cause brought new products into their homes—products that were otherwise difficult to obtain—and which, in their physical makeup, often represented a proud moment in their history.

This defining of consumer behavior as a collaborative statement about religious and racial identification took sharper form as black newspapers began to advise readers directly about how to minimize the problem of racism in the marketplace. Increasingly, editors served as guides to the politics of face-to-face shopping by alerting readers about merchants who treated blacks unfairly because of their skin color. In 1894, church leaders listed on the masthead of the *Baptist Vanguard* urged constituents to avoid reading any Arkansas white newspaper or patronizing its advertisers if it failed to oppose lynching or the recent expulsion of local blacks from the postal service.[18] They also transformed sections of their newspapers into abbreviated mail order catalogues. Editors now became limited brokers of the market, vouchsafing the quality and fair price of most items advertised in their pages and guaranteeing the buyer's full satisfaction with a money back guarantee.

Sometimes they even promised to secure fair terms of credit backed by the manufacturer. Interested readers mailed back an order with payment to the editors, who then contacted the wholesaler or manufacturer, arranged for delivery via an itinerant minister or the postal service, and sometimes pocketed a small commission on the sale.

Leading the way were the editors at the *Southwestern Christian Advocate,* who, taking advantage of their publishing house being based in New Orleans as well as their close ties to the white leaders of the ME Church, forged a series of relationships with local and national white manufacturers interested in finding new avenues to reach black consumers. They openly pitched their press as one of the most sensible and economical ways to shop. Subscribers learned that they could buy a twelve-volume encyclopedia at half the normal price and with no shipping cost if they placed an order through the newspaper.[19] If they wanted a new bell for their church, they could entrust their order to an editor who worked closely with a maker in New Orleans.[20] To quell any apprehensions about buying an item advertised through their paper, editors inserted a comforting pledge: "Our readers will please bear in mind that every organ, piano, bell or book purchased through us, helps to swell the profits of the Book Concern; and, further more, we can and do give purchasers better articles at lower prices than if sent elsewhere."[21]

In these examples, black newspaper editors offered a fresh opportunity for their constituents simultaneously to participate in the consumer economy and shore up the financial future of their spiritual organizations. Yet some took a more personal interest in selling and joined the ranks of the small but growing number of itinerant black ministers who literally scoured the countryside for converts with a Bible in one hand and a bag of consumer good advertisements and catalogues in the other. These ministers symbolized the growth of a distinctive breed of black entrepreneur in the post-Reconstruction South—that of the preacher as peddler. Following established preaching circuits or establishing new ones, they turned their pastoral visits into occasions both to save souls and to sell a narrow range of literary and consumer goods.

RELIGION AND MATERIAL CULTURE

To be sure, Delta blacks saw and bought only a few of the manufactured items made available to them through their preachers, churches, newspapers, and general stores because they usually lacked enough autonomy, money, and credit to acquire what they wanted on a regular basis. Their purchases were primarily limited to simple clothing, home furniture, Bibles, religious tracts, books, lithographs of scenes from the Old Testament, and visual images of black leaders. Still, they made these items the basis of an ideology of religious material culture that represented their evolving ideas about domesticity, family, and sacred space.

The crucial locale in the making of this new material culture of religion was the black Christian home. Although Delta blacks had always seen home life as vital in producing good Baptists and Methodists, the turn of the century witnessed a burgeoning interest in domestic spaces and specifically the ideological construction of the "black Christian home"—an idealized setting in which proper design and beautification theoretically nurtured the manners and morality of all who lived there. It was particularly important in the rearing of God-fearing children: here parents taught sons and daughters how to follow the Bible's precepts in their daily lives. The black Christian home was also an extension of the church, a place on whose walls hung images of black heroes and symbols of African American Protestantism and whose inhabitants dressed properly and behaved in a disciplined fashion.

At the heart of the concept of the black Christian home and religious material culture in general lay shifting ideas about black women. During the late nineteenth century, many black women echoed religious leaders and proclaimed themselves the chief curators of the black Christian home. They asserted primary responsibility for developing their households as symbols of sensible consumption, models of cleanliness, and schools for raising literate, law-abiding, and devout children. Their work, of course, promised tangible political benefits, such as overturning caricatures of African Americans as unruly profligates and teaching a new generation of blacks to read and write. But their labors carried a more personal payoff, too. By enhancing the cultural significance of their role in establishing the black Christian home and portraying its success as critical to the progress of the black community, black women created a fresh means of earning social and religious authority.[22]

Black women enhanced their new role as guardians of the black Christian home by claiming responsibility for inculcating the ethic of respectability in their families. Respectability emerged as a buzzword among many black religious and political leaders starting in the late nineteenth century. They widely defined it as a series of conservative moral values and attitudes whose main principles included sobriety, thrift, sexual purity, good hygiene, and politeness. Respectability, although not a universal remedy for poverty or racism, pledged to lift many burdens for its adherents. Chief among them was to improve prosperity and challenge popular images of blacks as unruly people incapable of responsibly exercising the privileges of freedom.[23]

Respectability influenced how Delta blacks interpreted the role of material culture in their religious lives by explicitly linking an ideal of disciplined character to frugal patterns of individual consumption. To convey a public image of economy and self-respect, blacks were encouraged to purchase simple clothing and keep themselves clean and well groomed. Conversely, proponents urged blacks never to throw away money on fads or fancies or spend beyond their means.[24] Only evil came to those who dressed fashionably, especially women, warned Laura Brown at a meeting of Arkansas Baptist mothers held in Pine Bluff in September 1894. "Many [of them] are homeless. Many are living in rented homes and on mortgaged farms because of fashionable dress. . . . It leads both men and women into debt."[25]

At the same time that Delta blacks created new standards for the decoration of their homes, they also reinvented norms of decoration for their churches. In both cases they invested commercial goods and styles of adornment with spiritual and social significance and created a religious material culture that registered their notions of beauty, respectability, and godliness. By the turn of the century, pastors and their flocks strove to create houses of worship whose size, design, and amenities represented the refinement of the community.

When crafting popular expectations of church beauty, Delta blacks took cues from changes in style and adornment occurring nationally. During the late nineteenth and early twentieth centuries, leading white and black evangelical congregations across the country built new churches and refurbished older ones with stained wood, wainscoting, moldings, cornices, frescos, wallpaper, carpet, upholstery, rich color schemes, and modern heating and lighting systems.[26] Delta blacks participated in a regional variation of the national trend of church adornment. Developing a local visual aesthetic for black Baptist and Methodist churches, they built new houses of worship or renovated old ones, embellished them with richly colored walls and ceilings, and outfitted them with a modest range of handsome furnishings and amenities.

Often the appearance of a black church in the Delta depended directly on the financial status of the congregation. In Little Rock, congregants at First Baptist Church, the oldest and wealthiest black church in the city, lavished attention upon the construction of a new building in the mid-1880s as part of a campaign to promote its venerable status. Through the addition of eye-catching architecture and new consumer goods, they publicly demonstrated the importance of their church and hoped to attract new members. They built the most ornate black Protestant church in the Delta, one constructed from red brick and outfitted "with two front entrances, spires on both sides, a pipe organ, beautifully engraved windows, steam heat, a pool gas, electric lights and fans, a balcony and a large bell that was [originally] purchased in 1869."[27]

Few black religious institutions in the Delta were so elaborately designed or decorated, of course. Instead congregants usually built simple houses of worship decorated with a few wall hangings and perhaps a set of electric lights. During his 1883 visit to the Mississippi Delta, New Yorker Clarence Deming, for instance, reported that "[a]long with every large plantation for hundreds of miles . . . goes the inevitable Negro church." Commonly the structure was a "rough, barn-like exterior, whitewashed, and with seating capacity for perhaps a hundred auditors. Within are coarse benches, cobwebbed board walls, a long desk and platform made of unfinished lumber, a dingy kerosene chandelier with one or two lights, and behind the so-called pulpit a line of tawdry colored prints pasted on the boards depicting scriptural themes like Moses and the burning bush, the ark on Ararat, and Daniel with the lions." Although most churches lacked a bell, it was an object greatly desired. One poor congregation wanted a bell so badly, Deming revealed, that church members improvised by "substitut[ing] a rusty buzz-saw hung by a rope [that], when stuck by a stone, g[ave] a . . . cracked note to summon worshippers together."[28]

THE EMERGENCE OF THE HOLINESS-PENTECOSTAL MOVEMENT

The changes that swept through the sacred world of Delta blacks living after Reconstruction were far-reaching but not universally accepted. Many black Christians came to view as blasphemers the thousands of men who sustained concurrent memberships in secret societies and churches, pledged undying loyalty to their lodges, and openly delighted in their fraternal uniforms, public parades, and insurances. They denounced the use of the consumer market to support the expansion of denominational institutions. To be sure, these critics approved of the rising level of literacy and education fueled by the growth of denominational churches and their presses. But they rejected preachers and newspaper editors seeking to fund these new projects by selling consumer goods. Equally condemnatory was the burgeoning popular interest in decorating black homes and churches with fine furnishings and expensive amenities. These behaviors struck protestors as idolatrous—as painful examples of men and women seeking value and power not in the word of God as recorded in the Bible but in man-made institutions and products.

In the late 1890s, critics mobilized a type of counter-reformation effort, the Holiness-Pentecostal movement. Leading the way was a new breed of black preacher in the Delta, men who were born in freedom, literate, highly mobile, and eager to explore new paths of spiritual growth. William Christian, Charles Price Jones, and Charles Harrison Mason spent much of their childhoods working on farms, received rudimentary schooling, and entered the Baptist ministry in their early teens only to publicly renounce it several years later. They shared a central message: that earthly comfort, security, and authority lay not in the teaching of any black Baptist or Methodist church but only in the acceptance of their new theology of moral perfectionism.[29] At its core lay the idea that Christians of any rank or station in life could suddenly be sanctified and forever cleansed of sin. Most denominational ministers embraced this belief as well, but only as an abstract doctrine of faith with little practical application to daily life. In contrast, Christian, Jones, and Mason confidently asserted that God readily and frequently imparted sanctification to his faithful. Those who experienced it were never the same because they earned a promise of eternal salvation and often a range of spiritual powers that recalled the gifts of Jesus' apostles, such as the ability to heal bodily ills, cast out evil spirits, testify, or prophesy.

The implications of basing a new religious movement on the radical experience of sanctification included practices that directly contradicted some recent reforms in Baptist and Methodist life. Sanctified Christians led visibly "holy lives." Placing faith in the Holy Spirit to provide for their needs and wants, they followed a strict disciplinary code characterized by an unswerving devotion to keeping the body pure and soul sinless. As a result, they avoided dancing, smoking, drinking alcohol, swearing, parading in public, wearing expensive clothes, and decorating their churches or their homes with costly goods. Breaking with long-standing tradition in black denominational churches, Holiness leaders also decreed that preachers only needed to be sanctified; formal education was no prerequisite. Women could serve in most high-ranking positions with the exception of pastor. Clerics and congregants alike could worship in a new style open to improvisation and spontaneity as men, women, and children reacted to being seized and shaken by the Holy Spirit.

The Holiness-Pentecostal movement quickly won thousands of converts and eventually spread east and west of the Mississippi River to become the fastest-growing form of organized black religion in the nation during the twentieth century.[30] It eventually divided into two branches, one led by Mason, which accepted his notion that the truly sanctified demonstrated their elect status by speaking in tongues; and the other directed by Christian and Jones, which rejected Mason's contention. Though initially criticized by Baptist and Methodist ministers, the Holiness-Pentecostal movement influenced the later development of denominational churches. By the 1930s, Baptist and Methodist preachers in the Delta and beyond welcomed into their churches the exuberant worship style of the Holiness-Pentecostal movement and its openness to women serving in formal leadership posts.

Although the African American Holiness-Pentecostal movement emerged as a direct response to the sweeping changes to black denominational life in the Delta after Reconstruction, it should not be analyzed apart from them. Its founders shared a common thread of spiritual experimentation and renewal with black Baptists and Methodists who reorganized their spiritual lives based on experiences with train travel, fraternal orders, and consumer markets under segregation. And when all of these developments in black religion are viewed collectively, they testify to a remarkable level of cultural innovation and syncretism during the years of Jim Crow little noticed by subsequent generations of scholars. Equally important, they bear witness to the fragile quality of history itself. In the black communities lining the Mississippi River today, stories of racial survival and religious adaptation abound but are rarely heard or investigated, victims perhaps of an enduring popular fascination with the here and now and larger dramas of national struggle. We tend to forget a simple lesson about discovering the past—namely, that by scrutinizing a small piece of American history we often realize larger themes central to the nation's story as a whole. In the case of studying black Delta religion in the post-Reconstruction era, we deepen our appreciation for the contested nature of segregation and the endlessly surprising ways that religion shaped African American identity.

NOTES

1. Department of Commerce, Bureau of the Census, *The Social and Economic Status of the Black Population in the United States: An Historical Overview, 1790–1978* (Washington, DC: Government Printing Office, 1979), Current Population Reports,

Special Studies Series P-23, no. 80 [1979], 13–20. In 1870, 91 percent of all black Americans lived in the South; in 1910, the number was 89 percent. For the purpose of their report, the Census Bureau defined the "South" as a region encompassing all of the former Confederacy plus Delaware, Maryland, West Virginia, Kentucky, Oklahoma, and the District of Columbia.

2. Bureau of the Census, *Negro Population, 1790–1915* (Washington, DC: Government Printing Office, 1918), 35–36, 46–49, 51, 115, 125, 127, 129, 131, 569–73, 777, 782, 784, 787–88. For population and agricultural census data for 1870–1920, I also relied on the University of Virginia Geospatial and Statistical Data Center's *United States Historical Census Data Browser,* online, 1998. Available: http://fisher.lib.virginia .edu/census/. Thanks to Patrick Murphy for his assistance in retrieving and tabulating this data.

3. Rayford W. Logan, *The Negro in American Life and Thought: The Nadir, 1877– 1901* (New York: Dial, 1954), is credited with dubbing *nadir* as a descriptive term for the lack of black cultural advancements during the post-Reconstruction era.

4. Nan Woodruff, *American Congo: The African American Freedom Struggle in the Delta* (Cambridge, MA: Harvard University Press, 2004), 10, 14, 23, 26, 32; Mikko Saikku, *This Delta, This Land: An Environmental History of the Yazoo-Mississippi Floodplain* (Athens: University of Georgia Press, 2005), 152, 154–56, who notes that by 1912 the levee system along the Mississippi and its tributaries was about fifteen hundred miles. See also John Wills, *Forgotten Time: The Yazoo-Mississippi Delta after the Civil War* (Charlottesville: University Press of Virginia, 2000), 6–8; Harris, *Deep Souths,* 42–43, 44, 47, 81, 213; Jeannie Whayne, *A New Plantation South: Land, Labor, and Federal Favor in the Twentieth Century* (Fayetteville: University of Arkansas Press, 1996), 1, 3, 14, 103, 116; and Thomas Foti, "The River's Gifts and Curses," in Jeannie Whayne and Willard B. Gatewood, eds., *The Arkansas Delta: Land of Paradox* (Fayetteville: University of Arkansas Press, 1993), 37, 42, 48.

5. "A.C.," 22 June 1898, *Southwestern Christian Advocate* [*SWCA*].

6. African Methodist Episcopal Church, box 435, folder 7, "Methodist," Works Project Administration–Historical Record Survey [WPA-HRS], University of Arkansas at Fayetteville [UAK-F]. In 1885, hoping to be "closer to the majority of the members," congregants of the Primitive Baptist Church in Salem, Arkansas, moved their original church on "Griggsby Ford Dirt Road where I[ndependent] M[oun]t[ain] R[ail]R[oad] crosses the same." "Primitive Baptist Church," box 416, folder 19, "Colored Primitive Baptist," WPA-HRS, UAK-F.

7. J. W. Spearman, "A Word to the Ministers," 16 January 1904, *Christian Index* [*CI*]. The *SWCA* openly praised the work of another black minister, Reverend Pierre Landry, pastor of St. Paul's Methodist Episcopal Church in Shreveport, Louisiana, for implementing a similar use of the idea of a railroad trip to develop a fund-raiser for a new church roof in 1890. Landry sold tickets to a fictitious "railroad excursion." These were no ordinary tickets, however, as purchasers found out upon examining them closely, but were actually printed cards that deftly combined references to the church's financial need, the story of Exodus, and experience of train travel. "We are now passing through the tunnel of Mount Indebtedness with one more river to cross. With your help we will soon bridge the same and extend this line over into the promised land of Free Deliverance. Fare for the round-trip. Pullman palace coaches, $20; vestibule palace coaches, $15; parlor reclining chair, $10; first-class passengers coaches, $5; second class passenger coaches, $1." Editorial [untitled] on Reverend Pierre Landry, 2 January 1890, *SWCA.* Similarly, Clifton Johnson records the presence of the railroad

in ex-slave religious narratives in *God Struck Me Dead: Voices of Ex-Slaves* (Cleveland: Pilgrim Press, 1993).

8. Letter to the Editor, 24 December 1904, *CI.*

9. Blind Lemon Jefferson, "All I Want Is That Pure Religion," in *Complete Recorded Works of Blind Lemon Jefferson, 1925-1929* (Vienna: Document Records, 1990), DOCD 8OCD 520, 3 compact disks, Blues Archive, University of Mississippi, Oxford.

10. On the relationship between fraternal orders and economic enterprise, see the classic statements by Booker T. Washington, *The Story of the Negro: The Rise of the Race from Slavery,* vol. 2 (New York: Doubleday, Page, 1909), 165–69, 170, 171; Carter G. Woodson, "Insurance Business among the Negroes" *Journal of Negro History* 14 (January 1929): 202; Edward Palmer, "Negro Secret Societies," *Social Forces* 23 (December 1944): 210, 211; E. Franklin Frazier, *The Negro in the United States* (New York: Macmillan, 1949), 370; August Meier, *Negro Thought in America: Racial Ideologies in the Age of Booker T. Washington* (Ann Arbor: University of Michigan Press, 1963), 121, 136, 137; and Joel Walker, "The Social Welfare Policies, Strategies, and Programs of Black Fraternal Orders in the Northeastern United States, 1896–1920" (PhD diss., Columbia University, 1985), introduction. Other authors who note the significance of economic enterprise of black fraternal orders to black life as part of wider studies include David T. Beito, "The Lodge Practice Evil Reconsidered: Medical Care through Fraternal Societies, 1900–1930," *Journal of Urban History* 23 (July 1997): 569–600; Dennis N. Minelich, "A Socioeconomic Portrait of Prince Hall Masonry in Nebraska, 1900–1920," *Great Plains Quarterly* 17 (Winter 1997): 35–47; David T. Beito, "Black Fraternal Hospitals in the Mississippi Delta, 1942–1967," *Journal of Southern History* 65 (February 1999): 109–40; David M. Fahey, *The Black Lodge in White America: "True Reformer" Browne and His Economic Strategy* (Dayton: Wright State University Press, 1994); Earl Lewis, *In Their Own Interests: Race, Class, and Power in Twentieth-Century Norfolk* (Berkeley: University of California Press, 1991); Joe William Trotter Jr., *Coal, Class, and Color: Blacks in Southern West Virginia, 1915–32* (Urbana: University of Illinois Press, 1990); Elsa Barkley Brown, "Womanist Consciousness: Maggie Lena Walker and the Independent Order of Saint Luke," *Signs: Journal of Women in Culture and Society* 14 (Spring 1989): 610–33; and David G. Hackett, "The Prince Hall Masons and the African American Church: The Labors of Grand Master and Bishop James Walker Hood, 1831–1918," *Church History* 69, no. 4 (December 2000): 770–802. Historians who treat the importance of black fraternal orders in larger works about postbellum black culture include Harry J. Walker, "Negro Benevolent Societies in New Orleans: A Study of Their Structure, Function, and Membership" (MA thesis, Fisk University, 1937); Hylan Lewis, *Blackways of Kent* (Chapel Hill: University of North Carolina Press, 1955); David Gerber, *Black Ohio and the Color Line, 1860–1915* (Urbana: University of Illinois Press, 1976); Peter I. Rachleff, *Black Labor in the South: Richmond, Virginia, 1865–1890* (Philadelphia: Temple University Press, 1984); Claude F. Jacobs, "Benevolent Societies of New Orleans during the Late Nineteenth and Early Twentieth Centuries," *Louisiana History* 29 (Winter 1988): 21–33; Fon Louise Gordon, *Caste & Class: The Black Experience in Arkansas, 1880–1920* (Athens: University of Georgia Press, 1995); J. William Harris, *Deep Souths: Delta, Piedmont, and Sea Islands Society in the Age of Segregation* (Baltimore: Johns Hopkins University Press, 2001); Woodruff, *American Congo;* and Steven Hahn, *A Nation under Our Feet: Black Political Struggles in the Rural South from Slavery to the Great Migration* (Cambridge, MA: Harvard University Press, 2003). On the relationship between fraternal orders and racial self-help, see specifically E. Franklin Frazier, *Black Bourgeois: The Rise of a New*

Middle Class in the United States (New York: Free Press, 1957), 87; William Muraskin, *Middle-Class Blacks in a White Society: Prince Hall Freemasonry in America* (Berkeley: University of California Press, 1975), 37; and Loretta J. Williams, *Black Freemasonry and Middle-Class Realities* (Columbia: University of Missouri Press, 1980).

11. Alferdteen Harrison, *A History of the Most Worshipful Stringer Grand Lodge: Our Heritage Is Our Challenge* (Jackson: Most Worshipful Stringer Grand Lodge Free and Accepted Masons Prince Hall Affiliate of the State of Mississippi, 1977), 28–31. Harrison is the only scholar to date who has gained access to the printed records of the Most Worshipful Stringer Grand Lodge. Her book contains numerous excerpts from those records, and I quote from them in this chapter.

12. I. S. Persons, "The Propriety of Closing the Doors of Various Churches," 16 May 1891, *CI*.

13. Editorial, "The Church and the Secret Society," 16 February 1889, *CI*.

14. Subscription advertisement featuring communion implements, 21 April 1896, *SWCA*; Subscription advertisement featuring calendar, 28 November 1895, *SWCA*.

15. Advertisement, "Prizes . . . Prizes," 23 September 1897, *SWCA*. See also "Further Inducements," 23 November 1893, *SWCA*.

16. Subscription advertisement featuring Bible, 30 July 1896 and 8 October 1896, *Baptist Vanguard [BV]*. In earlier years, editors offered new subscribers a copy of Webster's Dictionary for one dollar. "Do You Want a Dictionary?" 16 February 1893, *BV*.

17. Subscription advertisement featuring "Emancipation Chart," 6 April 1896, *BV*.

18. Editorial, "The Press and the Colored People," 14 July 1894, *BV*.

19. Advertisement for Chamber's American Encyclopedia, 20 July 1893, *SWCA*.

20. Advertisement for church bell, 29 October 1891, *SWCA*.

21. Editorial announcement, 20 June 1895, *SWCA*.

22. For a comparison with ideas of the white middle-class Christian home, see Colleen McDannell, *The Christian Home in Victorian America, 1840–1900* (Bloomington: Indiana University Press, 1986).

23. Evelyn Brooks Higginbotham, *Righteous Discontent: The Women's Movement in the Black Baptist Church, 1880–1920* (Cambridge, MA: Harvard University Press, 1993), 14–15, 145, 185–229. See also Evelyn Brooks Higginbotham, "African American Women's History and the Metalanguage of Race," *Signs: Journal of Women in Culture* 17 (Winter 1992): 257–67. On the views of whites and especially white landowners regarding the spending habits of blacks, see Ted Ownby, *American Dreams in Mississippi: Consumers, Poverty & Culture, 1830–1998* (Chapel Hill: University of North Carolina Press, 1999), 62.

24. For example, see Mrs. L. C. Thompson, "Women's Work in the Church," 14 November 1896, *CI*. See also the calls for cleanliness issued by members of the Baptist Women's Convention in 1905 in Higginbotham, *Righteous Discontent*, 193.

25. *Minutes of the Second Mothers' Conference Held in Pine Bluff, Arkansas, September 8th, 9th, & 10th, 1894* (Atlanta: Chas P. Byrd, 1894), 16–17, in "African-American Baptist Associations–Arkansas: 1867–1952," microfilm, roll 14, Arkansas Historical Commission, Little Rock, Arkansas.

26. Anne C. Loveland and Otis B. Wheeler, *From Meetinghouse to Megachurch: A Material and Cultural History* (Columbia: University of Missouri Press, 2003), 34, 46, 48, 53, 57; and Jeanne Kilde, *When Church Became Theatre: The Transformation of Evangelical Architecture and Worship in Nineteenth-Century America* (New York: Oxford University Press, 2002).

27. "First Baptist Church," box 417, F. 31, "Baptist," WPA-HRS, UAK-F.

28. Clarence Deming, *By-Ways of Nature and Life* (New York: G. P. Putnam's Sons, 1884), 359–60.

29. I use the term *Holiness* to describe the African American religious movement inspired by Christian, Jones, and Mason at the turn of the century in the Delta because it is the term that they generally employed themselves. Other scholars refer to the same movement as the sanctified church movement, in reference to the theology of radical sanctification preached by the three men and embraced by their disciples. See, for example, Cheryl Townsend Gilkes, "'Together and in the Harness': Women's Traditions in the Sanctified Church," *Signs: Journal of Woman in Culture* 10 (Summer 1985): 678–95; and Cheryl Townsend Gilkes, "The Role of Women in the Sanctified Church," *Journal of Religious Thought* 43, no.1 (Spring–Summer 1986): 25–28.

30. For general treatments of the relationship between the African American Holiness movement and southern society, see Paul Harvey, *Redeeming the South: Religious Cultures and Racial Identities among Southern Baptists, 1865–1925* (Chapel Hill: University of North Carolina Press, 1997), 93–95, 113, 116, 132–34, 239–40; Albert J. Raboteau, "The Black Church: Continuity within Change," in his *A Fire in the Bones: Reflections on African-American Religious History* (Boston: Beacon Press, 1995), 105–107; Edward Ayers, *The Promise of the New South: Life after Reconstruction* (New York: Oxford University Press, 1995), 398–408; Iain MacRobert, *The Black Roots and White Racism of Early Pentecostalism in the USA* (London: Macmillan, 1988), 28, 34, 37–42, 50–62; Vinson Synan, *The Holiness-Pentecostal Movement in the United States* (Grand Rapids, MI: Eerdmans Press, 1971), 78–80, 165–78; Charles Edwin Jones, *Black Holiness: A Guide to the Study of Black Participation in the Wesleyan Perfectionist and Glossolalic Pentecostal Movement* (Metuchen, NJ: Scarecrow Press, 1987), 45–47, 59–61, 63–64, 98; and Elmer T. Clark, *The Small Sects in America* (New York: Abingdon-Cokesbury Press, 1949), 116–23.

7

The Redemption of Souls and Soils

RELIGION AND THE RURAL CRISIS IN THE DELTA

Alison Collis Greene

On a December evening in 1935, Arkansan Lawrence Brooks Hays stood to address a New York City crowd on the theme "Farm Tenancy and the Christian Conscience." Most Arkansans knew Hays as a twice-failed gubernatorial candidate with a 350-member Sunday school class at Little Rock's Second Baptist Church. Members of the ecumenical, New York–based Christian Rural Fellowship invited the Arkansas New Dealer to talk about his weekday work as special assistant to the administrator of the Resettlement Administration. Speaking in both capacities, Hays described the devastation of southern soil even as he touted the benefits of redistributing worn-out land to displaced tenant farmers. "The Christian mind rebels against absentee ownership," Hays told his New York audience. "Religion is needed in the delicate task of bending the rigid rules of law pertaining to land, making the rules responsive to human needs."[1] In addition to deploring soil exhaustion brought on by poor farming methods, he lamented the loss of the family farm and the rise of corporate agriculture, such as the 38,000 acres of Mississippi earth held by the British-owned Delta Pine and Land Company, America's largest cotton plantation.[2]

Like many Americans, Hays worried that the Great Depression had precipitated a rural crisis. Farmers, miners, and mill workers struggled to make ends meet when prices were high, and by 1930 the raw materials they drew from the earth and processed on the assembly line were nearly worthless. Nowhere was the rural crisis more acute than in the Delta regions of Mississippi and Arkansas. More than 75 percent of the populations of the two states were classified as rural in 1930. They did not fare well. On a single day in 1932, nearly 44,000 Mississippi farm families lost their homes either to private loan agencies and mortgage holders or to the state. National media outlets quickly did the math, declaring "One-Fourth of a State Sold for Taxes." In the same year, Arkansas ran up $160 million in public debt, the highest per capita burden of any state in the nation.[3]

Most Southerners and New Dealers deemed the rural crisis an economic issue. But Brooks Hays and his New York audience, along with Christian reformers across the United States, argued that the rural crisis was also a moral and religious issue. Thus it demanded as powerful a response from the pulpit and pew as from the halls of Congress. Members of the Christian Rural Fellowship joined a range of progressive reformers who argued that the survival of rural churches depended on their ability to address both the material and spiritual needs of local communities. The church, they contended, had an essential role to play in the redemption of souls *and* soils.[4]

Disparate groups of activists determined to transform both the rural South and the rural church converged on the Delta. By the 1930s, the Delta was a region defined as much by the riverbed as by the river itself. The fecund topsoil, deposited over centuries by the river, made the Delta the richest cotton-growing land in the South, and this drew inevitable contrasts between the bountiful earth and the poor who worked it. With encouragement from reformers like Brooks Hays, researchers, denominational advocates, religious activists, and government agents descended on the region. Many hoped to make the Delta a laboratory for social and spiritual transformation. But if the Delta exemplified the nation's rural crisis, it presented unique challenges to those who sought to record and reshape its story.[5]

The Mississippi River no longer transported the majority of the Delta's residents and visitors, but it remained a powerful force in their lives. Despite human efforts to contain it, the river poured over levees in 1927 and again in 1937, displacing much of the region's population. Even in the years when the river remained within its banks, it served as both a reminder of the instability of farm life and a conduit for the region's most mobile and most despised population—what one reformer called "the itinerant share cropper." Both the local middle class and activists visiting the region drew a sharp distinction between this mobile population and "the real share cropper of the South," who presumably lived a stable, if humble, life on a single plantation. They expressed disdain for the former and sympathy for the latter.[6]

What neither local do-gooders nor outside reformers seemed to apprehend was that landless labor was inherently unstable and that this instability defined life for a vast number of Delta inhabitants. In the Delta, poor people moved, and they created social and religious structures that they could carry with them. Reformers struggled to understand the mobility of the men and women they sought to save, and they found it difficult to recognize the often-ephemeral institutions that those men and women established. Yet those who made the effort to understand and embrace the lives and religious worlds of the Delta's landless farmers outlasted those who refused to acknowledge the role of movement in shaping life along the Mississippi.

The Rural Crisis and the Rural Church

The Delta's problems reached crisis level during the Great Depression, but the previous decade had not been much better. A single-crop region dominated by vast cotton plantations on rich riverside soil, the Delta saw its fortunes tumble along with the nation's cotton prices after World War I. An agricultural depression kicked off the 1920s in the Delta, and the region's economy lurched through the decade, rising and falling in rhythm with increasingly erratic cotton prices.[7]

The only thing roaring in the Delta was the Mississippi River. In 1927, the river poured through the earthen levees built to contain it, backed up into its tributaries, and swept away Delta homes and businesses. In 1927, it seemed as though the rain would never stop. In 1930 and 1931, it seemed as though the rain would never return. The worst drought in the region's recorded history combined with record high temperatures to scorch tender cotton stalks as soon as they pushed through the parched ground. Even farmers allowed to grow food by their landlords salvaged only a few root vegetables in the heat of the summer. In January 1930, farmers outside England, Arkansas, made national headlines when they marched into town demanding food. Unable to scratch a livelihood from the burnt earth, many Delta farmers relied on the Red Cross to meet their basic needs.[8]

The notion that people could starve to death on American soil was hard enough for many citizens to grasp; the notion that, as one relief worker put it, "people could hunger with the bountiful soil immediately underfoot" was unfathomable. The same worker had just assumed that farmers had "only to decapitate another hen or pull up some produce from the garden." But the hens were starving, too, and those cotton farmers permitted by landlords and creditors to grow food crops watched their gardens shrivel in the dry heat. The combination of economic and environmental crisis made rural Arkansas and Mississippi as much a symbol of the Great Depression as a New York City breadline.[9]

Outside observers expressed dismay when they learned that most farmers in the Delta did not own so much as a square inch of soil. Unstable cotton prices and a credit system controlled by large planters and merchants drove many small farmers off their land and onto someone else's. By 1930, 55 percent of all southern farmers were landless, up from 36 percent in 1880. Black workers had once predominated among southern tenant farmers, but thousands of them left the Delta during the 1910s and 1920s to build new lives outside the grip of Jim Crow. Struggling white farmers joined the ranks of the landless in their place. In the South as a whole, and in pockets of the Delta, whites represented a majority of tenant farmers when the Depression began. Overall, 63 percent of Arkansas farmers and 72 percent of Mississippi farmers were without land in 1930. Those numbers grew even higher in the Delta. On the Arkansas side of the river, the tenancy rate was 80 percent, and in majority-black Delta counties like St. Francis, 95 percent of farmers worked someone else's land. Increasingly, that "someone else" was not an individual who lived nearby but an absentee owner or a corporation that managed vast tracts of land from afar.[10]

Franklin Roosevelt's New Deal promised relief to struggling farmers through the 1933 Agricultural Adjustment Act. The AAA provided subsidies for landholders to curb overproduction and rest the exhausted soil by plowing under their cotton crops. Ostensibly, plantation managers had to split their subsidies with their tenants, but many debt-burdened owners saw little sense in sharing their government checks with workers whose services they no longer needed. Landholders began to evict superfluous workers from their homes, replacing them as needed with cheaper wage labor and eventually with the tractors and cotton pickers that spelled the future of cotton farming. The AAA squeezed out the Delta's small farms to benefit its vast plantations and sped the shift toward corporate farming in the region. By the mid-1930s, thousands of farm families found themselves wandering the countryside homeless, landless, and hungry. The Delta had become an increasingly difficult place to make a life and a living for all but its wealthiest residents.[11]

While many men and women had no option but to leave the region during the Great Depression, a growing stream of researchers, government workers, and activists from across the United States made their way to the Delta for the first time. With a rich musical heritage, a collapsing labor system, and a growing reputation for poverty and violence, the region fascinated research-ers and reformers from across the nation. Comedian and social commentator Will Rogers, Catholic activist Dorothy Day, Protestant theologian Reinhold Niebuhr, Socialist Party leader Norman Thomas, anthropologists Hortense Powdermaker and John Dollard, musicologists John Work and Alan Lomax, and countless journalists spoke and wrote vividly about the days, and even weeks, they spent on Arkansas and Mississippi plantations. Outside observers and displaced Delta residents together introduced the region to thousands of Americans who had never set foot below the Mason-Dixon line.[12]

By the 1940s, scarcely a Delta institution had escaped scrutiny by a curi-ous investigator or activist. Hortense Powdermaker and John Dollard, both affiliated with Yale University's Institute of Human Relations, conducted eth-nographic studies in Indianola, Mississippi, in the middle of the decade. Pow-dermaker selected the location of her study with help from Charles Spurgeon Johnson, a sociologist at Fisk University who sent teams of researchers across the nation to study African American culture. Several of Johnson's studies either emphasized or included Sunflower, Bolivar, and Coahoma Counties in Mississippi and Poinsett County in Arkansas. The federal government sub-sidized Johnson's research into the problems of the cotton South, and it also funded local Works Progress Administration (WPA) researchers to conduct on-the-ground surveys.[13]

Nearly all these surveys touched on the region's rich religious heritage. Powdermaker, Dollard, and Johnson all conducted detailed studies of Del-ta religion. In Arkansas, WPA workers attempted to catalogue the history, appearance, and membership of every church in the state. Meanwhile, the region's denominations launched their own studies of local churches. Eight years before his New York speech to the Christian Rural Life Commission, Brooks Hays organized a rural life study among Southern Baptists in his home state of Arkansas. In 1934, he convened Arkansas educators and religious leaders for a conference on African American farm ownership. The Southern Baptist Women's Missionary Union in Arkansas launched its own study of ru-ral religion in 1938, focusing on successful denominational leaders with rural church roots. These studies promised to both illuminate and support the work of struggling rural churches.[14]

The academic, journalistic, and religious studies of the Delta during the Great Depression provide a glimpse of the relationship between the rural cri-sis and rural religion. These surveys of a region battered by economic and environmental crises reveal a population in perpetual motion and a religious world shaped by both the instability and the creativity of its inhabitants. They also reveal the stark separation of this world from the stable religious and social worlds of middle-class families.[15]

Even those reformers with personal ties to the Delta found it hard to understand the mobile men and women who inhabited the region's tenant shacks. Anna Weir Layne, a New Dealer who recorded her experiences interviewing white farmers for resettlement, expressed pride in her "knowledge of share croppers, acquired in my thirty years residence on the Mississippi river, at Helena Arkansas." Layne believed her Resettlement Administration work to be important, and she was generally sympathetic with the men and women she interviewed. But Layne selected only families that she believed would stay put once she moved them to their new homes. Thus she had little use for "the itinerant share cropper, floating down the river in a house boat," whom she deemed "the cause of much unpleasant publicity for the South." "They in no sense represent the real share cropper of the South," Layne claimed. Indeed, Layne recalled spending a day in a school "where the children of these people had been corralled for lessons." Despite her thirty years in Helena, Layne said, "It was just as tho I might have been flung in as a teacher in the Lower East Side of New York, where I would have no basis for understanding."[16] As far as Layne was concerned, neither the itinerant sharecroppers nor their children really belonged in the Delta—they had simply washed in from the river.

Most of the reformers did not link the "itinerant share cropper" to the river as directly as Layne, but the connection she draws between the two is telling. Sharecroppers all over the Delta—and all over the South—moved, whether they lived on the banks of the Mississippi or further inland where flooding rarely threatened their homes and crops. Yet Layne characterized those mobile workers as a "new class" that emerged during the Depression, "composed of the flotsam and jetsam drifting down the Mississippi and its tributaries." Unlike farmers native to the region, these itinerant workers were "mostly foreigners and labor agitators." Their outsider status meant that there was "no real basis for an understanding between them and land owners, and they cause no end of trouble." Layne neatly packaged itinerancy, agitation, and foreignness to the region together, and she blamed all three on the river.[17]

Indeed, the river's floodplains did host a particularly itinerant collection of men and women. The space between the river's banks and the levees, which Layne and other locals called "No Man's Land," provided a temporary home to many landless farmers. Yet most of these landless farmers had lived in the

Delta for some time, and many longed for more settled, permanent work. Layne was also right that the Depression (and the New Deal, though Layne did not mention it) had increased the proportion of itinerant workers in the region. But these workers were neither foreign nor a separate class from those who kept a toehold on a plot of land on a plantation. The river simply allowed the Delta's middle class to characterize those whose worlds they did not understand as outsiders and troublemakers, rather than as a product of problems endemic to the Delta's plantation culture.[18]

Although involvement in a religious community constituted one of the most universal experiences among residents of the Delta, churches and synagogues often cemented divisions of class, race, and geography. Plantation and mill workers rarely attended church with the men for whom they picked cotton or built furniture. Still sharper was the division between formal, established churches that served settled residents of all classes, and the informal, often temporary churches that brought together the region's large, highly mobile population of tenant farmers and wage laborers. Finally, black and white families that lived side by side, worked the same fields, and purchased goods at the same stores rarely worshipped together.[19]

Religious boundaries of class and race were difficult to bridge. A Mississippi Delta woman recalled that her mother, a prominent Methodist in the town of Sherard, "tried very hard to nurture the families" who worked at a local barrel stave mill and hoped "to assimilate them into the Sherard Church life." But the families "didn't want to come, and the establishment didn't want them either."[20] One Delta visitor noted that tenant farmers, like the millhands, were "considered mere outsiders, and are hardly recognized as a part of the community."[21] While settled working-class Deltans might feel at home in middle-class churches, the peripatetic workers that made up more than half the region's population formed temporary communities separate from and ignored by established community members. These religious communities only received attention when they challenged the status quo.[22]

For many Delta residents, the Depression was only a minor setback, and life continued much as before. These men and women congregated in village and town churches and were most often Baptist or Methodist. Larger Delta towns like Greenville, Mississippi, or Helena, Arkansas, were also home to Presbyterian, Episcopalian, Christian, Catholic, and Jewish congregations. Church social activities and societies often occupied their free time, and denominational distinctions mattered a great deal. "Now Mother loved the Sidon Methodist Church," recalled a woman who grew up in a small Delta town during the Depression. "She used to count the cars at the Baptist Church. She was a militant Methodist." Such church members both depended on and created stability in their religious lives, and for them "church" meant a solid building marked with religious symbols—usually a cross—on the outside, and with pews and a pulpit on the inside. "Church" also meant a predictable worship schedule, a stable community of believers, and a competitive sense of distinctiveness that compelled the Baptists and Methodists to count cars in their rivals' parking lots.[23]

A stable and predictable definition of church, however, required members who led stable and predictable lives. Middle-class Deltans assumed that the region's migratory labor force did not care for church. Even Christian socialist and tenant farmers' advocate Howard Kester lamented during his time in the region that "the great masses of cotton workers are unchurched."[24] Certainly, many cotton workers—like many middle-class Deltans—were "unchurched." Many also attended rural or village churches similar to their town counterparts, with Sunday school classes and regular services. But some simply did not live in a world where attending church in the traditional sense was possible. Fewer than 20 percent of Mississippi and Arkansas sharecroppers and tenant farmers stayed on the same plantation for five years or more, and more than 30 percent moved after only one year. Men and women on the move needed a religious life that they could carry with them.[25]

Disconnected even from the planters who employed them as short-term labor, some Delta tenant farmers and wage laborers had their own definition of "church." They created religious worlds that accommodated mobility but also lent stability to lives defined by economic uncertainty, exploitation, and illness. Mobile workers often cared little for denominational distinctions, and many affiliated with independent churches. Others called themselves Baptist, Methodist, or Pentecostal, but they rarely connected with larger denominational structures. Some tenant farmers attended church in solid frame buildings, perhaps funded in part by the plantation owner on whose land the church stood. Even those buildings might be Baptist one year and holiness the next—or both at the same time. The distinction mattered only on the rare Sundays when an itinerant pastor made an appearance, if it mattered at all. More frequently, religious services consisted primarily of hymn singing led by congregation members. Schools and vacant tenant cabins, as well as private homes or abandoned stores, also moonlighted as churches and operated independently from prying employers. Thus "church" for rural Delta workers often did not refer so much to a building as to a body of people who temporarily worshipped together. As Delta believers moved from one such church to another, they created a common canon of song and a shared worship style that bound them together in a larger religious community even as they parted ways with a particular church.[26]

In keeping with their emphasis on invisible community rather than visible structures, some Delta residents declined to attend church in a building at all. Drucilla Hall, the pastor of an Assemblies of God church in an Arkansas Delta community, explained to a WPA surveyor that her church had once worshipped with another organization, the Free Outside Pentecost. The Assemblies of God members, who met in a private residence before building a simple, unpainted frame church, grew frustrated with their co-worshippers not over theology but over construction. True to their name, adherents to the Free Outside Pentecost "did not believe in an organized church and would not keep any records." Most of the region's informal churches did not take such a firm stand against bricks and mortar, but many found that they could worship God just as well without walls.[27]

Many rural churches—like Drucilla Hall's—also found that they could worship just as well without men in the pulpit. Elder Ida M. Collins led congregations in two rural communities before moving to Jonesboro in 1930, where she became founder and pastor of the town's Original Church of God (Holiness) mission. Despite the church's small membership of twenty-five, the local newspaper featured photographs of seventy-two-year-old Collins and her church in a 1937 article that boasted, "Church of God Is One of Most Active Institutions in City." Collins's recognition in the local paper indicated that many locals were unfazed by the sight of a woman in the pulpit, although most of those women remained in informal churches. Collins was among a handful of female preachers who retained her position when she moved to a stable town church recognizable as such to the middle class.[28]

The WPA workers who catalogued Delta religious life in the 1930s found established churches like Collins's easiest to identify and understand. But they also provided a written record of an informal rural religious life that was virtually invisible to the region's middle class, which worried about both irreligion and religious enthusiasm among the lower classes. Mainline church leaders particularly feared losing influence to growing independent, holiness, and Pentecostal churches whose leaders they condemned as backward at best and heretical at worst. Charles Johnson echoed Hortense Powdermaker, John Dollard, and many middle-class reformers when he noted with some concern that "traditional congregations" in the rural South had begun to "disintegrate and reassemble as 'cult' churches." But the three researchers also revealed a more complex and dynamic religious world than the pejorative "cult" suggests.[29]

At the end of the 1930s, Johnson sent researchers across the rural South to study black teenage life, collecting surveys from approximately 2,000 high school students and then sending researchers into the field to interview some of them.[30] Some of Johnson's subjects lived in towns and had a stable place of residence even if they worked as tenant farmers. But many reported moving frequently for work, often leaving family behind. Jessie Henderson, a twenty-year-old sharecropper living in Jonestown, Mississippi, ran away from home at eighteen and had lived on his own since. When he left home, he lost his preaching job, one he had begun at age thirteen. Henderson recalled that he "got started at preachin'" not in church but as a result of family Bible-reading and prayers, and that he hoped to find another preaching job soon. Although his eighth-grade education meant that he had more schooling than many of his elders, Henderson's extreme youth would have disqualified him from most middle-class pulpits. His ability to find a rural church as a teenager may have been a function of the shortage of preachers, but it also demonstrated the willingness of rural and informal churches to flout standards that middle-class Delta churches took for granted. In part, it was rural believers' willingness to defy middle-class standards that led many reformers to see the rural church as a church in crisis.[31]

SOUTHERN DENOMINATIONS AND RURAL CHURCH REFORMERS

Middle-class concerns about the lack of control over rural churches arose long before the Great Depression. Theodore Roosevelt formalized progressive concerns about the limited educational opportunities and the prevalence of unorthodox religious practices in rural America when he established the Country Life Commission in 1908. He assigned experts to examine every aspect of the nation's rural life and, in the words of the Commission's chair, to propose recommendations "to make rural civilization as effective and satisfying as other civilization."[32] The Federal Council of Churches and several denominations soon established their own country life programs. Between 1909 and the onset of the Depression, rural church advocates produced mountains of literature recommending strategies to revitalize and rehabilitate rural religious life. Their efforts gained the most traction among urban-oriented northerners and scattered southern progressives.[33]

Rural church reformers based their recommendations on a few common observations: rural churches were too small and numerous, rural clergy lacked adequate training, and rural religion failed to respond to changes in rural life. Mainline progressives worried that rural believers were abandoning their faith or, worse, joining holiness and Pentecostal "sects" in a misguided search for meaningful religious experience. Correlating strength with size, reformers proposed uniting all rural Protestant churches into one "union church" in each community—or, in the South, two union churches divided by race. Such churches would operate as community centers. They would support and supplement local forms of social service and blend religious instruction with practical advice.[34] They would also solve myriad troubles of rural life by hiring well-educated ministers trained not only in theology but also in agriculture. As one reformer put it, rural ministers must teach "Erosion Control for Soils *and* Souls."[35]

Rural believers, at least in the South, were not impressed. If they acknowledged such recommendations at all, denominational leaders expressed outrage that outsiders expected Baptists, Methodists, and Presbyterians to merge their distinct denominational structures and to become agricultural extension agents to boot. For believers in the region's informal churches, the reformers' suggestions would have seemed equally ludicrous, reliant on community resources and a cross-class sense of unity that did not exist. Rural southerners snorted at the impracticality of outsiders' proposals to remake their churches.[36]

But during the Great Depression, federal studies of farm tenancy and rural poverty, fears of an uprising among the rural poor, and the anthropological studies that revealed the prevalence of nontraditional churches intensified local denominational leaders' concerns about the state of rural religion. If outside critiques were not enough to get their attention, financial concerns were. As southern denominations went broke in the Depression, they scaled back missionary support to poor churches. Only a few denominations cobbled together enough funds to maintain their missionary congregations. The Catholics were particularly determined. When Father Carl Wolf, the priest at the African American mission church and school in Greenville, Mississippi, discovered that the school needed immediate repairs to remain open, he wrote to his bishop. After a few months, the Church's national Negro and Indian Fund sent the necessary aid. Methodists were more numerous than Catholics in the countryside, and they too tried to maintain their work there despite reduced income. In 1936, the African American Upper Mississippi

Conference of the Methodist Episcopal Church (the northern Methodists) rescued four congregations in danger of losing their church buildings and disbanding. Such examples are rare, however, particularly among less centralized Protestant denominations. Many rural churches faced the Depression with declining resources, both from members and from denominational coffers.[37]

Denominations that worried about irreligion in the countryside created low-cost volunteer programs to expand their work in rural areas. Arkansas Episcopalians piloted a "Church on Wheels" program to serve rural communities outside the reach of its overwhelmingly town-based congregations. This program was even more mobile than the population it sought to serve, but Episcopalians had little success recruiting from the ranks of the rural poor.[38] Similarly, southern Presbyterians boasted of a new home missions experiment in Mississippi that deployed young women as evangelists to conduct Sunday schools and Bible classes in "needy and spiritually destitute communities." It was a brilliant tactic. Women eagerly accepted the opportunity to take over the traditionally male role of evangelist, but they also had to accept the much lower pay that the church offered them because of their gender.[39]

At the same time, the Presbyterians lamented their slow progress in the Delta. One local missionary reported "ten miles square with thousands of rural people without a Church or Sunday School" and "boys twelve and fourteen years of age who had never heard the name of Christ except in connection with an oath."[40] This unlikely claim reflected the scorn of middle-class churchgoers for the faith of the rural poor, whose informal churches and distinctive religious traditions bore little resemblance to the Sunday morning services in town churches. The reformers' inability to recognize the religious worlds of rural Delta inhabitants surely undercut the Presbyterians' oft-proclaimed vision of leading "a spiritual conquest of America."[41]

Southern Baptists, the best represented denomination among rural whites, also cut back their support for rural churches. Reeling from financial devastation, the Baptist State Convention of Arkansas replaced cash with counsel. It declared 1934 a "country church year" and then demanded that rural churches not only take care of themselves but also provide more consistent support to the denomination. This funding strategy capitalized on what convention leaders apparently presumed that rural people had in abundance: land. "We will promote a movement," state committeemen announced, "to induce farmers to plant an acre for the Lord, the fruits and proceeds of which are used for the work of the Lord." The God's Acre program, borrowed from a

similar Presbyterian experiment, might make use of church land or members'
own land, and farmers could share either the crop or the cash from it with the
church. The Baptists proposed splitting the "God's Acre" earnings evenly between the local church and the Cooperative Program, the denomination's centralized source of funding. Denominational leaders touted the spiritual as well
as the material benefits of the program. They promised, "The blessed effect of
the 'God's Acre Plan' upon the spiritual lives of the members, as they take God
into more intimate partnership with them in their farming, is great."[42]

Unfortunately, more than half of rural Arkansans already had an "intimate partnership" in their farming: they had landlords. Many tenant farmers
in the Delta and elsewhere would have been thrilled to own enough land to
plant an acre for the church. But often neither they nor their churches could
claim a square inch of soil as their own. Although middle-class Arkansans
dominated the Baptist State Convention's leadership, the denomination included many rural churches made up largely of tenant farmers. The broad
class representation among Southern Baptists could have been of benefit to
rural churchgoers had they been able to rely on contacts with middle-class
and working-class churches in town. But the denomination's congregational-
ist structure meant that most of its rural churches reported little connection
to the state convention and even less to Southern Baptists nationally. Indeed,
in 1929, 40 percent of Southern Baptist churches in Arkansas and 30 percent
of those in Mississippi made no report and gave no funds to the denomination's mission agencies.[43] Even more congregations withheld funds as church
members' financial struggles worsened. The denomination's desperate proposal for inducing these churches to support their clergy as well as Southern
Baptist missions and charities demonstrated a striking ignorance of the conditions in which their members lived and worked. The God's Acre program
did not translate to Arkansas conditions, and by 1936 it disappeared from the
Convention agenda.[44]

While leaders in the region's major denominations had little success
reaching rural Deltans, one of the nation's fast-growing Pentecostal denominations found a way to meet its rural members on their own terms and expand
the services available to them. Holmes County, Mississippi, was the birthplace
of the Church of God in Christ (COGIC), which began to build churches all
over the United States by the 1920s. Co-founder Charles H. Mason moved
the church headquarters from Holmes County to Memphis in 1907, but the
mother church still stood just outside the small town of Lexington. Shortly
before the Depression, Mason sent a young church member from Illinois to

St. Paul's Church to help operate its tiny school. For the next decade, educator and activist Arenia Mallory worked with local leaders to transform Saints Industrial School from a haphazard operation in a tumbledown shack into one of the most successful African American schools in Mississippi.[45]

Like their mainline counterparts, COGIC leaders struggled to make ends meet during the Depression, and the denomination sent Mallory to its fledgling school because it could not send money. A Lexington churchwoman had started Saints School in 1918 as an extension of the St. Paul's Bible Band, teaching biblical and functional literacy to tenant farmers' children. Educational opportunities in Depression era Mississippi were minimal for whites and almost nonexistent for the African Americans who made up most of COGIC's membership. Mason and other church leaders recognized that Saints School met an important need in the community, and he entrusted its future to Mallory. She built relationships with black and white religious leaders and education officials both inside and outside Mississippi. She also organized her students into a gospel-singing band modeled on the Fisk Jubilee Harmonizers and trucked them all over the United States to sing for potential donors. At the same time, Mallory enforced the school's strict dress code and its emphasis on frequent and fervent prayer, honoring the faith of the rural church members who entrusted their children to her care. Sometimes controversial, her methods nonetheless allowed Saints Industrial School to construct several new buildings, hire additional teachers, and establish a statewide reputation for quality education.[46]

A significant factor in the school's success was its ability to house students on campus. Their families might move regularly, but as long as they could live without the children's labor—by no means a given—the children could remain at the school. Although other private African American boarding schools operated in Mississippi as well, the degree to which Saints Industrial School stood out from its counterparts in the state was clear by the end of the decade. A teenager who participated in the Charles Johnson study in Clarksdale, nearly one hundred miles northeast of Lexington, reported that if she had all the money in the world, her first expenditure would be tuition to Saints Industrial School. The school succeeded because Mallory bridged the gap between middle-class values and networking skills and tenant farmers' mobile lifestyles and distinctive religious worlds.[47]

A few southern and midwestern advocates of church reform with rural backgrounds proposed yet a different vision of the ideal rural church. They drew on the earlier proposals of their northern counterparts, but they also expressed interest in learning more about rural churches before proposing ways to transform them. While Delta residents showed little inclination to merge churches of different denominations, many rural congregations were accustomed to sharing buildings and resources across denominational lines. Rural reformers in the South recognized the cooperation among rural churchgoers and looked for ways to expand it. Programs for rural clergy grew more popular as well, and Disciples of Christ minister and professor Alva Taylor contributed to a particularly successful summer program for rural ministers at Vanderbilt University in Nashville. The African Methodist Episcopal Church also operated programs for rural clergy, North and South. During the 1930s, southern reformers resurrected the argument that rural ministers should take courses in rural agriculture and educate their parishioners about cooperative land use and sustainable farming practices. These reformers began to experiment with cooperative, collectively owned farms as the solution to the tenancy crisis, designating clergy as the spiritual and practical leaders of the farms.[48]

Other southern reformers envisioned a more modest role for the churches. Still religious in orientation, men and women like Anna Layne and Brooks Hays of Arkansas emphasized the importance of addressing the structural problems that created and perpetuated the plantation system. These reformers argued that southern believers had a responsibility to advocate for state and federal policies that would rebuild southern communities by minimizing farm tenancy and restoring land to the dispossessed. As Hays explained in his speech before the Christian Rural Fellowship, "The Christian mind rebels against the widespread corporate ownership of land when operated solely for profit." Politically active since the 1920s, Hays joined the Resettlement Administration upon its establishment in 1935. He committed himself to its mission of reestablishing landless farmers in experimental cooperative communities, and he became an advocate for the dispossessed tenant farmers in the Delta.[49]

The Southern Christian Left Meets Delta Radicalism

As he worked on behalf of Delta tenant farmers, Hays encountered a number of Christian radicals who agreed that the rural crisis demanded a response that extended beyond the walls of the church. They also agreed that middle-class reformers and working-class believers both had unique contributions to make to the salvation of rural America. Vanderbilt graduates Ward Rodgers and Howard Kester, along with Claude Williams, once a student in

Alva Taylor's rural church summer program, deemed it their religious duty to campaign for social, economic, and racial justice alongside southern workers. They warned that the nation's churches and religious leaders had abandoned prophetic Christianity for middle-class platitudes. As Howard Kester put it, "To attempt to emancipate the mass of white and Negro workers in the South . . . only through the methods of goodwill, moral suasion and education is to invite the continued exploitation, misery and suffering of generations yet unborn." These radicals charged that the New Deal's policies fell short of meeting the needs of working Americans, shoring up a corrupt capitalist system rather than supporting more just alternatives.[50]

The Vanderbilt activists called for a peaceful revolution led by workers, and they devoted their time to labor organizing and interracial activism across the South in hopes of finding laborers ready to lead the charge. In July 1934, an interracial coalition of homegrown socialists, local preachers, and tenant farmers in eastern Arkansas formed a labor union that combined deeply Christian rhetoric with largely political purposes. The Southern Tenant Farmers' Union (STFU) quickly won support from Rodgers, Kester, and Williams, who in turn drew in a broad range of political and religious activists from across the nation. The most creative response to the Great Depression in the Delta thus brought together local cotton workers and outside middle-class activists.[51]

The founders of the STFU first met in a schoolhouse in Marked Tree, Arkansas, near a plantation whose owner had evicted twenty-three families just after they planted the year's cotton crop. The seventeen black and white men who assembled in the schoolhouse began to discuss dividing the union by race immediately upon founding it. But local white socialist leader and union organizer Harry Leland Mitchell and Isaac Shaw, an elderly veteran of an African American farm labor union, pointed out that landlords depended on a racially divided labor force. Tenant farmers of both races had little in common with their employers, but they recognized that they shared with each other the perpetual insecurity of the mobile poor. Persuaded that a successful union must be interracial, the group elected a white chairman, a black vice chairman, and a white secretary. They also appointed a black holiness preacher as union chaplain.[52]

If the union's vision was bold, its first demands were modest. The STFU constitution expressed members' desire "to establish a co-operative order of society." It proposed a socialist policy regarding property, emphasizing use rather than ownership: "Since the earth is the common heritage of all, we maintain that the use and occupancy of the land should be the sole title." No claim could have more clearly summarized the distinct perspectives of the families who worked the land from the men who owned it. The tenant farmers argued that their labor gave them as much right to the land as a title owned by a distant corporation or a man who patrolled the fields he hired others to tend. Yet STFU members knew that this vision was not readily attainable, and they made only practical demands. Members requested adequate pay for their labor, freedom to buy supplies where they chose, security from eviction, humane treatment from planters, and a union contract recognizing their legitimacy.[53]

The STFU did not claim to be a religious organization, but its structure and membership drew on the unique rural Christianity of the Delta. H. L. Mitchell recalled that one early member told him when she first heard of the union, "I thought it was a new church."[54] The mistake was an easy one to make, because union meetings revealed the deep religious faith and the common religious context that black and white cotton workers shared. Preachers—some of them itinerant evangelists whose work was invisible to the stable middle class—often led STFU locals, their mobility now an advantage in uniting men and women across the communities they served.[55]

It was the union's religious bent that attracted many middle-class reformers, including Howard Kester, who joined the effort in 1935. Kester contributed his networking and fund-raising skills to bring national attention to the miserable condition of southern farm laborers. He joined his Vanderbilt colleague Ward Rodgers, who had helped the union's organizing efforts from its founding, and soon Claude Williams pitched in as well. With both external support and internal organizing work, the STFU grew rapidly. It claimed 2,500 members by the time of its first convention in February 1935 and 25,000 members by January 1936.[56]

Union meetings often took place in black churches, in many cases the only buildings from which members were not banned. As interracial crowds sat together in the pews, they listened to union leaders, often ministers, speak from the pulpit. Meetings opened with the union song, "We Shall Not Be Moved," followed by devotional services and prayer. Its original meaning was symbolic, but the old spiritual took on literal meaning for tenant farmers fighting eviction from their land. Union members traded the individual "I" of the original spiritual for the collective "We." "We shall not be moved," they sang at their meetings and during their protests. "Just like a tree planted by the water / We shall not be moved."[57] With those words, union members connected faith to protest, vowed to stand firm, and imagined a world in which they could put down roots and "not be moved." One union member believed that the song "sprung from our lips with the mind of God." Indeed, it "refered my mind Back to the time when Moses was Leading the children of irsel [and] i believe that [it] was Handed Down for this Day."[58]

Union members found special meaning in the story of the Israelites' exile from their homeland, as well as in the many biblical passages that favored the poor and the dispossessed. Two hand-painted signs in the union office boasted verses from Isaiah. "What mean ye that crush my people and grind the faces of the poor?" read one. The other provided a biblical condemnation of large landowners: "Woe unto them that join house to house, that lay field to field till there be no room, and ye be made to dwell alone in the midst of the land." These passages come from a version of the Bible common in divinity schools and perhaps reflect the influence of Howard Kester, who had just begun to learn that the STFU's distinctive religious orientation resulted as much from its members' migratory lifestyles as from their class backgrounds.[59]

Outside reformers praised the union's radical, biblically based theology, but locals feared it. When reformers like Anna Layne characterized new sharecroppers alien to the culture of the region as "mostly foreigners and labor agitators," they implied—and sometimes declared outright—that the landless farmers who dared complain about their situation did not really belong in the Delta anyway. The constant movement of tenant farmers made new faces a common sight in the Delta, and planters had long experimented with foreign labor. But it was the new unity, not the new faces, among tenant farmers that worried the Delta's settled middle class. Even when they sympathized with cotton workers' troubles, middle-class Deltans feared that the region's underclass would disrupt their otherwise orderly lives.[60]

Abner Sage, pastor of the planter-controlled Methodist Church in Marked Tree, shared the darker opinion of many townspeople that black and white tenant farmers were dirty, lazy, and generally worthless. A ringleader of the planter backlash against the STFU, Sage told a *New York Times* reporter who traveled to the area, "It would have been better to have a few no-account shiftless people like that killed at the start than to have had all this fuss raised up." Particularly concerned with "the mistering of all these niggers and stirring them up to think the government was agoin' to give them each forty acres," Sage organized the Marked Tree Co-operative Association in 1935.[61] Offering custodial work for a dollar a day in wages to any white tenant farmer who renounced the union, Sage tried to crack the STFU's racial unity and prevent union members from receiving federal relief. He did so by targeting the most threatening and unifying institution the tenant farmers had—their churches. Sage took credit for organizing a group he called the Nightriders, which torched black churches and terrorized union members—particularly ministers—by night. According to a member of Sage's congregation, the church's planters soon raised Sage's salary "in recognition of his work in fighting the Southern Tenant Farmers' Union." The STFU rendered visible and threatening the multitude of cotton workers whose labor provided the foundation for middle-class stability in the Delta. Sage and his allies were determined to repel that threat.[62]

Shortly after Sage organized his pseudo-relief association, Marked Tree tenant farmers met to draft a response. "Poverty and misery have existed in our midst for months and years. We have seen our children and our children's children go to bed night after night without food," they wrote. Yet their defiance was more powerful than their suffering: "We are hungry tonight, but we will eat the grass of the field rather than take the miserable charity of those who have dispossessed, disinherited, and enslaved us."[63]

In 1934 and 1935, union members endured poverty, violence, and intimidation. Outraged planters and their allies repeatedly attacked STFU organizers. Arthur Brookins, union chaplain, and E. B. McKinney, union vice president, fled to Memphis after vigilantes rained bullets into their homes. Brookins reported, "Several hundred shots went through my home, one of which went through the hair of my thirteen year old daughter, taking a little skin off her scalp." The gunmen missed McKinney, but shot two of his friends at his home. When McKinney vanished, the vigilantes advertised that they would give "$25.00 a pound for his meat."[64]

The union's middle-class supporters did not escape harassment. On a January evening in 1936, Howard Kester stood before a crowd of 450 black and white tenant farmers in an African Methodist Episcopal church near the town of Earle when a mob of armed men broke through the doors. Union members identified "planters, officers of the law and townspeople" in the armed mob, which attacked men and women alike with ax handles and billy clubs. A group of men kidnapped Kester and the union attorney, drove them to the county line, and warned them never to return. The next night, a planter in Cross County evicted one hundred people, twenty-eight of them children, from his plantation in an attempt to rid his property of the union. The winter of 1936 was a cold one, and Howard Kester reported after the eviction, "Scores of our people are sitting on the roadside today as a blanket of snow covers the earth." The union aided the evicted farmers as best it could, securing tents and clothing from donors outside the region.[65]

Eventually, violence and evictions took their toll. Many of the union's most effective organizers, like E. B. McKinney, fled the Delta, knowing that to return was a death sentence. McKinney continued working for the union from Memphis, but the union missed his on-the-ground skills. Several more union members sat in jail awaiting trial. The constant migration that characterized life in the Delta intensified with the mass evictions, and the union found it difficult to keep track of its membership. Delta cotton workers had created religious structures that accommodated the perpetual flow of new people and places through their lives, but the union had more concrete, worldly goals, and it required a stable membership base to meet them.[66]

Long-standing internal divisions and new concerns about the union's political allegiance further crippled its work. After suffering disproportionately for their organizing work, McKinney and other black union members began to question the union's interracial commitments. Many STFU locals remained segregated, and black union members bore the brunt of planter violence while white members held more prominent leadership roles. As local leaders fled for safety, outside activists like Kester took on greater responsibilities. For all their good intentions, these outsiders failed to bring together the region's mobile population as effectively as organizers like McKinney had done. Seeking access to a stable source of power, the union joined a CIO-affiliated agricultural union in 1937, but disagreements over the STFU's autonomy under the alliance led to sharp disputes between the STFU's communist members and its socialist-leaning, Democratic, and Republican members. Socialist Howard Kester stopped working with the STFU in 1937, disillusioned by what he believed to be a hostile takeover on the part of communists, including his former friend Claude Williams. The union's radical vision remained, but its support had begun to disintegrate and its heyday had passed. In the 1940s, the union faded into obscurity as the expansion of corporate agriculture, mechanization, and migrant wage labor rendered tenant farming obsolete.[67]

The men and women who deemed the rural crisis a religious issue in the 1930s persisted in their efforts to address the crisis after the Depression ended. Residents of the Delta continued to build meaningful religious lives in the midst of a rapidly changing world. During World War II, black and white Deltans flocked to new jobs available in Memphis, Chicago, Detroit, and elsewhere, and they carried their religious commitments and creativity with them. Southern denominations expanded their outreach to rural churches and rural clergy. Brooks Hays served as a congressman from 1943 to 1958 and then as president of the Southern Baptist Convention. He moved rightward as his career progressed, and in 1981 he published a memoir whose title summed up his approach to faith: *Politics Is My Parish*. In it, Hays defended both his work among tenant farmers and a 1956 decision to sign the segregationist Southern Manifesto. The members of the STFU and the outside radicals who worked with them had gone their separate ways by the 1940s, although both groups continued to argue that religious belief demanded action in the face of injustice.[68]

The Southern Tenant Farmers' Union represented the most significant attempt at cooperation between middle-class reformers and Delta workers who lived on the move. The Union's brief success against tremendous odds resulted in large part from its members' ability to draw on a collective religious tradition distinct from that of their settled middle-class and working-class counterparts in the region. Its failure resulted from fierce repression, internal dissension, and the refusal of the region's middle class to acknowledge the full humanity of the Delta's mobile workforce. But the union also demonstrated the potentially transformative power of a coalition of grassroots organizers and outside activists who sought common ground in faith and politics.

NOTES

1. Brooks Hays, "Farm Tenancy and the Christian Conscience," *Christian Rural Fellowship Bulletin*, no. 9 (February 1936): 4, folder 5, box 24, subseries 1, series 2, Lawrence Brooks Hays Papers, MS #H334, Arkansas Collection, Special Collections, University of Arkansas Libraries, Fayetteville (hereafter Hays Papers, Arkansas Collection); James Thomas Baker, *Brooks Hays* (Macon, GA: Mercer University Press, 1989), 35–36; Brooks Hays, *Politics Is My Parish: An Autobiography* (Baton Rouge: Louisiana State University Press, 1981), 72.

2. Hays, "Farm Tenancy and the Christian Conscience"; Lawrence J. Nelson, "Oscar Johnston, the New Deal, and the Cotton Subsidy Payments Controversy, 1936–1937," *Journal of Southern History* 40, no. 3 (August 1974): 399–416 (400); Nan Elizabeth Woodruff, *American Congo: The African American Freedom Struggle in the Delta* (Cambridge, MA: Harvard University Press, 2003), 23–37.

3. Bureau of the Census, *Fifteenth Census of the United States, 1930* (Washington, DC: Government Printing Office, 1932); "One-fourth of a State Sold for Taxes," *Literary Digest*, May 7, 1932, 10; "Other People's Money," *New Republic*, January 24, 1934, 308; Ben F. Johnson, *Arkansas in Modern America, 1930–1999* (Fayetteville: University of Arkansas Press, 2000), 14. The *Literary Digest* article qualified its title claim, explaining that some families would be allowed to remain in their homes for the short

term and try to repurchase them. Nonetheless, the state and private insurance and mortgage companies claimed control of much of the land and auctioned off the rest.

4. William J. Atto, "Brooks Hays and the New Deal," *Arkansas Historical Quarterly* 67, no. 2 (Summer 2008); Baker, *Brooks Hays,* 35–36. On the Christian Rural Fellowship and for a history of rural missions and rural church reform, see Mark Rich, *The Rural Church Movement* (Columbia, MO: Juniper Knoll Press, 1957), 133–34. On the rural church crisis and the Depression, see Samuel C. Kincheloe, *Research Memorandum on Religion in the Depression* (New York: Social Science Research Council, 1937); Edmund de Schweinitz Brunner and J. H. Kolb, *Rural Social Trends* (New York: McGraw-Hill, 1933); Edmund de Schweinitz Brunner and Irving Lorge, *Rural Trends in Depression Years: A Survey of Village-Centered Agricultural Communities, 1930–1936* (New York: Columbia University Press, 1937); and Charles S. Johnson, *Growing Up in the Black Belt: Negro Youth in the Rural South* (Washington, DC: American Council on Education, 1941).

5. James C. Cobb, *The Most Southern Place on Earth: The Mississippi Delta and the Roots of Regional Identity* (New York: Oxford University Press, 1992), 1–6, 98–208; Jeannie M. Whayne, *A New Plantation South: Land, Labor, and Federal Favor in Twentieth-Century Arkansas* (Charlottesville: University Press of Virginia, 1996), 138–218.

6. Anna Weir Layne, Family Selection Specialist, preface to "A Portfolio of Little Stories of Folks in Arkansas," p. 1, for the Resettlement Administration, U.S. Resettlement Administration–Arkansas, Eleanor Roosevelt Pamphlet Collection, Franklin D. Roosevelt Presidential Library, Hyde Park, NY. On the floods of 1927 and 1937, see John M. Barry, *Rising Tide: The Great Mississippi Flood of 1927 and How It Changed America* (New York: Simon & Schuster, 1997); Pete Daniel, *Deep'n as It Come: The 1927 Mississippi River Flood* (Fayetteville: University of Arkansas Press, 1996); American Red Cross, *The Ohio-Mississippi Valley Flood Disaster of 1937: Report of Relief Operations of the American Red Cross* (Washington, DC, 1938).

7. On the agricultural depression Delta of the 1920s, see Gilbert Courtland Fite, *Cotton Fields No More: Southern Agriculture, 1865–1980* (Lexington: University Press of Kentucky, 1984), 91–119; George Brown Tindall, *The Emergence of the New South, 1913–1945* (Baton Rouge: Louisiana State University Press, 1967), 111–15; Donald Holley, "The Plantation Heritage: Agriculture in the Arkansas Delta," in *The Arkansas Delta: Land of Paradox,* ed. Jeannie Whayne and Willard B. Gatewood (Fayetteville: University of Arkansas Press, 1993), 238–77; Whayne, *A New Plantation South,* 138–46; and Woodruff, *American Congo,* 74–151.

8. On the flood of 1927, see Barry, *Rising Tide;* Daniel, *Deep'n as It Come.* On the drought of 1930–31, see "Drought: Field Reports from Five of the States Most Seriously Affected," *New Republic,* February 25, 1931, 37–41; and Nan Elizabeth Woodruff, *As Rare as Rain: Federal Relief in the Great Southern Drought of 1930–31* (Urbana: University of Illinois Press, 1985), 3–139. On the England riot, see "The Week," *New Republic,* January 14, 1931, 228–29; "An Arkansas Farmer Speaks," *New Republic,* May 27, 1931, 40–41; "From Mr. Coney of England, Arkansas," *New Republic,* July 1, 1931, 182; Woodruff, *As Rare as Rain,* 56–65; Donald Holley, *Uncle Sam's Farmers: The New Deal Communities in the Lower Mississippi Valley* (Urbana: University of Illinois Press, 1975), 3–14.

9. "Red Cross Remains in Field to Assist Drought-Hit Areas," *Washington Post,* March 15, 1931, M15; Woodruff, *As Rare as Rain,* 66–99.

10. Charles Spurgeon Johnson, Edwin R. Embree, and W. W. Alexander, *The Collapse of Cotton Tenancy* (Chapel Hill: University of North Carolina Press, 1935),

4–5, 25–38; Holley, "The Plantation Heritage," 257–58; H. A. Turner, *A Graphic Summary of Farm Tenure: United States Department of Agriculture Miscellaneous Publication no. 261* (Washington, DC: Department of Agriculture, 1936); Bureau of the Census, *Fifteenth Census of the United States,1930, Agriculture* (Washington, DC: Government Printing Office, 1932); James N. Gregory, *The Southern Diaspora: How the Great Migrations of Black and White Southerners Transformed America* (Chapel Hill: University of North Carolina Press, 2005); and James R. Grossman, *Land of Hope: Chicago, Black Southerners, and the Great Migration* (Chicago: University of Chicago Press, 1991). I have opted to use the term tenant farming to include both tenant farmers and sharecroppers, following the example set by the Southern Tenant Farmers' Union. Technically, tenant farmers had a little more independence than sharecroppers, although the nature of tenant farming varied from place to place, and boundaries between tenant farming and sharecropping were often unclear. Tenant farmers generally paid for the land they rented either with cash or part of their crop and supplied most of their own tools and livestock. If they had leftover crops after paying rent, they could sell them as they chose. Sharecroppers borrowed tools and livestock on credit from owners and planted crops as they were told, often under harsh supervision from plantation managers. The farmer took the cotton to market and paid sharecroppers for any leftover produce after subtracting money for rent, tools, medical care, and housing, with interest. Many tenant farmers and sharecroppers ended a year of hard work with nothing but debt to the planter, and those who made money often had to accept payment in company scrip, redeemable only at the high-priced plantation commissary. Arkansas plantations were particularly notorious for using only company scrip. See Alex Lichtenstein, "Introduction: The Southern Tenant Farmers' Union: A Movement for Social Emancipation," in *Revolt among the Sharecroppers,* 2nd ed., ed. Howard Kester (Knoxville: University of Tennessee Press, 1997), 27–29.

11. On the AAA in the Delta, see Cobb, *The Most Southern Place on Earth,* 184–96; David Eugene Conrad, *The Forgotten Farmers: The Story of Sharecroppers in the New Deal* (Urbana: University of Illinois Press, 1965); Daniel, *Breaking the Land,* 91–109; Fite, *Cotton Fields No More,* 128–62; Jack Temple Kirby, *Rural Worlds Lost: The American South, 1920–1960* (Baton Rouge: Louisiana State University Press, 1987), 60–79; and Keith J. Volanto, "The AAA Cotton Plow-Up Campaign in Arkansas," *Arkansas Historical Quarterly* 59, no. 4 (Winter 2000). On mechanization, see George B. Ellenberg, *Mule South to Tractor South: Mules, Machines, and the Transformation of the Cotton South* (Tuscaloosa: University of Alabama Press, 2007).

12. "Will Rogers Reports on Visit to Arkansas Drought Area," *New York Times,* January 24, 1931, 16; Dorothy Day, "Sharecropper," 1936, Southern Tenant Farmers' Union Papers, 1934–70 (Glen Rock, NJ: Microfilming Corporation of America, 1971), reel A (hereafter STFU Papers); Reinhold Niebuhr, "Meditations from Mississippi," *Christian Century* 54 (February 10, 1937): 183–84; Norman Thomas, *The Plight of the Sharecropper* (New York: League for Industrial Democracy, 1934); Hortense Powdermaker, *After Freedom: A Cultural Study in the Deep South* (New York: Viking Press, 1939); John Dollard, *Caste and Class in a Southern Town,* 3rd ed. (Garden City, NY: Doubleday, 1957); John W. Work, Lewis Wade Jones, and Samuel C. Adams, *Lost Delta Found: Rediscovering the Fisk University–Library of Congress Coahoma County Study, 1941–1942,* ed. Robert Gordon and Bruce Nemerov (Nashville: Vanderbilt University Press, 2005); and Jonathan Daniels, *A Southerner Discovers the South* (New York, Da Capo Press, 1970).

13. Dollard, *Caste and Class;* Powdermaker, *After Freedom;* Work et al., *Lost Delta Found;* Jane Adams and D. Gorton, "Southern Trauma: Revisiting Caste and Class in the Mississippi Delta," *American Anthropologist* 106, no. 2 (January 7, 2008): 334–45; Johnson, *Growing Up in the Black Belt;* Johnson, *The Economic Status of Negroes: Summary and Analysis of the Materials Presented at the Conference on the Economic Status of the Negro Held in Washington, D.C., May 11–13, 1933, under the Sponsorship of the Julius Rosenwald Fund* (Nashville: Fisk University Press, 1933).

14. Powdermaker, *After Freedom,* 223–96; Dollard, *Caste and Class,* 220–49; Johnson, *Growing Up in the Black Belt,* vii–ix, 135–69, boxes 411–67, Historical Records Survey–Arkansas–Group H–Church Records (MS H62), Special Collections, University of Arkansas Libraries, Fayetteville (hereafter Arkansas Church Records); Hays, *Politics Is My Parish,* 73; "Report of Rural Church Commission," *Arkansas Baptist Advance,* December 12, 1929, 6–7; "Minutes of the Conference held at Hendrix College, Conway, Arkansas," April 28, 1934, folder 14, box 24, Hays Papers; and *Our Fields and Fruits: A Study of the Country Church,* Women's Baptist Missionary Union of Mississippi, 1938, Pamphlet 103, Pamphlet Collection, Southern Baptist History Library and Archives, Nashville (hereafter SBHLA).

15. Other historians have mined some of these sources to produce excellent portraits of rural church life in the Delta. See Anthea D. Butler, *Women in the Church of God in Christ: Making a Sanctified World* (Chapel Hill: University of North Carolina Press, 2007); John M. Giggie, *After Redemption: Jim Crow and the Transformation of African American Religion in the Delta, 1875–1915* (New York: Oxford University Press, 2007); Grossman, *Land of Hope;* Milton Sernett, *Bound for the Promised Land: African American Religion and the Great Migration* (Durham, NC: Duke University Press, 1997); and Whayne, *A New Plantation South,* 193–194.

16. Layne, preface to "A Portfolio of Little Stories of Folks in Arkansas," 1.

17. Layne, "The Scion of an Ancient Family," from "A Portfolio of Little Stories of Folks in Arkansas," 6.

18. Ibid. See also James C. Cobb, ed., *The Mississippi Delta and the World: The Memoirs of David L. Cohn* (Baton Rouge: Louisiana State University Press, 1995), 98–103.

19. On the importance of class and race to the character of southern churches, see Bettye Collier-Thomas, *Jesus, Jobs, and Justice: African American Women and Religion* (New York: Knopf, 2010); Richard J. Callahan Jr., *Work and Faith in the Kentucky Coal Fields: Subject to Dust* (Indianapolis: Indiana University Press, 2009); Joe Creech, *Righteous Indignation: Religion and the Populist Revolution* (Urbana: University of Illinois Press, 2006); Wayne Flynt, "Religion for the Blues: Evangelicalism, Poor Whites, and the Great Depression," *Journal of Southern History* 71 (February 2005): 3–38; Wayne Flynt, *Dixie's Forgotten People: The South's Poor Whites,* 2nd ed. (Bloomington: Indiana University Press, 2004); Paul Harvey, *Freedom's Coming: Religious Culture and the Shaping of the South from the Civil War through the Civil Rights Era* (Chapel Hill: University of North Carolina Press, 2005), 47–168; John Hayes, "Hard, Hard Religion: The Invisible Institution of the New South," *Journal of Southern Religion* 10 (2007): 1–24; Jarod Roll, *Spirit of Rebellion: Labor and Religion in the New Cotton South* (Urbana: University of Illinois Press, 2010); Erik S. Gellman and Jarod H. Roll, "Owen Whitfield and the Gospel of the Working Class in New Deal America, 1936–1946," *Journal of Southern History* 72 (May 2006): 303–48; and Erik S. Gellman and Jarod H. Roll, *The Gospel of the Working Class: Labor's Southern Prophets in New Deal America* (Urbana: University of Illinois Press, 2011).

20. Mamie Lee Ratliff Finger, "Cora Rodman Ratliff, 1891–1958: A Woman of Courage and Vision," September 1989, p. 5, Mamie Lee Ratliff Finger Collection, folder 1, SMMSS #93-3, Department of Archives and Special Collections, J. D. Williams Library, University of Mississippi.

21. Howard Snyder, "Negro Migration and the Cotton Crop," *North American Review* 219, no. 818 (January 1924): 25.

22. Margaret Jones Bolsterli, *During Wind and Rain: The Jones Family Farm in the Arkansas Delta, 1848–2006* (Fayetteville: University of Arkansas Press, 2008), 94–101; Kirby, *Rural Worlds Lost,* 181–85. John Hayes and Paul Harvey have argued that black and white working-class churchgoers crossed racial boundaries more frequently than their middle-class counterparts. This was sometimes the case in the Delta, but such boundary-crossing was not the norm. See Hayes, "Hard, Hard Religion"; and Harvey, *Freedom's Coming,* 107–68.

23. Interview with Captain Viola Brown Sanders by Shana Walton, August 12, 1999, Cleveland, Mississippi, transcript, p. 540, Delta State University Oral Histories, Charles W. Capps Archives and Museum, Delta State University, Cleveland, MS. This characterization roughly pairs with Tom Tweed's description of "dwelling" and "homemaking" as one component of religious life. Tweed describes stasis and motion, or "dwelling" and "crossing," as intertwined elements of religious practice. I agree with Tweed that both dwelling and crossing are, in the end, kinetic, but I argue that the emphasis on dwelling among the middle class in the Delta prevented its recognition of the more kinetic faith of their neighbors. John Giggie has also noted the influence of movement on Delta religious life in his study of African Americans in the Delta before the Depression. Thomas A. Tweed, *Crossing and Dwelling: A Theory of Religion* (Cambridge, MA: Harvard University Press, 2006), 54–163; and Giggie, *After Redemption,* 23–58.

24. Kester, *Revolt among the Sharecroppers,* 47.

25. Turner, *A Graphic Summary of Farm Tenure,* 47–48; and T. J. Woofter Jr., *Landlord and Tenant on the Cotton Plantation* (Washington, DC: Works Progress Administration, 1936), 107–24.

26. A survey of the Arkansas Church Records demonstrates the fluid membership and affiliations of Delta churches. See, for example, White Hall Missionary Baptist Church, Hilleman, Woodruff County, folder 18, box 415, Arkansas Church Records; and Church of God (Cleveland), Haynes, Lee County, folder 104, box 427, Arkansas Church Records. John Hayes also notes the disregard of many rural churches for denominational structures: Hayes, "Hard, Hard Religion," 16–17. On informal churches in the mobile South and the nature of rural churches, see Michael Berger, *The Devil Wagon in God's Country: The Automobile and Social Change in Rural America, 1893–1929* (Hamden, CT.: Archon Books, 1979), 128–30; Benson Y. Landis and George Edmund Haynes, *Cotton-Growing Communities Study Number 2: Case Studies of 10 Rural Communities and 10 Plantations in Arkansas* (New York: Department of Race Relations, Federal Council of Churches of Christ in America, 1935); Work et al., *Lost Delta Found,* 229, 237–46; and Lawrence J. Nelson, "Welfare Capitalism on a Mississippi Plantation in the Great Depression," *Journal of Southern History* 50, no. 2 (May 1984): 225–50.

27. "Assembly of God Pentecost, Greenfield, Poinsett County," folder 11, box 412, Arkansas Church Records.

28. Ibid., "Original Church of God (Holiness), Jonesboro, Craighead County, folder 119, box 429, Arkansas Church Records. See also Assembly of God, Wynne

(1020 Union Street), Cross County, folder 7, box 411, Arkansas Church Records. On the role of women in southern churches, see Butler, *Women in the Church of God in Christ;* Cheryl Townsend Gilkes, *If It Wasn't for the Women: Black Women's Experience and Womanist Culture in Church and Community* (Maryknoll, NY: Orbis Books, 2001); Glenda Elizabeth Gilmore, *Gender and Jim Crow: Women and the Politics of White Supremacy in North Carolina, 1896–1920* (Chapel Hill: University of North Carolina Press, 1996); Evelyn Brooks Higginbotham, *Righteous Discontent: The Women's Movement in the Black Baptist Church, 1880–1920* (Cambridge, MA: Harvard University Press, 1993); John Patrick McDowell, *The Social Gospel in the South: The Woman's Home Mission Movement in the Methodist Episcopal Church, South, 1886–1939* (Baton Rouge: Louisiana State University Press, 1982); Mrs. W. D. Pye, *The Yield of the Golden Years: A History of the Baptist Woman's Missionary Union of Arkansas, Written to Commemorate the Golden Jubilee, 1900–1938* (n.p., n.d.); and Baptist Woman's Missionary Union of Mississippi, *Hearts the Lord Opened: The History of Mississippi Woman's Missionary Union* (Jackson, MS: Purser Brothers, 1954).

29. Johnson, *Growing Up in the Black Belt,* 169. See also Powdermaker, *After Freedom,* 223–96; and Dollard, *Caste and Class,* 220–49. On the growth of independent, holiness, and Pentecostal churches in the 1910s–1930s, see Joel A. Carpenter, *Revive Us Again: The Reawakening of American Fundamentalism* (New York: Oxford University Press, 1997); Giggie, *After Redemption;* Vinson Synan, *The Holiness-Pentecostal Tradition: Charismatic Movements in the Twentieth Century* (Grand Rapids, MI: W. B. Eerdmans, 1997 [1971]); Sernett, *Bound for the Promised Land;* Randall J. Stephens, *The Fire Spreads: Holiness and Pentecostalism in the American South* (Cambridge, MA: Harvard University Press, 2007); Matthew Avery Sutton, *Aimee Semple McPherson and the Resurrection of Christian America* (Cambridge, MA: Harvard University Press, 2007); and Grant Wacker, *Heaven Below: Early Pentecostals and American Culture* (Cambridge, MA: Harvard University Press, 2001).

30. Johnson, *Growing Up in the Black Belt,* xiii–xxiii, 163

31. Interview with Jessie Henderson by Lincoln A. Sawyer, n.d., Jonestown, MS, transcript, pp. 6–8, folder 3, box 214, Coahoma and Bolivar County Studies, Charles Spurgeon Johnson Collection, Fisk University Archives, John Hope and Aurelia E. Franklin Library, Fisk University, Nashville (hereafter Johnson Collection).

32. Liberty Hyde Bailey, *The Country-Life Movement in the United States* (New York: Macmillan, 1911), 1.33. "The Seed Bed of the Church," *Minutes of the General Assembly of the Presbyterian Church in the U.S.A., Part II* (Philadelphia: Office of the General Assembly, 1936), 113; and Rich, *The Rural Church Movement,* 64–71. A sampling of the Depression era rural church studies includes C. Luther Fry, *The U.S. Looks at Its Churches* (New York: Institute of Social and Religious Research, 1930); Elizabeth R. Hooker, *Hinterlands of the Church* (New York: Institute of Social and Religious Research, 1931); Benjamin E. Mays and Joseph William Nicholson, *The Negro's Church* (New York: Institute of Social and Religious Research, 1933); John William Jent, *Rural Church Problems* (Shawnee: Oklahoma Baptist University Press, 1935); Paul H. Landis, *Rural Life in Process* (New York: McGraw-Hill, 1940); and Brunner and Lorge, *Rural Trends in Depression Years.* For other historical examinations of the rural church, see Hayes, "Hard, Hard Religion," 13–17; James H. Madison, "Reformers and the Rural Church, 1900–1950," *Journal of American History* 73 (December 1986): 645–68; Scott J. Peters and Paul A. Morgan, "The Country Life Commission: Reconsidering a Milestone in American Agricultural History," *Agricul-

tural History 78, no. 3 (Summer 2004): 289–316; Leigh Eric Schmidt, "From Arbor Day to the Environmental Sabbath: Nature, Liturgy, and American Protestantism," *Harvard Theological Review* 84, no. 3 (July 1991): 299–323; Sernett, *Bound for the Promised Land,* 210–40; Karen Aaron Stone, "Rescue the Perishing: The Southern Baptist Convention and the Rural Church Movement" (PhD diss., Auburn University, 1998); Merwin Swanson, "The 'Country Life Movement' and the American Churches," *Church History* 46 (September 1977): 358–73; and Robert P. Swierenga, "The Little White Church: Religion in Rural America," *Agricultural History* 71, no. 4 (Autumn 1997): 415–41.

34. Kenyon L. Butterfield, *The Country Church and the Rural Problem: The Carew Lectures at Hartford Theological Seminary, 1909* (Chicago: University of Chicago Press, 1917), 109–28; Garland A. Bricker, ed., *Solving the Country Church Problem* (Cincinnati: Jennings and Graham, 1913); and Charles Otis Gill and Gifford Pinchot, *The Country Church: The Decline of Its Influence and the Remedy* (New York: Macmillan, 1913).

35. Albion L. Holsey, "Erosion Control for Soils and Souls," *Opportunity* 15 (February 1937), 45–47. Emphasis mine.

36. John William Jent, *The Challenge of the Country Church* (Nashville: Sunday School Board of the Southern Baptist Convention, 1924); "Erroneous Suggestions for the Development of Southern Baptist Rural Churches," *Mississippi Baptist Record,* June 19, 1930, 2; and "Where Is the Country Church of Yesterday?" *Mississippi Baptist Record,* June 11, 1931, 2.

37. Bishop Richard Gerow's notes on correspondence with Carl Wolf, January 19 and December 13, 1933, Wolf, file 11, Catholic Diocese of Mississippi, Jackson; John H. Graham, *Mississippi Circuit Riders, 1865–1965* (Nashville: Parthenon Press, 1967), 166–67; and Nancy Britton, *Two Centuries of Methodism in Arkansas, 1800–2000* (Little Rock: August House, n.d.), 171–218.

38. Margaret Simms McDonald, *White Already to Harvest: The Episcopal Church in Arkansas, 1838–1971* (Sewanee, TN: University Press of Sewanee, 1975), 218–21.

39. Presbyterian Church in the United States, Committee on Assembly's Work, Department of Home Missions, *Sixty-fifth Annual Report,* Montreat, NC, May 28, 1931, 18, Special Collections, John Bulow Campbell Library, Columbia Theological Seminary, Atlanta (hereafter CTS).

40. Presbyterian Church in the United States, Committee on Assembly's Work, Department of Home Missions *Sixty-fourth Annual Report,* Charlottesville, Virginia, May 22, 1930, 10–11, CTS.

41. Presbyterian Church in the United States, Committee on Assembly's Work, Department of Home Missions, *Sixty-second Annual Report,* Atlanta, May 17, 1928, 4, CTS. For additional examples of this call with slightly different phrasing, see Presbyterian Church in the United States, Committee on Assembly's Work, Department of Home Missions, *Seventieth Annual Report,* Augusta, May 21, 1936, 6, CTS; and Presbyterian Church in the United States, Committee on Assembly's Work, Department of Home Missions, *Seventy-second Annual Report,* Meridian, MS, May 19, 1938, 5, CTS.

42. "Seven Necessities for 1934," *Arkansas Baptist,* January 4, 1934, 8; and "Sowing and Reaping for the Lord," *Arkansas Baptist,* February 15, 1934, 16. On Southern Baptist struggles in Arkansas, see C. Fred Williams, S. Ray Granade, and Kenneth M. Startup, *A System and Plan: Arkansas Baptist State Convention, 1848–1998* (Franklin, TN: Providence House, 1998), 203–23. A minister in Asheville, NC, introduced the Lord's Acre program in 1930. *The Country Church Needs the Lord's Acre Plan,* folder 20,

box 14, Social Ethics Pamphlet Collection, RG #73, Yale Divinity School Library, New Haven, CT; Rich, *The Rural Church Movement,* 128–29; and "Religion: Lord's Acre," *Time,* September 1, 1924, 17.

43. E. P. Alldredge, *Southern Baptist Handbook, 1930,* 10–15, 45, 63, 79. Southern Baptist handbooks focused on a different denominational issue or agency each year. In 1930, the focus was on stewardship and the large number of "do-nothing" churches. The precise percentages of "do-nothing" churches are Arkansas, 41.8, and Mississippi, 31.82.

44. *Proceedings of the Arkansas Baptist State Convention in This Eighty-first Annual Session,* Pine Bluff, January 22–25, 1935, 52–53, SBHLA; and *Proceedings of the Arkansas Baptist State Convention in This Eighty-second Annual Session,* Hot Springs, January 21–24, 1936, 56–58, SBHLA.

45. On the history of COGIC and Mallory's work in the church, see Butler, *Women in the Church of God in Christ,* 96–116; Dovie Marie Simmons and Olivia L. Martin, *Down behind the Sun: The Story of Arenia Cornelia Mallory* (Memphis: Riverside Press, 1983); Calvin White Jr., "In the Beginning, There Stood Two: Arkansas Roots of the Black Holiness Movement," *Arkansas Historical Quarterly* 68, no. 1 (Spring 2009): 1–22; Elton Hal Weaver, "'Mark the Perfect Man': The Rise of Bishop C. H. Mason and the Church of God in Christ" (PhD diss., University of Memphis, 2007); and Ithiel C. Clemmons, *Bishop C. H. Mason and the Roots of the Church of God in Christ* (Lanham, MD: Pneuma Life, 1996).

46. "Do Not Fail to Read This," *The Whole Truth,* 1982 Souvenir Edition, reprint of an edition from late 1932, p. 6, folder 4, box 5, Dupree African American Pentecostal and Holiness Collection, Schomburg Center for Research in Black Culture, New York (hereafter Dupree Collection); Simmons and Martin, *Down behind the Sun,* 13–21, 27–33, 69; and Butler, *Women in the Church of God in Christ,* 96–116. On education in Mississippi and the South during the Depression, see James D. Anderson, *The Education of Blacks in the South, 1860–1935* (Chapel Hill: University of North Carolina Press, 1988), 109–85; Katherine Mellen Charron, *Freedom's Teacher: The Life of Septima Clark* (Chapel Hill: University of North Carolina Press, 2010); Ann Short Chirhart, *Torches of Light: Georgia Teachers and the Coming of the Modern South* (Athens: University of Georgia Press, 2005); Adam Fairclough, *A Class of Their Own: Black Teachers in the Segregated South* (Cambridge, MA: Belknap Press, 2007); Sylvia Reedy Gist, *Educating a Rural Southern Community: A History of Schooling for Blacks in Holmes County, Mississippi, 1870 to 1993* (Pelham, AL: Productivity Unlimited, 1995), 1–97; and Neil R. McMillen, *Dark Journey: Black Mississippians in the Age of Jim Crow* (Urbana: University of Illinois Press, 1989), 72–108.

47. Interview with Carrie Randolph by Hortense Powdermaker, n.d., Clarksdale, MS, transcript, p. 12–13, folder 4, box 216, Coahoma and Bolivar County Studies, Johnson Collection. On other schools in the period, see Claire Nee Nelson, "Louise Thompson Patterson and the Southern Roots of the Popular Front," in *Women Shaping the South: Creating and Confronting Change,* ed. Angela Boswell and Judith N. McArthur (Columbia: University of Missouri Press, 2006), 204–28; and Alferdteen B. Harrison, *Piney Woods School: An Oral History* (Jackson: University of Mississippi Press, 2005).

48. Benson Y. Landis and John D. Willard, *Rural Adult Education* (New York: Macmillan, 1933), 118–20; and Sernett, *Bound for the Promised Land,* 218. The Arkansas Church Records abound with examples of rural churches working together.

See, for example, Liberty Baptist Church, Lake City, AR, Craighead County, folder 4, box 413. For an example of a successful rural church merger (two Southern Baptist churches), see E. P. Alldredge, *100 Successful Country Churches: First Fruits of the Southern Baptist Country Church Survey,* 12–14, Pamphlet 3954, Pamphlet Collection, SBHLA. The most notable examples of rural reformers who supported cooperatives as a solution to farm tenancy are Sam Franklin, Sherwood Eddy, and William Amberson, who hatched the idea for the Delta and Providence Cooperative Farms. See Fred C. Smith, *Shadows over Goshen: Plain Whites, Progressives, and Paternalism in the Depression South* (Hattiesburg: University of Southern Mississippi, 2008), 235–51.

49. Hays, "Farm Tenancy and the Christian Conscience," 4; Hays, *Politics Is My Parish,* 120–35; Baker, *Brooks Hays,* 55–61; and "Memorandum for Mr. Porter" (1935), folder 1, box 24, Hays Papers. Hays cautiously supported the STFU, and he grew more conservative after the Depression. Nonetheless, STFU leader H. L. Mitchell considered him an ally in the 1930s. See H. L. Mitchell, "The Founding and Early History of the Southern Tenant Farmers' Union," *Arkansas Historical Quarterly* 32, no. 4 (Winter 1973): 363.

50. "Annual Report of Howard Kester, Southern Secretary, Annual Conference of the Fellowship of Reconciliation," October 1933, folder F314, box 9, Howard Anderson Kester Papers #3834, Southern Historical Collection, Wilson Library, University of North Carolina at Chapel Hill (hereafter Kester Papers, SHC); and "Conference of Younger Churchmen of the South Findings," Monteagle, TN, May 27–29, 1934, folder 328, box 9, Kester Papers. On the southern Christian left, see Anthony P. Dunbar, *Against the Grain: Southern Radicals and Prophets, 1929–1959* (Charlottesville: University Press of Virginia, 1981); Robert Francis Martin, *Howard Kester and the Struggle for Social Justice in the South, 1904–1977* (Charlottesville: University Press of Virginia, 1991); Cedric Belfrage, *A Faith to Free the People* (New York: Dryden Press, 1944); and Roll and Gellman, "Owen Whitfield and the Gospel of the Working Class." On the Southern left in the 1930s, see Glenda Elizabeth Gilmore, *Defying Dixie: The Radical Roots of Civil Rights, 1919–1950* (New York: W. W. Norton, 2008), and John Egerton, *Speak Now against the Day: The Generation before the Civil Rights Movement in the South* (New York: Knopf, 1994).

51. On the history of the STFU, see Donald H. Grubbs, *Cry from the Cotton: The Southern Tenant Farmers' Union and the New Deal* (Fayetteville: University of Arkansas Press, 1999); Kester, *Revolt among the Sharecroppers;* Jason Manthorne, "The View from the Cotton: Reconsidering the Southern Tenant Farmers' Union," *Agricultural History* 84, no. 1 (Winter 2010): 20–45; Mitchell, *Mean Things Happening in This Land: The Life and Times of H. L. Mitchell, Cofounder of the Southern Tenant Farmers' Union* (Montclair, NJ: Allanheld, Osmun, 1979); Elizabeth Payne, "The Lady Was a Sharecropper: Myrtle Lawrence and the Southern Tenant Farmers' Union," *Southern Cultures* 4, no. 2 (Summer 1998): 5–27; Roll, *Spirit of Rebellion;* Whayne, *A New Plantation South,* 184–218; Woodruff, *American Congo,* 152–90; and Joshua C. Youngblood, "Realistic Religion and Radical Prophets: The STFU, the Social Gospel, and the American Left in the 1930s" (MA thesis, Florida State University, 2004), 47–70.

52. Untitled history of the STFU dated 1935–36, reel 1, STFU Papers; Mitchell, *Mean Things Happening in This Land,* 47–49; Kester, *Revolt among the Sharecroppers,* 55–57; Clay East, interviewed by Sue Thrasher, September 22, 1973, Interview E-0003, transcript, p. 12, 75–76; and Southern Oral History Program Collection (#4007), SHC.

Versions of the founding of the STFU differ from Kester to Mitchell to the untitled history.

53. Kester, *Revolt among the Sharecroppers,* 86–95; "Declaration of Principles and Constitution," STFU Papers, reel 1; and "A Program for Action," STFU Papers, reel 1.

54. Grubbs, *Cry from the Cotton,* 64; and Mitchell, *Mean Things Happening in This Land,* 33, 48.

55. H. L. Mitchell, "Organizing Southern Share-Croppers," *New Republic,* October 3, 1934, 217–18; Clay East interview, 10, 94; Grubbs, *Cry from the Cotton,* 64–65; and Mitchell, *Mean Things Happening in This Land,* 49, 52, 64, 82–83. Several historians have particularly emphasized the religious nature of the STFU. See Dunbar, *Against the Grain;* Roll, *Spirit of Rebellion;* and Youngblood, "Realistic Religion and Radical Prophets."

56. Kester, *Revolt among the Sharecroppers;* Martin, *Howard Kester,* 86–108; Gellman and Roll, *The Gospel of the Working Class,* 52–57; H. L. Mitchell, "The Southern Tenant Farmers' Union in 1935," p. 1, reel 1, STFU Papers; and *Southern Tenant Farmers' Union Convention Proceedings: Official Report of Second Annual Convention,* January 3–6, 1936, Labor Temple, Little Rock, p. 1, reel 1, STFU Papers. Because of threats of violence, the union membership remained somewhat secret. Organizers later acknowledged that they generously inflated the membership numbers (Mitchell, *Mean Things Happening in This Land,* 82).

57. John Herling, "Field Notes from Arkansas," *The Nation,* April 10, 1935, 419; and *STFU Song Book,* n.d., 16, Delta Cooperative Farm Records, MS 13, MVC.

58. J. W. Washington to H. L. Mitchell, January 19, 1936, reel 1, STFU Papers.

59. Dorothy Day, "Sharecroppers," 1936, reel A, STFU Papers; Isaiah 3:15 and Isaiah 5:8, American Standard Version; "Southern Tenant Farmers' Union Convention Proceedings: Official Report of Second Annual Convention," January 3–5, 1936, Labor Temple, Little Rock, reel 1, STFU Papers; and Mitchell, *Means Things Happening in This Land,* 38–86.

60. Layne, "The Scion of an Ancient Family," 5–6.

61. "Arkansas Violence Laid to Landlords," *New York Times,* April 16, 1935, 18;

62. "Norman Thomas Visits the Cotton Fields," March 13–15, 1935, STFU Papers, reel 1; Kester, *Revolt,* 75–76; and Mitchell, *Mean Things,* 36.

63. Statement adopted in STFU meeting in Marked Tree, AR, March 6, 1935, reel 1, STFU Papers.

64. Howard Kester, "Acts of Tyranny and Terror Committed against Innocent Men, Women and Children of the Southern Tenant Farmers' Union in Northeast Arkansas," 1935, reel 1, STFU Papers; and "Affidavit of Arthur Brookings [*sic*] of Memphis, Tenn," 1935, reel 1, STFU Papers.

65. "For Immediate Release," STFU notice, Memphis, January 18, 1936, reel 1, STFU Papers; and H. L. Mitchell and Howard Kester to the Editor of *Nation,* January 16, 1936, reel 1, STFU Papers.

66. Howard Kester, "Acts of Tyranny and Terror Committed against Innocent Men, Women, and Children of the Southern Tenant Farmers' Union in Northeast Arkansas," 1935, reel 1, STFU Papers; and E. B. McKinney to H. L. Mitchell, March 8, 1936, reel 1, STFU Papers.

67. H. L. Mitchell to Aaron Gilmartin, March 18, 1936, reel 1, STFU Papers; H. L. Mitchell to Bryne L. Ray, March 23, 1936, reel 1, STFU Papers; Martin, *Howard Kester,* 70–96; Grubbs, *Cry from the Cotton,* 162–92; Manthorne, "The View from the Cotton," 5–27; Mitchell, *Mean Things Happening in This Land,* 156–82; and Roll, *Spirit*

of Rebellion, 115–76. The agricultural union the STFU joined was the United Cannery, Agricultural, Packing, and Allied Workers of America (UCAPAWA).

68. Wallace D. Best, *Passionately Human, No Less Divine: Religion and Culture in Black Chicago, 1915–1952* (Princeton, NJ: Princeton University Press, 2005); Laurie B. Green, *Battling the Plantation Mentality: Memphis and the Black Freedom Struggle* (Chapel Hill: University of North Carolina Press, 2007); Hays, *Politics Is My Parish,* 145–78; and Dunbar, *Against the Grain,* 199–258.

8

---◆---

Bonfires on the Levee

PLACE, MEMORY, AND THE SACRED IN
RIVER ROAD CATHOLICISM

Justin D. Poché

In June 1988, members of a local historical society in St. James Parish, Louisiana, traveled to Alsace, France, to uncover the roots of the annual Christmas bonfire celebrations atop the Mississippi River levee. For decades, residents of this largely French and German Catholic community along the "River Road" between Baton Rouge and New Orleans embraced the practice even as they held conflicting views about its origin and purpose.[1] Some argued that Acadian refugees from Nova Scotia as early as the 1780s brought the fires to welcome the arrival of "Papa Noël," or Santa Claus. Others traced its roots to the New Year's celebrations of early French settlers who later moved it to Christmas Eve to light the path to midnight Mass.[2] Explanations ranged widely. Yet for over a century, as Catholics created a distinct religious and multiethnic culture along the River Road, they assigned their own place to the bonfires. For one woman growing up on the west bank of the Mississippi in the late nineteenth century, the nighttime glow reflecting across the river advertised the prestige of wealthy plantation families on "l'autre bord." Leading into World War II, the building of fires atop the levees offered young men a rite of passage. As boys spent weeks gathering wood from the riverbank to show off to friends and family, shared stories of strong currents and destructive floods offered a sense of mastery over the river.[3]

But in the 1950s, this modest smattering of fires to gather the community on the levee developed into a major tourist attraction. Hundreds of fires, many as high as twenty feet, lit up the river through the Christmas season.[4]

Local business and industry promoted the event with unprecedented fervor over the next two decades, drawing tourists from around the region to participate in the ritual. In 1975, the state of Louisiana even declared St. James Parish the "bonfire capital of the world."[5] The bonfires continued to bolster a struggling tourist economy through the next decade even as some residents expressed concern over the effects of smoke pollution and bonfire construction on the wooded riverbanks that protected levees from erosion. By the time the historical society traveled to Alsace, the ritual offered a vague connection to the Old World. The group discovered similar fires along the Rhine, rooted in early pagan and Christian practice. Yet in describing a scene "richer in symbolism" than their own, they reflected an anxiety over the ritual's meaning.[6] In their efforts to reclaim the public memory of the annual rite and redefine the levee as an ethnic space, the society joined a centuries-long conflict over the meaning of the river and the land that has struggled to contain it.

From the early settlement of the lower Mississippi valley to the twentieth century, outside investors and longtime residents brought competing visions of an economic, cultural, and social order to bear on the river and the surrounding landscape. Man-made levees prevented annual flooding and empowered sugar cane planters with access to the river and the global market that it connected. But the river, as both a natural and socioeconomic current, continuously challenged the social and economic boundaries that defined the plantation South. Constrained by the levees, it channeled faster and higher water over the decades and threatened entire communities with destruction. It also brought into contact a variety of peoples that would interact and transform the River Road after the Civil War. Slave emancipation forced white landowners to accommodate black mobility while maintaining a steady labor force in the region. Northern investment in lumber, sugar, and tobacco industries created a new landscape of towns and small farms flanked by river and railroad. The growth of commerce through the first half of the twentieth century paved the way for the emergence of the petrochemical industry, which dramatically altered the environment and reconfigured the human and cultural landscape of the River Road after the 1950s. As fires of a different kind lit up the river on a nightly basis, offering vigils to a gospel of prosperity that gripped southeast Louisiana, the contrasts between old and new worlds impressed regional promoters and critics alike. "On the trip up the Mississippi River from New Orleans, one is struck by two developments," one analyst noted. "First, the burgeoning industry on the riverbanks, and second, the corresponding decay of many well-loved structures which formerly dated [dotted] the countryside. This somewhat curious juxtaposition accounts for both the problems and potentials of growth and development."[7]

Adapting to these changes and to the constant dangers of both river and industry, residents laid claim to the collective meaning and memory of the land. In the shadows of New South development, white tourist promoters sought to preserve and create relics of the "Old South." Beginning in the 1970s, state funding and sponsorship by petroleum companies rebuilt the region's historic plantation homes, offering a sense of permanence to the once transient and volatile plantation society. Nonetheless, as these groups superimposed a plantation geography upon the River Road, the selective and hotly contested creation of a mythic and therapeutic southern past competed with the shared histories and ritual spaces that communities—black and white, Protestant and Catholic, farmer and field laborer—had developed along the river for more than a century.[8] Through social customs, religious rituals, and shared narratives of struggle and survival that accompanied the construction of religious sites, communities mapped important ritual spaces and social boundaries that patterned life in the region and made sense of the often dangerous and ever-shifting physical and social landscape.[9]

The interaction of place and memory for one particularly prominent community along Louisiana's River Road is my subject here. From the Lourdes grotto at St. Michael's Church in Convent to annual cemetery visits along the river, Lenten rosaries on front porches, and prayer services on the levee to stave off looming floods, German and French Catholic communities in Louisiana created a network of formal and informal religious spaces that patterned life and infused the river and the land with religious meaning. Through shared rituals and narratives that sustained these places and practices, Catholics along the River Road created what many scholars have termed a distinct "moral geography" through which they understood, adapted, and sometimes resisted social, economic, and environmental change throughout the twentieth century.[10] In using this interpretive lens, I highlight the role of sacred spaces in shaping the ways the community has coped with social and physical change. The creation of sacred spaces (processes of creating, demarcating, and narrating the places around which people tied their identity and made sense of their physical and social circumstances) involves rituals of both inclusion and exclusion. Indeed, in addition to being "storied" and "significant" places, sacred space is inherently political and contested. As Philip Sheldrake notes, "it is occupied by some people's stories but not by others."[11] Tensions between competing moral and economic geographies, the ways different social groups

understood the meaning and purpose of the land, involved careful negotia-
tion between the demands of modernity and the desire of competing social
groups for cultural permanence in an impermanent landscape.

The process of "sacralizing" the landscape embodied both the aspirations
and anxieties of people as they moved about in their daily lives and both reflected and shaped communal understandings of race and economic conflict.
In exploring the significance of place in these conflicts, I hope to offer some
insight into the lived experience of social and environmental transformation
in an area that, much like New Orleans and the coastal wetlands bearing the
brunt of hurricanes and a recent oil spill, remains in the national conversation as much for its tragic potential as for its cultural vitality. Indeed, when
not characterized by the idyllic "River Road plantations" or the "saints on the
river," referring to the St. James, St. Charles, and St. John civil parishes that
encompass the region, outsiders have tagged the area as the nation's "petrochemical corridor" or, as often, "Cancer Alley." Both names suggest a dramatic re-narration of the surrounding landscape. The economic potential and
environmental consequences of development have waged a heavy toll on the
human health and welfare of the region. Lost in these modern economic and
epidemiological geographies that place industry at the center are the hidden
narratives and geographies of community and belonging that have shaped
experience there. In the process of assaying the economic and environmental
volatility of the region, both sides of the "jobs vs. environment" debate have
remapped the landscape in ways that compete with the meanings that residents of this multiracial, multiethnic, and intensely religious space assign to
the surrounding landscape.[12]

While not comprehensive, this brief study seeks to unearth these religious sites and the corresponding, though often conflicting, narratives that
gave them significance. It is driven by a basic assertion: while therapeutic narratives of the Old South promoted by the tourist and petrochemical industries
alike have come to dominate the terrain and adapt residents and outsiders
to the region's industrial development, deep and interwoven stories of faith,
ritual, and place offer the potential for a common identity that is both culturally and politically meaningful as the community faces future environmental
and economic challenges.

In 1876, around the time small bonfires began appearing on the levee in St.
James Parish, the Marist Fathers of St. Michael's Church in Convent erected
a replica of the Grotto of Our Lady of Lourdes.[13] Building it only eighteen

years after the original report of an apparition of the Virgin Mary in France, the Marists and the Archdiocese of New Orleans hoped to connect the community to the devotional life of the larger church. Throughout the twentieth century the Catholic Church in Louisiana promoted pilgrimages to the site, offering special indulgences to those visiting St. Michael's.[14] As locals attributed miracles to the grotto, they revealed their daily concerns and struggles against the dangerous landscape. Several accounts tell the story of a young man named Vasseur Webre who wandered into the swamplands beyond the plantations, remaining lost for several days. According to the legend, Webre promised a special honor to Our Lady of Lourdes if he were found. Locals discovered him after four days of starvation and torture by mosquitoes. Attributing his good fortune to the spiritual intervention that it brought to the land, he placed an ex voto above the Grotto.[15]

In creating the Lourdes replica, the Catholic community of the River Road not only sought a devotional bridge to the universal church but also staked a claim to the changing human and cultural geography of the postbellum South. As refugees from French anticlericalism, Marists offered the Lourdes replica as a transnational symbol of Catholic spiritual and political power against the rise of European secularism. The construction and occupation of Lourdes grottoes in prayer and devotion, Colleen McDannell suggests, brought local communities into a larger Catholic narrative of spiritual struggle and survival, one "emotionally engaged with the sacred past."[16] Yet in this process, River Road Catholics also translated the significance of Lourdes to their own local experience by drawing on the region's economic and cultural symbolism. In the process they crafted a distinctive *southern* past as much as a Catholic present.[17] The designer, Christophe Colombe Jr., the son of wealthy planter Marius Pons Bringier, constructed the site out of a large sugar kettle over the altar and burnt cane pulp known as bagasse to create the rocky texture. In consecrating the plantation past within the ritual space of the grotto, the community symbolically reinforced a social and economic structure built by the river and the plantation system it nurtured through the nineteenth century. The Lourdes Grotto at St. Michael's offered an "ordered and meaningful" space within an increasingly uncertain socioeconomic landscape through the turn of the century.[18]

The eighteenth-century construction of a levee system to prevent annual flooding cycles had created the sugar plantation system that defined the region's antebellum landscape. Mastery over the river's movement empowered wealthy planters who created a highly centralized and brutal gang labor system for harvesting sugar cane. Within this geography of domination, spaces along the river brought power and prestige to planters. Yet as the long band of plantation territory widened away from the river to the swampland, the conditions of the "back of the plantation" space reinforced the low social status of African American slaves and poor Acadians and freedmen who made a modest living from all plots of land and the woodcutting trade. While for Vasseur Webre the swampland demanded constant vigilance and the intervention of Our Lady of Lourdes, it offered slaves a sense of potential freedom and autonomy as they nurtured a community in the shadows of the plantations. Nonetheless, the danger and uncertainty of this wilderness created a natural barrier against escape and bound them to the land.[19]

The Civil War and Reconstruction significantly altered this landscape. As the increased global supply of sugar lowered prices and constrained postwar recovery, the river's currents and the rise of the railroad brought new communities of Sicilian, Irish, and northern "carpetbaggers" who sought to engage in new trades. Additionally, planters faced the challenges of freed slaves who demanded both economic autonomy and geographic mobility. Unlike the cotton South where plantations often split into sharecropping and tenancy systems to meet freedmen's demand for land, sugar harvesting and refining demanded a centralized labor system. Planter efforts to preserve plantation regimens against the demands of black laborers culminated in the violent labor strike of 1887 in the Thibodaux region west of the river parishes.[20] But in the years both before and after this event, the demands of "free labor" and the freedman's ability to "go & come as he pleased," as one planter lamented, challenged the geography of domination that developed in the antebellum period.[21] In the wake of emancipation, former slaves established settlements and developed a moral geography centered upon public ritual and institutional life. Protestant river baptisms and funeral processions that, according to one participant, brought "sometimes violent emotions," unlike the more "subdued" Catholic processions, asserted black ownership of the river landscape and reconfigured the levee and the surrounding land.[22]

While planters implemented a wage system and recovered the hierarchies of sugar cane production by the turn of the century, the emergence of the railroad and the growth of black institutions challenged the ways whites exerted dominance. As with the rise of Jim Crow elsewhere in the South, whites in this rural region created more intricate and fluid racial geographies that accommodated black physical movement while minimizing social mobility. In a 1920s article titled "Keeping the Negroes Home," a group of Louisiana sugar planters supported the construction of black social spaces like movie theaters and dance halls. In the process, planters sought "a sound and sane solution" to black demands. Such a method, they argued, "will be more effective than to try to compete with the wage scale of the northern factories, as the payment of high wages merely results in the negro laborer working fewer days per week."[23] Cultural histories of Jim Crow demonstrate the important ways in which southern whites created and policed new spaces of black and white interaction and exclusion through an elaborate system of laws, customs, and manners. In the absence of legal distinctions between slave and free, whites reinforced social and psychological boundaries through rituals of violence, exclusion, paternal interaction, and invention of black "otherness."[24]

Throughout Catholic Louisiana, churches played a crucial role in this process. While the grotto's creation did not explicitly enact a system of racial exclusion, over time it nonetheless anchored a church space in which white Catholics both ritualized and affirmed the rise of Jim Crow. St. Michael's supported roughly five hundred African Americans by the 1920s. While the parish built a special school for black children and insisted upon "the same spiritual care as the white," the latter nonetheless sought to control access to Catholic spaces and rituals. Like most churches throughout Louisiana, St. Michael's had implemented segregated seating at the turn of the century. Throughout the state, whites translated a Catholic orthodoxy of order and place to their understanding of society at large. At one rural parish west of the River Road, several parishioners evicted a "very white colored man" who had approached the altar rail with whites to receive Holy Communion. At another church, a white man attacked a boy for putting his finger in the holy water font before the man's wife could do so. The following Easter Sunday, another boy brushed past a white woman in a crowded service, inciting another fight outside after Mass. When priests attempted to change the status quo, they often met fierce resistance from white parishioners.[25] At St. Michael's in 1924, the congregation reprimanded a local Marist priest who attempted to move African Americans into the regular pews toward the front of the church. "The admirable zeal, the sincerity and devotion of that man will destroy the good results governing the proper places of people," one group reported to the archbishop of New Orleans. While blacks certainly deserved "all religious advantages" accorded them as Christians, spiritual progress, they insisted, would not come "at the price of social equality."[26]

While churches and the Mass itself offered an important venue for white assertions of dominance, physical separation was merely one component of a larger worldview developing through the first half of the twentieth century. Particularly in the rural sugar cane belt where the economy demanded the maintenance of a steady black labor force and constant interaction between races, white rituals constructed images of black "otherness" to reinforce social boundaries. For River Road Catholics well into the 1950s, the local Mothers' Club of St. Michael's and nearby St. Joseph's hosted the annual "Black and Tan Minstrel."[27] In addition to these racial narratives, parish histories of St. Michael's invoke images of the church's black sacristan, Pierre Duhon, who, "like an old land-mark," dutifully served the church through the first half of the century.[28] White narrations of black life, whether in the performance of minstrels or the celebration of the "loyal negro," sought to supplant black narratives of freedom and struggle. The latter's stories, refashioning the freedmen's own geography of social and spiritual struggle, have only recently been recovered.

Yet as many scholars note, the culture of Jim Crow was built as much on racial interaction as separation. Growing up in the St. Michael's congregation, Louis Poché reflected upon the racial boundaries that shaped his moral and social upbringing along the River Road. Like many southern children who "learned race" from an early age, he came to understand the nuanced system of social deference and manners, personal kindnesses, and debts that ordered society and lent a sense of givenness to racial inequality in the region.[29] As a boy he knew that "our actions in their regard, inspired as they were by the compassion and generosity of our parents, may often have brought relief, at times perhaps even life and joy, but we rarely questioned, and we certainly never challenged, the opprobrious customs and laws."[30] The small acts of charity by whites, he argued, demanded habits of deference both in church and daily life. Throughout his stories, the ritual segregation of blacks within the parish seemed to belie the intimate interactions of daily life. Between Sundays, the levees, yards, back porches, and gardens offered shared spaces where the young Poché interacted with the families that "lived in the back of us." On the riverbank behind the levee, the farmhand taught him to ride a horse. On the back steps the same man took away and buried the remains of his mother's miscarriage. Such interactions "have never allowed me to forget the sincere concern that reached across racial lines to walk extra miles with us."[31]

The experiences of Poché, a future Jesuit, revealed a deep sense of interconnection among people bound inevitably by the difficult conditions of their physical environment. For many whose recollections of Catholic life serve as both reclamation of the landscape and a reaffirmation of a religious and social identity that it nurtured, the river itself played a key, if not defining, role in creating important social and religious boundaries. The river's "calm serenity," the early historian Lillian Bourgeois noted, belied "the disastrous tricks which the great river has some times played on St. James."[32] While Catholic memories of struggle and survival were invariably mediated through white structures and perceptions of power and place, the river became a great equalizer, drawing people of the River Road together in a common narrative of survival. Dramatic accounts of floods underscored this dependency, even if black actors remained impersonal and even indifferent to tragedy. Bourgeois' retelling of the "la crevasse Nita" story, for instance, offered one example. Referring to the Nita plantation home where the levee broke, the story involved an "old Negro" (known only as "Neega") who left a funeral wake around midnight and was forced to walk along the railroad tracks because of rising water. When he rushed into a nearby store to announce the imminent flood, a group of men continued their tite partie (high stakes card game), insisting that "such things were not uncommon." Their disregard proved devastating when the levee finally broke at 2 AM. The entire wake service scrambled home, "leaving the sorrowing mother alone in vigil over her dead daughter." The story returned primarily to the devastation of the Nita plantation itself, where Madame Flagil's servants were forced to drag the weeping matron away before the water collapsed the house "like a flimsy deck of cards."[33]

As "great floods" occurred over generations, they punctuated life on the Mississippi and designated the river and levee as dangerous sacred spaces that required constant, prayerful vigilance. "The mightiest of all rivers cuts through St. James Parish like a saber," Leonce Haydel recalled of community life at the river's edge. "We have learned to live with it and take from it what it offers, yet we all know that when it gets ready to take from us, it will."[34] At such moments, levees became the central religious site where residents gathered to pray against the rising waters.[35] In St. John the Baptist Parish, the parents of Grace Populas warned that the river would soon "drown New Orleans" if the levee ever broke. "And they would go on the levee with Notre Dame de Bon Secours—a statue of her—and pray to her. The day they really thought it was going to bust, they started walking on the levee with that statue and saying the rosary, and in a day or two the water went down."[36] During one particularly dangerous season, Louis Poché's mother escorted her family to the top of the levee as the floodwaters began to rise. "There she gave us a small religious medal which my brothers and I inserted into a piece of driftwood and cast into the waters. 'Mister River, you just stay right where you are.'"[37]

While levees served to stave off annual flooding and offered an important social space, locals never ignored their complicity in the river's violent behaviors as well as the struggles between communities. On good days levees functioned as promenades where planters hosted social functions and asserted their status within the community. On bad days, the levee focused social conflict as much as spiritual reflection. Breaks in the levee sent guards running down the road firing guns in the air and echoing the familiar but haunting "Crevasse! Crevasse!"[38] According to Marcia G. Gaudet, the physical divisions created by the river generated resentment between peoples on the "east bank" and "west bank." "St. John the Baptist and neighboring parishes are cut into two sections by the river," Henry Yoes noted, "and each half considers the other half made up of obstinate people, peculiar people."[39] During flooding threats, residents often posted guards to keep downriver communities from dynamiting portions of the levee to prevent flooding in their own neighborhoods. In such conflicts, like the bonfires during peaceful times, the levee became a distinctly male space where men performed their ownership and protection of the vulnerable community. The ritual of "walking the levee" brought men to the riverbanks carrying guns and lanterns to inspect the structure for weak spots and to ward off persons seeking to blow the levee to protect their own homes across the way.[40]

Nonetheless, at the river's most peaceful moments, rituals along the River Road drew upon the intimate reliance that people had on the Mississippi for both survival and social identity. "The mighty river has taken a lot from St. James Parish over the years," Haydel noted. "It has also given a lot." The riverbanks offered boys a place to play and gather wood for upcoming bonfires. On early summer mornings the river offered passage for black men eking out a living before the sugar cane cutting season. According to Poché, "men rowed a skiff across the Mississippi at 3:00 a.m. to cut in the rice fields in St. James."[41] Signifying both a sense of limitation and transcendence, social rituals invoking a language of "crossing the river" usually marked significant events and connections in a person's life, one shaped by a dual sense of tragedy and possibility. The practice of charivari, for instance, involved the communal celebration at the home of a newly married couple. "The requirement for the serenade was that either one or both be a widow or widower," according to Claudia Montz Cambre. At the beginning of the ritual, a "caller" would announce his arrival from "across the river" by exhorting the crowd in front of the house to "repeter les bourgeau," or "repeat the racket," until the couple allowed the crowd to enter.[42]

On certain Sundays and holy days of obligation, Leonce Haydel's family crossed over to the west bank to visit cemeteries and relatives. The difficulty and weeks of planning that went into the ritual led his father to name the task "making The Way of the Cross." On "l'autre bord," as he termed it, "Everybody had to be visited, so it meant short visits at each house." Despite some of the tensions that many felt between those on the "other side" of the river, he later realized, "I can't go ten feet along the river without claiming relationships with a Haydel, Tregre, Berthelot, or any other 'River Road name."[43] Along with many River Road Catholics, Haydel traversed a complex geography where river, levee, and road tied religious spaces of cemeteries, churches, and homes together and forged important familial and spiritual ties.

As white ethnic Catholics identified the sacred spaces and boundaries that commanded reverence and became locations for the reinforcement of a shared history and identity, they developed gendered understandings of place and religious authority. As "female spaces," homes and front porches along the River Road variously shaped and challenged formal Catholic practice. Catholic women along the River Road nurtured intimate links between the formal and informal sites of religious practice.[44] Poché's aptly named memoir, *Sins My Mother Taught Me,* underscores the formative role of laywomen in the transmission of Catholic piety. "My own first confession was made from a short list of sins that my mother patiently helped me to memorize."[45] Lydia Keller Poché "taught us the rules" of formal Catholicism, "and she never forced on us any religious or devotional 'extras.'" Nonetheless, her "deep and intelligent faith" nurtured a religious imagination that moved him beyond the boundaries of formal church practice. One of his memories came in the construction of a nativity scene for the Christmas season for which each of the boys received a sheep to move progressively closer to the crib. "Good behavior on our part would send the animals up one step each day . . . the winner of the race to Bethlehem would have the honor of bringing all the nickels [family donation] to the big crèche at St. Michael's on Christmas day."[46]

Poché's experience, along with Gerard Arthur Becnel, reveals not only the extent to which Catholic children on the River Road learned to "materialize the sacred" in the spaces of homes, churches, and levees but also how children themselves became, as Robert Orsi notes, "privileged media for giving substance to religious meaning."[47] As adult Catholics placed upon children their own anxieties and aspirations for their own religious and cultural survival, they made children the representatives of familial identity and piety. Gerard Arthur Becnel's fascinating and often humorous journey through the historical landscape of the River Road reveals the ways children, in the formal space of the church, performed the religious duties of families. Special feast days drew entire communities to the church where white-clad children took center stage. "Our being all in white signified, of course, how pure we all were—or at least were presumed to be at the time—in mind and spirit," recalled Becnel. "Our group could process into church, recess out of church, genuflect, sit, kneel, rise, etc., with unit coordination some Marine Corps drill instructors and even the Rockettes dance master might admire. No verbal instructions were given or needed." Only once did the kindly French priest have to tell the Sunday congregation "Hier, les petits était comme des animaux! (Yesterday the children acted like animals)."[48] Such moments invited swift inquisitions back home.

For Becnel, Haydel, and other Catholics growing up along the levee, the female-centered space of the front porch offered a crucial site of religious and cultural transmission. Porches gathered people and stories "[i]n all but the coldest weather," for Becnel's family. "Later, much later, Mama mentioned to us that her knowledge about people and events stemmed partly from porch talk. . . . Without resorting to any notes at all, she could and did give very accurate information about births, deaths, and marriages of relatives and others of the 1850s and 1860s. All from porch talk."[49] While "gossip" also frequented Becnel's porch, families could be found on the front porches during Lent holding rosary services. On Holy Saturday, the ringing of the Angelus at the nearby church would bring expressions of relief and celebration. "Since everybody gave up something for Lent it, was always a welcome sound when the church bell rang on Saturday."[50] Memoirs also note the significance of church bells in River Road Catholicism for the ways they reflected the order and discipline of the plantation between the 1870s and the 1930s. According to Claudia Montz Cambre, bells "kept the system in perfect operation," calling workers to the fields at 4 a.m. and signaling the final cut of cane at the end of the day. The symbolic transformation of plantation discipline to liturgical discipline was reflected in the donation of bells to churches, such as the one from Woodland Plantation to St. Joan of Arc Parish.[51]

Becnel laments the impact of television and air-conditioning on the decline of the front porch. This decline significantly altered southerners' historical consciousness, kinship, and "a strong sense of place," according to historian Raymond Arsenault.[52] But if the porch's role in the transmission of family memory and religious practice has declined, cemeteries have remained crucial cultural and spiritual anchors for both current and former residents.

Within the dangerous and uncertain River Road landscape, Catholics who built, maintained, and visited family grave sites sought tangible control over the ultimate fate of themselves and their loved ones. All Saints' Day brought relatives from throughout the countryside to visit cemeteries. Families often kept vigil through the night as they prepared the family gravestones. "Woe to the person who does not clean the family gravesite or places a cheap bouquet in the vase," Haydel remembered. "St Jamesians are as a whole great 'cemetery-goers' all year round, but even most of those who don't attend all year appear for All Saints' Day. They might allow their house to look shabby but never the family grave site."[53] Becnel described how " we moved along among the tombs and graves, exchanging greetings with others doing the same. At selected tombs or graves . . . Mama would pause, close her eyes, and move her lips in prayer. I followed suit." As the family moved through the site, she also shared stories of the deceased with young Gerard. Becnel recalled that "there wasn't anything maudlin or depressing or glum about being in a cemetery on All Saint's Day. . . . We met people we knew, we reminisced, and we talked and laughed in the bright sunshine."[54]

Like churches, cemeteries offered material evidence of the Christian promise of salvation and resisted the tragic potential of other spaces where flooding, disease, and social conflict threatened both spiritual and physical harm. Yet while the Second Vatican Council transformed Catholic orientations to space within the church, cemeteries remained lay-controlled spaces through which French and German Catholics preserved a historically and geographically rooted faith amid the "modernization" of Catholic practice. They became the most vital centers of a Catholic moral geography increasingly at odds with the emerging economic, cultural, and physical landscape. Whereas levees and homes once offered places in which individuals assigned larger cosmic meanings to their experiences of opportunity and loss along the river, the reduction of flooding threats through technological innovation and the movement of peoples both in and out of the land shifted the moral landscape. Cemeteries marked off the sacred from the increasingly "profane spaces" of an emerging cultural and industrial landscape in the 1960s and 1970s.[55]

The recent reenactment of old burial rites and the persistence of All Saints' Day celebrations along the River Road reveal a certain anxiety. Memoirs offer an important text for understanding the ways different groups craft a shared memory of a place not only to gain a sense of personal identity but also to accommodate and resist transformations of the space. Invoking rich memories of the cemeteries, levees, front porches, and sanctuaries, Catholics unearth and reassert a spiritual landscape that competes with the current industrialization of the region's physical and historical resources. While memoirs often gloss over or dismiss these changes, moments of cultural and social tension emerge. Becnel's journey through St. James Parish balances a sense of cultural loss with a passing acknowledgment of change wrought by modern industry. For Becnel, where once the river was "any number of things at once," including a "dreamland" for youth seeking adventure, few venture into the waters. "Maybe the reason is that people are more aware of how polluted the river is with the comparatively recent addition of industrial wastes."[56]

Claudia Montz Cambre criticized the naming of the town of La Place, the center of St. John the Baptist Parish. The region had once thrived as the 3,900-acre Laplace Plantation, Cambre reminded locals, and changing the spelling tampered with the historic identity of the region, "depriving a person's innate right to his name and stripping the town of its heritage and background, dating back to 1870." Cambre's memorial of the Laplace Plantation reflected larger anxieties over the region's social and cultural transformation. In reasserting the memory of the orderly plantation system, the author sought to make sense of conflicts arising from the 1960s movements for civil and economic rights. Repeated concern for the preservation of the Laplace name and the memory of the plantation labor system framed a critique of what Cambre saw as a passing of the days when "everybody pulled his weight" and "there were no so-called 'poor people' riding in automobiles and paying half price for commodities, or better yet, paying nothing."[57] As the social, cultural, and economic tensions of the 1960s gripped the river parishes, Cambre joined a larger ongoing project to identify and assert the storied landscape of the Old South.

Along the River Road, community efforts to desegregate schools and express the common interests of an economically vulnerable multiracial community raised the stakes for many whites who sought to reassert power through their ability to define the cultural and historical meaning of the landscape. As many southern historians have noted, a new tacit resistance to social change arose in the 1970s South. According to historian David R. Goldfield, southerners abandoned the explicit language of race for one of "past, place, and manners."[58] In restoring the plantation spaces of the "Old South," historical societies and their supporters sought to influence perceptions of the landscape by both outsiders and longtime residents. In the 1970s and 1980s, the River Road Historical Society raised public funds and private company donations to resurrect plantation buildings. Most notably through this period, the Destrehan Plantation offered "an interpretive museum of life on the Mississippi River" between early settlement and the Civil War.[59]

By superimposing a plantation geography upon the River Road, both residents and outsiders created a therapeutic memory that accommodated ongoing changes in the landscape. In their efforts to identify southern sacred spaces, historical societies and civic leaders forged a productive but uneasy alliance with local industries. Companies such as Kaiser Aluminum, Amoco, DuPont, and Marathon Oil took a vested interest in identifying plantations and reconstituting them as markers of the region's cultural distinctiveness.[60] Industries purchased land and sponsored rebuilding efforts. Along similar lines, they put advertisements in local newspapers that promoted the region's bonfire heritage and encouraged tourist pilgrimages.[61]

Nonetheless, by the time the state declared St. James Parish the "bonfire capital of the world," intense conflicts arose between industry and community over the right to identify and locate sites of southern remembrance. As the state promoted heritage tourism along the River Road, companies that purchased land made significant decisions over which spaces deserved remembering and which might be redeveloped as industrial land. Some, like Oak Alley with its immaculate tree-lined walkways, emerged as stand-ins for the mythical South. Others, like Welham Plantation, became casualties of industrial growth.

When Marathon Oil purchased Welham Plantation in 1975, it launched a wave of concerns over the future of the site. A year later, parish officials passed a resolution requesting that Marathon donate the plantation to the River Road Historical Society. However, one morning in 1979, the community awoke to the sound of the house's destruction. The event sparked an outcry among residents. "Greed Triumphs," one article read in the local paper. "Conniving like some thief in the night, Marathon not only committed a crime against history and heritage, it committed a crime against our parish."[62] Response to the destruction of Welham revealed significant anxieties about the future of the parish. One editorial deemed Welham "the last page in the open book of our past." The community also used it as a moment to reflect on the effects of industry. "Maybe it's time to look more closely at those industries proposing to come into our parish and to put a halt to those transgressions we have had to suffer because of their taking more than they give."[63]

By the early 1980s, as the remapping of the plantation societies neared completion, a guidebook touted the "Ruhr valley of Louisiana" where "the landscape offers visions of sugar cane fields, stately plantation mansions, and sleek industrial installations co-existing side by side."[64] Despite the successful efforts to map the historical geography of the region around the plantation homes, new efforts have emerged to challenge these narratives. Not long after the historical society of St. James traveled to Europe, Kathe Hambrick returned to the River Road to reinfuse the landscape with her own lost narratives of suffering, struggle, and salvation. In 1991, Hambrick stood on the levee where she had a "spiritual awakening," as she describes it. On a trip from California, "I found myself looking at one of God's greatest creations, the Mississippi River. . . . As I turned my back to the mighty river and looked across the River Road, I saw the Tezcuco Plantation yard scattered with live oak trees and the fence lined with rows of sugarcane. . . . I could see African people standing under the big oak trees and in the cane fields. . . . It seems the ancestors were trying to tell me something."[65] Hambrick's awakening fueled her desire to erect a museum of African American history on the River Road. The museum staff have not only resurrected stories of growing up black in the river parishes of St. James, Ascension, and St. John the Baptist but also recovered endangered worship spaces. These spaces demarcate a persistent African American moral geography that resists the symbolic annihilation of slave experience seen in plantation museums.

Hambrick's efforts, along with those of the Catholic historical society that sought out the bonfires across the Atlantic, reveal a renewed attention to unearthing the hidden narratives of life and struggle along the River Road, narratives that are often subsumed in efforts to reconstruct antebellum plantation spaces. The definition of the land as plantation space not only masks these hidden narratives but also mitigates efforts to reconcile those narratives in ways that help residents deal productively with the effects of environmental change. In examining the history of racial conflict and the appropriation of the land for industrial use, it is important to note that competing black and white Catholic visions of the land and their identity within it have, of course, not been mutually exclusive. These spiritual and mental maps intersect and help craft a common identity. Lamentably, however, this shared identity has all too often failed to generate a sense of shared struggle as communities face the unintended consequences of modernization. White manipulations of space and the attachment of racial identities to them have reinforced a paternalistic attitude toward the region's African American population. This process has undermined what has become a religious cause among many African Americans in "Cancer Alley" to seek out justice for vulnerable communities.

It should come as no exaggeration in the present day that southern Louisianans seem to live between catastrophic events. The yellow fever epidemic of 1853 and the repeated flooding of the lower Mississippi valley, highlighted most dramatically in 1927, Hurricane Betsy in 1965, and Hurricane Katrina in 2005, have all cast light on the vulnerability of Louisiana communities. Yet long before Katrina, River Road neighborhoods faced constant threats from surrounding chemical plants. Memories of plant explosions punctuate experience and highlight the ongoing hazards of life in these historically rooted places. Prompted by these catastrophes, communities recognize the definition of power not as the ability to prevent these events but rather as the right to define the meaning of a place in the wake of their violence. Throughout the century, residents have made sense of these dangers through story and ritual. As a socially constructed space, the River Road itself embodies a multiplicity of emotions, meanings, narratives, and obligations. It is to be hoped that examining the creation of a Catholic moral geography in St. James will provide a useful cultural and religious context for understanding the larger social, economic, and political history of the region through its postwar transformations into the present day.

Notes

1. River Road is the stretch of highway that parallels the Mississippi River on both sides between Baton Rouge and New Orleans. The largely rural civil districts that occupy this region are often referred to as the "river parishes" and include Ascension, St. James, St. John the Baptist, and St. Charles Parishes. Certain people identify them as "the saints on the river."

2. Most anecdotal evidence suggests that no bonfires were lit until the 1880s. Small fires were lit on the batture, the stretch of land between the river and the levee, before moving to the top of the levee. Marcia G. Gaudet, *Tales from the Levee: The Folklore of St. John the Baptist Parish* (Lafayette: Center for Louisiana Studies, 1984), 9–11; Lillian C. Bourgeois, *Cabanocey: The History, Customs, and Folklore of St. James Parish* (New Orleans: Pelican, 1957).

3. Emily Chenet Guidry, *Bonfires on the Levee: Christmas Eve Tradition along the River Road* (Lutcher: St. James Historical Society, 1994).

4. Ibid.

5. A scan of local papers from the 1940s forward reveals no mention of the fires until 1956, when the practice moved from Convent to the growing industrial towns of Lutcher and Gramercy. Evidence suggests that the practice had been gradually building in the 1950s, but enjoyed unprecedented attention at the turn of the decade. St. James *News-Examiner,* 27 December 1968, 17 July 1975.

6. Guidry, *Bonfires on the Levee,* 2.

7. "River Road: An Analysis," in "Highways-River Road," n.d., vertical file, Louisiana Collection, Jones Hall, Tulane University Special Collections.

8. This current work attempts to bring these concepts into an understanding of social and environmental change in the twentieth-century South. On the interaction of place and memory in the New South, see Stephanie Yuhl, *A Golden Haze of Memory: The Making of Historic Charleston* (Chapel Hill: University of North Carolina Press, 2005).

9. By "mapping" I depend upon Thomas A. Tweed's definition as "the ways that groups orient themselves in a natural landscape and social terrain, transforming both in the process." Tweed, *Our Lady of the Exile: Diasporic Religion at a Cuban Catholic Shrine in Miami* (New York: Oxford University Press, 1997). Amy DeRogatis employs this definition in her study of both the literal and "metaphorical mapping" of the old Northwest by Protestant missionaries. DeRogatis, *Moral Geography: Maps, Missionaries, and the American Frontier* (New York: Columbia University Press, 2003).

10. For insight on "moral geography," I am indebted to several scholars whose work on early America has helped shape my own thinking about the dynamics of power and place along the River Road. In addition to DeRogatis, see Tracy Neal Leavelle, "Geographies of Encounter: Religion and Contested Spaces in Colonial North America," *American Quarterly* 56, no. 4 (December 2004): 913–43; Philip Sheldrake, *Spaces for the Sacred: Place, Memory, and Identity* (Baltimore: Johns Hopkins University Press, 2001); and Belden Lane, *Landscapes of the Sacred: Geography and Narrative in American Spirituality* (Baltimore: Johns Hopkins University Press, 1988, 2001). Historians of modern American religion have also examined how competing theological understandings of place have shaped larger social forces in the late twentieth century. See Gerald Gamm's *Urban Exodus: Why the Jews Left Boston and the Catholics Stayed* (Cambridge, MA: Harvard University Press, 1999). In *Parish Boundaries: The Catholic Encounter with Race in the Twentieth Century Urban North* (Chicago: University of Chicago Press, 1996), John T. McGreevy discusses the sacred "orbit" of the neighborhood parish and its role in shaping racial conflict in the urban north. Robert Orsi's *Madonna of 115th Street* offers insight into a more home-centered spirituality often at odds with the formal Catholic practice inculcated in parish churches. Orsi underscores the dynamic interplay of the priest-centered church and female-centered home through the landscape of rural Louisiana.

11. David Chidester and Edward Linenthal, eds., *American Sacred Space* (Bloomington: Indiana University Press, 1995).

12. Several excellent studies of "Cancer Alley" tap into modern concerns over the safety and sustainability of neighborhoods in the vicinity of chemical plants. See Barbara L. Allen, *Uneasy Alchemy: Citizens and Experts in Louisiana's Petrochemical Corridor Disputes* (Cambridge, MA: MIT Press, 2003); and Steve Lerner, *Diamond: A Struggle for Environmental Justice in Louisiana's Petrochemical Corridor* (Cambridge, MA: MIT Press, 2006). In both these studies, religion plays an important organizational role while only occasionally emerging as a source of interpretation. While modest in its scope, my article suggests an approach that takes these spiritual understandings of landscape and social boundaries into consideration as they shaped the larger community's response to environmental and cultural transformation.

13. Bourgeois, *Cabanocey*, 45; Roger Baudier, *The Catholic Church in Louisiana*. Local histories claim that it was the first replica grotto in the United States.

14. St. James *News-Examiner*, 31 January 1958, 7 February 1958.

15. Bourgeois, *Cabanocey*, 45.

16. Colleen McDannell, *Material Christianity: Religion and Popular Culture in America* (New Haven, CT: Yale University Press, 1995), 161.

17. For a good discussion of the relationship between material culture and collective memory, see W. Fitzhugh Brundage, ed., *Where These Memories Grow: History, Memory, and Southern Identity* (Chapel Hill: University of North Carolina Press, 2000). From the immediate post-emancipation era into the late twentieth century, southerners built monuments and preserved historical homes and other sites and objects that, Brundage notes, "anchor their memories in space and time. Objects become infused with commemorative qualities, and thereby serve as physical markers of memory that preserve the past in the present" (8).

18. McDannell, *Material Christianity,* 161; Lillian Bourgeois, *Cabanocey,* 44–45. Recent accounts attest to the importance of the material structure itself. See Frank M. Uter, *Stones beside a River: A History of the Catholic Church on the East Bank of St. James Parish, 1809–2009* (2006).

19. On plantation landscapes in the sugar region before and after emancipation, see Rebecca Scott, *Degrees of Freedom: Louisiana and Cuba after Slavery* (Cambridge, MA: Harvard University Press, 2005), 12–14; and Roderick A. McDonald, *The Economy and Material Culture of Slaves: Goods and Chattels on the Sugar Plantations of Jamaica and Louisiana* (Baton Rouge: Louisiana State University Press, 1993).

20. John C. Rodrigue, *Reconstruction in the Cane Fields: From Slavery to Free Labor in Louisiana's Sugar Parishes, 1862–1880* (Baton Rouge: Louisiana State University Press, 2001), 7, 68–76, 104. See also Rebecca Scott, "Fault Lines, Color Lines, and Party Lines: Race, Labor, and Collective Action in Louisiana and Cuba, 1862–1912," in *Beyond Slavery: Explorations of Race, Labor, and Citizenship in Post-Emancipation Societies,* ed. Frederick Cooper and Rebecca J. Scott (Chapel Hill: University of North Carolina Press, 2000), 65–83. Scott discusses the massive cane labor strike of 1887 amid the restructuring of plantation agriculture throughout this period. John C. Rodrigue, "Labor Militancy and Black Grassroots Political Mobilization in the Louisiana Sugar Region, 1865–1868," *Journal of Southern History* 67 (February 2001): 115–42.

21. Planter quoted in Rodrigue, *Reconstruction in the Cane Fields,* 69.

22. See Curtis Johnson, *How We Will Know It's Us* (copy in African American River Road Museum) discussing African American Protestant religious rituals, particularly wakes and baptisms. He compares the "subdued" Catholic funerals with the "sometimes violent emotions" expressed during Protestant funeral processions. See also Thomas Durant, *Our Roots Run Deep: A History of the River Road African American Museum* (Virginia Beach: Donning, 2002).

23. "Keeping the Negroes Home," reprinted from "Facts about Sugar" in St. James *Voice,* 15 December 1923.

24. See Grace Elizabeth Hale, *Making Whiteness: The Culture of Segregation in the South, 1890–1940* (New York: Pantheon Books, 1998).

25. Annals of the Sisters of the Blessed Sacrament 22 (1925): 113, Archives of the Sisters of the Blessed Sacrament, Bensalem, PA.

26. Twelve parishioners of St. Michael's Parish to Father Henri de la Chapelle, S.M., Provincial, in Marist Files, Archives of the Archdiocese of New Orleans. I am grateful to Father Frank M. Uter, S.M., at St. Michael's Church in Convent for this reference.

27. St. James *News Examiner,* 12 December 1947, 5 April 1957. Nearby St. Joseph's Church hosted the annual "Darktown Follies" in the town of Paulina. Copies of

programs can be found in Jules A. Dornier Papers, box 1, folder 11, Lower Mississippi Valley Collection, Louisiana State University Special Collections.

28. Bourgeois, *Cabanocey,* 45.

29. On the ways southern society socialized children, see Jennifer Ritterhouse, *Growing Up Jim Crow: How Black and White Southern Children Learned Race* (Chapel Hill: University of North Carolina Press, 2006). Of the voluminous body of work on southern paternalism, both before and after emancipation, see Eugene Genovese, *Roll Jordan Roll: The World the Slaves Made* (New York: Pantheon Books, 1974); and Peggy Hargis, "For the Love of Place: From Paternalism and Patronage in the Georgia Low-country, 1865–1898," *Journal of Southern History* 70 (November 2004): 825–64, which offers an interesting perspective on one family's experience of emancipation and the survival of paternalist labor arrangements.

30. Louis A. Poché, S.J., *Sins My Mother Taught Me,* published by the author, 35.

31. Ibid., 35.

32. Bourgeois, *Cabanhocey,* 95.

33. Ibid., 96–97.

34. Leonce Haydel, *Stories from the River Road* (Lutcher, LA: Ruhr Valley Press, 1992), 54.

35. The historian Mary Ann Sternberg notes that prayer services on the levee were a common occurrence during floods. Sternberg, *Along the River Road: Past and Present on Louisiana's Historic Byway* (Baton Rouge: Louisiana State University Press, 1996).

36. Marcia G. Gaudet, *Tales from the Levee: The Folklore of St. John the Baptist Parish* (Lafayette: University of Southwestern Louisiana Press, 1984), 27.

37. Poché, *Sins My Mother Taught Me,* 22.

38. Gaudet, *Tales from the Levee,* 27.

39. Yoes quoted in ibid., 25.

40. Ibid., 26.

41. Poché, *Sins My Mother Taught Me,* 35.

42. Claudia Montz Cambre, *History and Heritage of the Saints on the River* (La-Place, LA: Cambre Press, 1979), 152.

43. Haydel, *Stories from the River Road.*

44. Robert Orsi, *Madonna of 115th Street: Faith and Community in Italian Harlem* (New Haven, CT: Yale University Press, 1985), 75–106.

45. Poché, *Sins My Mother Taught Me,* 30.

46. Ibid., 22.

47. Robert Orsi, "Material Children: Making God's Presence Real for Catholic Boys and Girls and for the Adults in Relations to Them," in Orsi, *Between Heaven and Earth: The Religious Worlds People Make and the Scholars Who Study Them* (Princeton: Princeton University Press, 2005), 73–109.

48. Gerard Arthur Becnel, *River Road Moments: Growing Up in the 1930s and 1940s* (Lake Charles, LA: G. Becnel, 1999), 43–44.

49. Ibid., 40.

50. Haydel, *Stories from the River Road,* 55–56.

51. Cambre, *History and Heritage,* 121.

52. Raymond Arsenault, "The End of the Long Hot Summer: The Air Conditioner and Southern Culture," *Journal of Southern History* 50 (November 1984), 597–628.

53. Leonce Haydel, *Stories from the River Road,* 73.

54. Becnel, *River Road Moments,* 49–50.

55. For analysis of the transformation of Catholic "place" in the post-1960s church, see John T. McGreevy, *Parish Boundaries: The Catholic Encounter with the Twentieth-Century Urban North* (Chicago: Chicago University Press, 1996), and Gerald H. Gamm, *Urban Exodus: Why the Jews Left Boston and the Catholics Stayed* (Cambridge, MA: Harvard University Press, 1999).

56. Becnel, *River Road Moments,* 13.

57. Cambre, *History and Heritage,* 17, 30.

58. David R. Goldfield, *Black, White, and Southern: Race Relations in Southern Culture, 1940 to the Present* (Baton Rouge: Louisiana State University Press, 1990), 170. See also James C. Cobb, "Searching for Southernness: Community and Identity in the Contemporary South," in *Redefining Southern Culture: Mind & Identity in the Modern South,* ed. Cobb (Athens: University of Georgia Press, 1999), 125–49.

59. River Road Historical Society *Newsletter,* January 1984, in Louisiana Collection, Tulane University Special Collections. For in-depth analysis of plantation museums, including Destrehan, as sites of "symbolic annihilation" of black presence, see Jennifer L. Eichstedt and Stephen Small, *Representations of Slavery: Race and Ideology in Southern Plantation Museums* (Washington, DC: Smithsonian Institution Press, 2002).

60. Stephanie Yuhl, *A Golden Haze of Memory: The Making of Historic Charleston* (Chapel Hill: University of North Carolina Press, 2005), 9–10. Yuhl examines the ways that "self-interested constituencies . . . deploy historical memory for a variety of ends: to organize society; to regulate access to or exclusion from political, social, and economic power; to create and resist consensus identities; to invent tradition; and to control or challenge public discourse."

61. St. James *News-Examiner,* 24 December 1970.

62. Ibid., 1 May 1975; Judy Lucia, "Greed Triumphs," *Le Communique,* newsletter of the River Road Historical Society (May 1979), in Louisiana Collection, Tulane University Special Collections.

63. Judy Lucia, "Greed Triumphs," *Le Communique,* May 1979.

64. "St. James Parish, Louisiana: Where Industry and Agriculture Meet, Work Together, and Prosper," in "St. James Parish" vertical file, in Louisiana Collection, Tulane University Special Collections.

65. Quoted in Durant, *Our Roots Run Deep,* 13.

9

"Big River"

JOHNNY CASH AND THE CURRENTS OF HISTORY

John Hayes

In the 2003 video for Johnny Cash's cover of the alternative song "Hurt," the floodwaters of the Mississippi River raged, seeming to sweep away everything in their wake in a dizzying array of visual imagery. The symbolism was germane: Cash had grown up near the mighty river, in Mississippi County in the Arkansas Delta, lived in Memphis for five years in the mid-1950s (where he began his long career as a singer and performer), and spent much of his adult life in a house on Old Hickory Lake outside Nashville, a lake created from one of the Mississippi's major tributaries, the Cumberland. He had memorialized the Mississippi in a variety of songs, most notably 1957's "Big River," where the river became a frame for a love affair gone awry, 1959's "Five Feet High and Rising," which evoked the terror of a catastrophic flood in his youth, and 1970's "Mississippi Delta Land," which told of how hard agricultural labor in the rural South yielded little more than "a mind that knows the truth."

Now in "Hurt," as the piano boomed and the song reached its crescendo, Cash dramatically signified what exactly that hard-won "truth" was. Staring straight out at the viewer and asking in song, "What have I become?" his trembling hand poured a goblet of wine all over a festal banquet table. Like detritus in the Mississippi floodwaters and wasted, wine-soaked banquet food, the trappings of fame shown in the video—awards, honors, memorabilia in the defunct House of Cash museum—were imagined as a hollow, ultimately ephemeral "empire of dirt." To this hollow empire of dirt and destruction was contrasted, in a variety of elusive imagery, the redemptive suffering of Christianity. The video opened with a crucifix on the wall of Cash's house, moved on to a Victorian Protestant painting of Jesus, evoked Eucharistic imagery in its ornate festal banquet, and came to a dizzying, dramatic conclusion with images of the Crucifixion from Cash's own 1973 life-of-Jesus film, *The Gospel Road*. The symbols all suggested an arc of return in Cash's life, from the religion of his Delta youth, away from it into American popular culture, and then imaginatively back home, back to his deepest cultural roots in the faith of his upbringing.

The "Hurt" video brought Cash considerable publicity that year, winning the Country Music Association's Single of the Year award, playing over and over again on MTV and VH-1, and generating considerable public discussion. The video-single sold over two million copies, officially becoming Cash's best-selling single shortly after its debut.[1] Cash's core audience of aging country fans watched the video and talked about it, but so did teenagers who knew little about country music and typically did not listen to anyone over thirty. The video showed Cash as a badly aged seventy-year-old man, candidly displaying his severe physical decline. But when he died in September, some six months after the video's premiere, it came to serve with striking serendipity as a kind of self-penned epitaph on his long public career.

In the months after Cash's death, as "Hurt" was in continual replay, scores of tributes and eulogies poured forth from a wide variety of sources, from Bob Dylan to *Christianity Today*, from the *Nation* to *National Review*, all offering different forms of praise for a performer who had spent almost fifty years on the public stage, whose persona already seemed mythic and semi-legendary. In a reflective tribute in the *Nation* called, suggestively, "JC's Resurrection," Benjamin Hedin argued that no one else in American popular music "possessed the sort of obsession, or waged the same struggle, with faith."[2] Certainly "Hurt" displayed that struggle recently and vividly, and so did the title track of the million-selling double-album that "Hurt" appeared on, a booming epic of the apocalypse and the risen Christ that Cash wrote called "The Man Comes Around." So also did the posthumously released *My Mother's Hymn Book* (2004), an album of old gospel hymns and folk songs that Cash had learned from his mother in his Delta childhood.

Cash's artistic statements of faith coincided with a heightened presence of Protestant Christianity in American politics and culture. The Republican Party triumphed in the November 2004 presidential and congressional elections, and the dominant analysis claimed "evangelical Christian" voters, with their concern for "moral values," to be the decisive force in the elections. One well-circulated cartoon sought a geographic home for these evangelicals, by depicting a red-state "Jesusland" encompassing the South and Midwest, with Cash's Mississippi County near its demographic center. On the march, hawk-ish, and inspired by pre-1960s social norms, evangelicals seemed to be the largest and most politically potent religious bloc in the early twenty-first century. A quite different Protestant Christianity appeared in the phenomenally popular 2000 film *O Brother, Where Art Thou?* and the subsequent musical tours it spawned. With a soundtrack stocked with archaic music from the 1920s and 1930s (much of which Cash had personally grown up with), the film imagined a mythic, mysterious, gothic South, somewhere on the border of the Mississippi Delta and the hill country. This South was not an evangelical Jesusland, but rather Flannery O'Connor's "Christ-haunted" region. In music critic Greil Marcus's phrase, the film presented the South as "old, weird America," and many people seemed intrigued by its oldness and weirdness as a way to make sense of their twenty-first-century lives.[3] Such people also made Johnny Cash's late-in-life art some of the most popular of his career.

Johnny Cash lived an unusually long life in the public eye—from his first hit single in 1956 to the volley of attention garnered by "Hurt" and "The Man Comes Around" in 2002–2003—and that long public life took many shapes: from early rock and roll to the folk revival, from the country mainstream to alt.country, from network television to his self-produced *The Gospel Road,* from Folsom Prison to the White House and Billy Graham Crusades, from American Indian Movement protest to master of ceremonies at the nation's Bicentennial. Amidst the panoply and variety, though, Cash was unmistakably a religious figure, and the host of eulogies and tributes sought to narrate his life in religious categories. Two distinct strands of religious narrative could be discerned in the volley of postmortem commentary and appraisal.

One was a gendered story of fall, redemption, and triumph. In this narrative Cash was a classic manly hell-raiser, a wild, self-destructive outlaw who destroyed motel rooms, cars, footlights at the Grand Ole Opry, and himself—through no-holds-barred binges with drugs and alcohol—until he was finally rescued by the self-sacrificing, unfailingly loyal, ever-hopeful love of the pious, God-fearing June Carter, whom he married in 1968. She saved his life, and then showed him the path of salvation, in a long, committed marriage, the rediscovery of his Christian faith, and his stature as a respectable, reigning patriarch of country music. This was the basic plot in a host of tributes, and it gained wide visibility as the frame in the 2004 authorized biography *The Man Called Cash* and the 2005 Hollywood biopic *Walk the Line.* It was the story told by the country song "Today's the Day When Johnny Met June" (about their reuniting in heaven), and it appears in flagrant form in the marquee of one Johnny and June's Country Saloon, where a massive photographic poster of bad man Johnny giving the finger is juxtaposed with an angelic, almost-haloed, gently smiling June Carter. Perhaps the most succinct instance of this narrative appeared in the eulogy in *Time,* which honored Cash with the cover story. Richard Corliss argued that in place of mourning, people "could segue into celebration over a difficult life made exemplary, an outlaw redeemed by a woman's devotion. Besides, if you believe, the Man in Black is now garbed in white, and the doting husband has eternity to spend with his beloved."[4]

A rather different story imagined Cash as a paradoxical figure, a man of constant struggle, who saw the light amidst the darkness of his own soul. This story lionized Cash not for his ultimate triumph over his demons but rather for his refreshing candor about his own sins. Rather than the sequential narrative suggested above, this story shunned neat moralisms and gendered distinctions and portrayed Cash as perpetually a person of rival impulses, as both a violently destructive wild child and an earnest Christian seeking to be faithful. Cash's Christianity, in this story, was less something injected into his life by June Carter and more the deep imprint of his upbringing, something that was an intrinsic part of him even in his darkest moments. Many of Cash's musical colleagues told this story, most notably in a tribute concert at Nashville's Ryman Auditorium and a series of eulogies in *Rolling Stone,* but it also appeared in the more reflective analyses published in the spring after Cash's death. Two academic works on Cash, theologian Rodney Clapp's *Johnny Cash and the Great American Contradiction* and literary scholar Leigh Edwards's *Johnny Cash and the Paradox of American Identity,* emphasized Cash's dialectical persona, and so did a T-shirt depicting gaunt, drugged-out, chain-smoking Johnny standing in front of a stark, gothic church straight out of O'Connor's "Christ-haunted" South. The most succinct version of this story came in the terse, often-repeated lines from Kris Kristofferson's 1971 song about Cash, "The Pilgrim, Chapter 33": "He's a pilgrim and a preacher / and a problem when he's stoned / he's a walking contradiction / partly truth and partly fiction / takin' every wrong direction / on his lonely way back home."[5]

This essay seeks to unravel the genealogies behind these two stories of Johnny Cash, in the process gaining a clearer analysis of two quite different religious cultures, one national in scope, politically powerful, and very much in the flow of the twentieth-century cultural mainstream; the other definitely regional, of the poor and marginalized, a product of creative ferment in the back eddies and countercurrents of national life in the late nineteenth and early twentieth centuries. One religious culture, Neo-Evangelicalism, flourished most notably in the exploding suburbs of post–World War II America, in the sprawling metropolises connected by interstate highways. Another religious culture, southern Folk Religion, thrived in the New South era, especially in impoverished areas of the countryside, like the hard world of Cash's own Mississippi County.

The early 1940s may be understood as a symbolic dividing point for these two cultures. In 1942, in the Mississippi River metropolis of St. Louis, a small cohort formed a new organization, the National Association of Evangelicals. They were excited about the nation's future and wanted to shape it, and as it turned out, this St. Louis meeting marked the beginning of a very popular religious movement—Neo-Evangelicalism. In 1944, in the waters of a tributary of the Mississippi, the muddy Tyronza, twelve-year-old Johnny Cash was baptized by immersion, signifying his adult appropriation of the religion of his elders—a religion, it also turned out, that was beginning to fade as the ground from which it grew showed signs of fatal erosion. But as we will see, Cash came full circle, from the southern Folk Religion into which he was baptized, to Neo-Evangelicalism, and back to Folk Religion again. The "truth" he ultimately wanted to claim was the truth he had absorbed in his youth, in a specific, particular context shaped by fertile Delta soil, cotton, and the mighty and dangerous elemental river.

Cash was both a real person, with ideals and aspirations of his own, and a persona in popular culture, a prism through which people, as audiences and consumers of his art, could publicly grapple with their own ideals and aspirations. Analyzing the religious contexts behind Johnny Cash, both the person and the persona, therefore allows us to better understand the power of different religious cultures, not only for Cash himself, but also for significant segments of the American population. In Cash's story we can trace the scope, geographic locus, and cultural power of distinct Protestant forms. We can better understand and interpret the popular appeal of religious cultures that, alternately, were in the ascendancy and the decline, one that, beginning in the 1940s, was picking up more in its course like the Mississippi on its way to the Gulf of Mexico, the other which that same decade was becoming an isolated backwater forgotten by the main stream's mighty flow.

Before May 1970, when he appeared at a Billy Graham Crusade in Knoxville, Tennessee, Johnny Cash did not stand out as a religious persona. He had recorded three albums of gospel songs, both his own compositions and covers, as *Hymns by Johnny Cash* (1959), *Hymns from the Heart* (1962), and *The Holy Land* (1968). In concerts he often closed the night with a set of gospel songs, like "Were You There When They Crucified My Lord?" and "Peace in the Valley," a pattern that can be heard on the very popular concert albums *At Folsom Prison* (1968) and *At San Quentin* (1969). From his performing beginnings in 1955 to the Folsom Prison album, Cash was a major figure in the relatively circumscribed world of country music, and his religious cultural productions were well within normative parameters of the genre. Many a country performer recorded the occasional gospel album or wove gospel songs into their performing repertoire. As country music historian Bill Malone argues, these productions make sense less as statements of present belief and more as evocations of a fondly remembered religious past, as "tributes to [the performer's and audience's] parents and their world."[6] A Capitol Records advertisement for Buck Owens's 1970 gospel album, *Your Mother's Prayer,* made this nostalgic recollection explicit: "Buck Owens sings the beloved melodies of simpler days, when evenings were spent with the family, gathered around the piano, sharing songs of faith and belief."[7]

Only with his appearance at Graham's Knoxville Crusade did Cash distinguish himself as a country performer who wanted to demonstrate his own faith and belief, not merely recollect the (allegedly) simpler days of the bygone past. Beginning with Knoxville, Cash became a regular speaker and singer at Graham's Crusades—and at the rallies staged by Neo-Evangelical preachers James Robison and Rex Humbard and by Neo-Evangelical groups Campus Crusade for Christ and Youth for Christ. Cash became personal friends with Graham in particular, writing and recording a duet with him, "The Preacher Said, 'Jesus Said,'" which he premiered on his television variety show in 1971. Less publicly than these personal appearances, Cash in 1971 became a member of Neo-Evangelical preacher Jimmy Snow's Evangel Temple in the Nashville suburbs, a church Snow (son of country singer Hank Snow) founded in 1967 as a mission to people in the country music scene. Evangel Temple's choir sang back-up on Cash's 1972 hit song "A Thing Called Love," and Jimmy Snow played Pontius Pilate in *The Gospel Road,* a life-of-Jesus film that Cash poured his time and savings into in the years 1971–73, writing and producing the film. After its mediocre theater run, it was picked up for distribution by the Billy Graham Evangelistic Association. In 1972 Cash headlined the inaugural show of *Grand Ole Gospel Hour,* a country gospel show taped at Nashville's Ryman Auditorium and hosted by Jimmy Snow. For the Neo-Evangelical press Zondervan, Cash wrote his memoir *Man in Black* in 1975, and the following year Spire Christian Comics (a Neo-Evangelical series of conversion narratives turned into comic strips) depicted the story of Cash's life and (seemingly) newfound faith. Outside the public gaze entirely, Cash and June Carter in the mid-1970s took correspondence courses in the Bible from the San Antonio–based Christian International Bible College, a small school in the circuit of Fundamentalist colleges and seminaries. Cash wrote laudatory forewords to James Robison's 1976 *America: Garden of the Gods* and Jimmy Snow's 1977 *I Cannot Go Back.* Closing out this decade of considerable Neo-Evangelical activity, Cash in 1979 received Youth for Christ's "Man of the Year" award, the same year that his double-album of gospel songs, *A Believer Sings the Truth,* sought to make it clear that his faith was not mere nostalgia but a personally felt force in the present.

Cash personally and publicly identified with Neo-Evangelicalism in the very decade of its massive expansion in American life. The form took shape in the early 1940s, as a young cohort of Fundamentalists sought new methods of cultural engagement. They replaced the rigid theology that had brought Fundamentalism shame in the 1925 "Scopes Monkey Trial" with a new pietistic emphasis on individual feeling and experience. They formed new transdenominational organizations like the National Association of Evangelicals, Youth for Christ, Campus Crusade for Christ, Inter-Varsity Christian Fellowship, Young Life, and the Fellowship of Christian Athletes. They organized seminaries and colleges, publishing houses, and recording companies, and they began publishing their own periodical, *Christianity Today.* Beginning with his 1949 mass meetings in Los Angeles, Billy Graham became the leading face of Neo-Evangelicalism. In his preaching Graham continually emphasized the necessity of a "born-again" experience, and he brought his Crusades to a climax by inviting individual listeners to make their own, inescapably personal "decision for Christ."[8]

Cash's story suggests reasons for the appeal of Neo-Evangelicalism in its period of massive expansion. In 1972 he played a major role in Explo '72, a four-day rally in Dallas organized by Campus Crusade for Christ. Billy Graham preached to the predominantly young crowd, and Cash closed the event with an open-air concert attended by some 150,000. *Life* gave the rally prominent billing as a cover story and quoted some of Cash's comments to the concert audience. "I have tried drugs and a little of everything else," Cash testified, "and there is nothing more soul-satisfying than having the kingdom of God building inside you and growing."[9] This, in a nutshell, expressed the distinct appeal of Neo-Evangelicalism.

In their drive for cultural engagement, Neo-Evangelicals learned to speak in the idioms of the dominant culture, particularly the consumerist and therapeutic paradigms of the post–World War II decades. People came to think of themselves as consumers—of automobiles, electrical appliances, homes, popular culture, and government services. With the rapid expansion of medicine, and particularly of psychology and psychiatry, they also came to think of themselves as patients who needed tangible forms of healing and guidance, of therapy and counseling. Neo-Evangelicals framed their Protestant Christianity in these consumerist, therapeutic idioms. Christianity was a "personal relationship with Jesus Christ," a pietistic array of experiences that gave the faithful something they lacked before they had "got Jesus." Cash at Explo '72 was speaking as a newly minted Neo-Evangelical when he described the kingdom as a kind of inward possession that gave true satisfaction to his soul.

Neo-Evangelical writer Charles Paul Conn echoed Cash's testimony in his 1973 biography, *The New Johnny Cash:*

> The vibrations that he sends out when he talks and sings today testify to something of much greater substance than merely the personality of a good and decent man. They speak of a personal, vibrant acquaintance with a living Christ, and of a single-minded absorption in the work of his kingdom. That is the *new* Johnny Cash.

Conn then turned to the reader with an invitation:

> If your life is empty, Jesus Christ can fill it. . . . Like Cash, you can know Jesus Christ personally, so that He becomes an exciting, powerful presence in your life. And when that happens, when you come to know Him for yourself, you will experience the same newness of life that this man in black has found.[10]

Conn's summons highlighted a critical factor in Neo-Evangelicalism's appeal: its resolute emphasis on newness and a resultant near-denial of both an individual's past and an inherited collective tradition. When the Christian appropriated Christ in the inwardness of pietistic experience, a sharp break was made with the past. The Christian was born again, and the narrative of life gained not a new chapter but rather a new plot altogether, one that properly began with conversion and never looked back. It was a radically ahistorical form of religion.

Historian Martin Marty clarifies a second critical factor in Neo-Evangelicalism's appeal. "Evangelicals are the pioneer religious moderns," Marty argues, and in an era of confusing flux, when people are plagued by anomic questions like "who am I?" and "to whom do I belong?" they offer the self-evident guarantee of inward experience, sanctioned by a far-flung group of fellow-believers who signify their own similar experiences through a vocabulary of pietism in a consumerist, therapeutic grammar.[11] As moderns, they speak to the isolated individual—unable to rest securely in local community, family, tradition, nation, or land—and they hold out the promise of the present immediacy of experience, in the unassailable depths of individual inwardness. In a world where so much seems uncertain and insecure, the anomic individual can know one thing with unmistakable clarity—"Jesus Christ personally," in Conn's words.

When Cash told his Neo-Evangelical conversion story in *Man in Black,* it was in this individualist frame. He recounted the guilt and grief he had felt when his older brother Jack was killed in a work accident, when Jack was fourteen and Johnny was twelve. He went on to write at length about how, just as his musical career took off in the late 1950s, he fell into an all-consuming drug addiction. It spiraled destructively in the 1960s, and Cash wrote of how he effectively abandoned his first wife, Vivian, and their four daughters, of how he destroyed all manner of property (motel rooms, automobiles, endangered yellow condors, etc.), of how he alienated everyone who knew him, of how he went on violent binges where he had bizarre delusions and did severe damage to his body. Some elements of this story were known in the country music world of the 1960s. Bill Malone writes that "Cash appears to have been the first country singer to be identified as a bad boy . . . a hell-raiser."[12] The country trade press revealed some of Cash's hell-raising stories, and many spread by word-of-mouth. Anyone attending a Cash show, or looking casually at certain album covers (particularly 1967's *Carryin' On* and 1968's *From Sea to Shining Sea*) could see that the large-framed Cash was looking like a ravaged, hollowed-out skeleton.

Neo-Evangelicalism held out the promise of wiping the slate clean. It offered not a path of penance for accumulated guilt but rather a radical new break and a history-free new beginning. In a climactic scene in *Man in Black,* Cash recounted what he felt in a spring 1971 service at Evangel Temple. Listening to gospel songs, he realized that "the future was the important thing now. What I did with my life from now on was all that mattered. I had learned a lot from my mistakes, and I'd learned the tempering, steeling hard way." Cash came forward at Snow's altar call, told Snow that he wanted to join the church, and felt inside a major purging: "I had learned the long-suffering and complete forgiveness of God. What a joy to know that He'd clean the slate for all those years."[13] On the heels of this, Cash in an interview drew sharp divisions between two eras in his life: "I don't have a career anymore. What I have now is a ministry. Everything I have and everything I do is given completely to Jesus Christ now. I've lived all my life for the devil up 'til now, and from here on I'm going to live it for the Lord."[14]

Neo-Evangelicals, in their drive for cultural engagement, were thrilled to have the new Cash in their ranks. Campus Crusade for Christ and Billy Graham organized Explo '72 with the explicit goal of reaching out to the youthful counterculture, and Cash was given a prominent position as the rally's closing word.[15] Zondervan's book jacket for *Man in Black* dubbed Cash "God's superstar," and Neo-Evangelical writers some thirty years later memorialized Cash as a pop culture icon who was on their side. "Against all popular wisdom," Ted Olson wrote in *Christianity Today,* Cash "became a celebrity's celebrity while singing more explicitly about Jesus than many contemporary Christian music favorites."[16] Official biographer Steve Turner argued that Cash was "a Christian with traditional evangelical beliefs who was revered by icons of the subculture," and Turner noted that Cash once called his first appearance at a Billy Graham Crusade "the pinnacle of my career."[17] Cash's was a double-edged story of triumph: both his own clean break with his destructive past and his subsequent successful testifying to the power of Neo-Evangelical faith.

As these statements from the years after Cash's death suggest, the Neo-Evangelical narrative of Cash's life, generated in the 1970s, had durable staying power. For many, Cash is known as a Christian because of his Neo-Evangelical activity, particularly his friendship with Billy Graham. Cash's Neo-Evangelicalism made him stand out from the religious nostalgia of country music, in open affirmation of a heartfelt contemporary faith. Yet the Neo-Evangelical story of Cash's life—and by extension, Neo-Evangelicalism's cultural power—has its limits. The religious narrative of Johnny and Jesus was dampened down into the more secular, distinctly gendered story of Johnny and June. She was the angelic presence, the pious Christian, who rescued Cash from his self-destructive behavior. Less the inward, pietistic presence of Jesus, it was more the human, self-giving love of a strong woman that saved Cash. The clear break between one pattern of life and another was there, but the decisive moment was not a Graham Crusade in 1970 or Evangel Temple in 1971, but rather Johnny and June's marriage in 1968. From that decisive moment on, Cash was a new man.

This popular narrative of Cash's life (the first one noted above) has a Neo-Evangelical plot, but the actual characters and setting are more generically human and secularized. This suggests that though Neo-Evangelicals have become *the* dominant face of American Christianity in the past forty years, their goal of cultural engagement has been only partially realized. Indeed, it may be precisely their sense of limited cultural power that has pushed them into political activity: if you cannot convert people through individual evangelism, perhaps at the policy level you can craft a more Christianized polity. By this logic, the 2004 elections would be, ironically, evidence of the limitation of Neo-Evangelical cultural transformation.

The future will answer this hypothesis, but the past offers clues for Neo-Evangelicalism's major expansion. Cash and the Neo-Evangelicals narrated his story in a modernist fashion, as the personal journey of a troubled, deliverance-seeking individual. But there are historical and contextual factors that suggest reasons for the appeal of Neo-Evangelicalism as a religious option. Not every Neo-Evangelical convert was a pop culture figure, and not everyone lived a wild, hell-raising life as a prelude. But, like Cash, a whole generation lived through sweeping transformations in American life from the 1940s to the 1970s. A widespread consumer-based economy came to touch every corner of the nation, as peripheral regions like the South and the West became fully integrated into the national economy. Millions of people left the countryside for the exploding cities and suburbs, and the automobile came to thoroughly reshape the experienced landscape. Through the new media of radio and television, a far-reaching popular culture brought a national audience together with normative fashions and codes of behavior. African American activism challenged the presumed justice of the status quo and inspired social change in a variety of fronts—among women, students, Native Americans, prisoners, and Chicano migrant workers. Cash embodied many of these transformations: as his native South was agriculturally revolutionized, he left the farm for good, finding a new life in Sunbelt metropolises (Memphis, Los Angeles, Nashville), made a living in a popular culture medium that presupposed spending money and the dissemination of art through recording technology, and at points put social protest into song (for Native Americans, in 1964's *Bitter Tears,* and for prisoners in *At Folsom* and *At San Quentin*).

Though many gained from these transformations in tangible ways—ways measurable by standard-of-living indexes and income-per-capita charts—the transformations could also be psychologically unsettling. Amidst the prosperity and good times of the postwar "consumers' republic," culture shock and anomie plagued people on the inside. Binx Bolling, the main character of Walker Percy's 1961 novel *The Moviegoer,* narrated these unsettling inward dislocations. A successful stockbroker and veteran of the Korean War, Binx lived in a suburb of New Orleans and was an inveterate watcher of movies. Yet he came to feel, amidst the evident comfortability, that he was "infested with malaise," "sunk in the everydayness," and the dark impression grew on him "that everyone is dead."[18] To this feeling of inward hollowness and dislocation, Neo-Evangelicalism offered the promise of resolute inner certainty, of a powerfully felt inward sense of belonging. The outer world might be changing in unsettling ways, but at the end of the day, what truly mattered was what was inside the individual, securely immune from history.

In the 1970s, as the forces that we now call globalization and the information revolution began to make themselves felt, Americans' outward security began to unravel, as global competition revived and the prosperous consumers' republic began to show growing divisions of wealth. The sense of unsettling dislocation accelerated, and it was in this decade, after expanding in the previous three, that Neo-Evangelicalism began a period of rapid growth and expansion. As the outer world became even less certain and less secure, the appeal of an ahistorical, experiential religion accelerated. Zondervan's book jacket advertisement for *Man in Black* tersely expressed the social, contextual appeal of Neo-Evangelicalism. "This book," the advertising beckoned, "reveals how a solid faith makes it possible to live serenely in the vortex of a sometimes chaotic whirl."[19]

Neo-Evangelicalism was Cash's solid rock in the 1970s—but really only in the 1970s. By the 1980s his appearances at rallies had trailed off considerably, he and June Carter stopped attending Evangel Temple, and his zealous "ministry" seemed to be merely a country music career again (and a lackluster one at that, as the hits and record sales slowed considerably). Personally, Cash was flailing, falling deeply into old habits of self-destructive drug use and erratic behavior. Marshall Grant, Cash's longtime bass player and de facto personal manager, recalled of the early 1980s that Cash "was in terrible condition, as bad as I've ever seen any man at any time in my life. And it was getting to the point that he couldn't perform, couldn't do anything. He was just staying totally blown away all of the time. . . . It's impossible to explain just how ridiculous John's behavior was."[20] Matters came to a head in 1983, when Cash's family organized an intervention, insisting that he seek institutional help for his raging drug addiction. Cash checked into the Betty Ford Clinic late that year, and newspaper accounts were the first public cracks in the surface of the Neo-Evangelical image of the redeemed, rescued, "new" Johnny Cash. As it turned out, for the next twenty years, sometimes in the public eye but often out of it and only hinted at by press stories of "hospital visits," Cash would struggle with drug addiction and the violent, self-destructive behavior that came with it.

This was an embarrassing reversal in Cash's narrative of Neo-Evangelical deliverance, and it certainly seemed to belie bold pronouncements of personal triumph and wholesale rebirth. In this time of crisis and confusion, Cash sought guidance in his roots, and he went back imaginatively to a more limited, regionally specific form of Protestantism, the southern Folk Religion he had absorbed in his Mississippi County youth. This was not nostalgia but rather tradition in the genuine sense—finding orientation for the present and future by working within parameters inherited from the past. It was a distinctly non-evangelical move of going back to what was old, of seeking authority and clarity not in contemporary inward experience but in a received, collective body of religious belief and practice.

Though its presence was obscured and even erased in the Neo-Evangelical narrative of his life, southern Folk Religion had been Cash's religious cultural influence in his youth. From ages three to eighteen (1935–50), Cash was the third child of tenant farmers who struggled to acquire their own land, in the fertile, gray-black soil of the Arkansas Delta. A huge expanse of land extending westward from the Mississippi River some 250 miles from north (Missouri) to south (Louisiana), the Arkansas Delta was utterly flat, broken only in a few places by a notable ridge, originally thickly wooded, and drained by innumerable rivers and creeks that all flowed into the Mississippi. Mississippi County, where Cash grew up, lies in the northeast corner of the state, with the big river on the east and Missouri's boot heel just north. Mississippi and adjoining counties were the last frontier of the New South, the southern economic order defined by intensification of land use, aggressive extraction of resources, full market connectivity through railroads, and town- and village-building. Cash's father and older brother cleared the land they farmed (only once cutover by timber companies), and a railroad spur at the just-built town of Dyess carried the produce of the land to distant markets. That produce, for Cash and his family, was cotton. Backbreaking labor in the cotton field defined Cash's early life, and in a 1997 memoir he reflected on its pervasiveness and on its distance from what came afterwards. "Inside me," he wrote in his *Cash: The Autobiography,*

> My boyhood feels so close, but when I look around, it sometimes seems to belong to a vanished world. In the United States in the late 1990s, is it really possible to imagine whole families, boys and girls of eight to eighteen at

their parents' sides in the cotton fields, working through the July heat from dawn to dusk, driving away exhaustion with songs of the spirit?[21]

In this reflection Cash succinctly expressed the two staples of his youth: labor and religion.

Through his family, through the churches he attended in Dyess, through radio shows and through stories he heard, Cash was initiated into a distinct form of Protestantism. From his mother, Carrie, a gifted singer and musician, he learned a wide body of songs, old songs from the early nineteenth-century camp meetings like "I Am Bound for the Promised Land" and "I Am a Pilgrim," and newer songs from the gospel hymn genre like "Let the Lower Lights Be Burning" and "I'll Fly Away." From his storytelling father, Ray, he absorbed tales of his grandfather, William Henry Cash, a farmer and Baptist preacher who traveled on his horse with a Bible and a gun. Cash's older brother, Jack, surely absorbed these stories, too, because when he was thirteen he experienced a "call to preach" and began to fervently study the Bible in preparation for his vocation. Jack's mystical deathbed visions, an array of images from the book of Revelation, left a deep imprint on Cash into his very last year. In the painful months after Jack's death, young Johnny listened to his mother pray, lament, and sometimes break down with grief during family labor in the cotton field. He also listened to his father preach a sermon in the local Baptist church when the regular preacher was absent. The Cashes, like many people in the rural South, routinely attended churches of different denominational affiliation. In Dyess, emblematic of much of the rural South, the differences were fairly limited: Baptist, Methodist, Church of Christ, and Church of God. In these churches Cash absorbed sermons of spontaneous oral composition, communal practices like a mass baptism, and a more extensive body of songs. He also soaked up songs from the inexpensive battery-powered radio the family bought from Sears Roebuck. He listened especially closely to the gospel songs of "hillbilly" musicians like the Louvin Brothers and the "race" musician Sister Rosetta Tharpe. From seasonal workers, drifters, and neighboring tenant families, Cash soaked up a variety of stories, tales, and legends.

In these predominantly auditory ways, Cash was initiated into southern Folk Religion. The form took shape in the late nineteenth century, as the once-separate cultures of slave religion and plain-folk faith came together in a new synthesis for the New South. In the 1880s and 1890s, as the economic horizons of millions of descendants of slaves and of plain-folk shrank, and debt, landlessness, and a confining poverty came to blanket the region, the poor of both races spoke and listened to one another. The resultant borrowing and fusion of once-distinct traditions was Folk Religion.[22] Unlike Neo-Evangelicalism's founders—solid members of the nation's middle class, living in major cities from Boston to Pasadena—the people that crafted Folk Religion were obscure, impoverished, southern, usually rural, and they left scarce written records. They were not a small cohort but rather disparate communities of faith, who codified normative beliefs and practices through performance and perpetuation. While Neo-Evangelicals used the latest technology in their drive for cultural engagement, the practitioners of Folk Religion lived in an almost entirely oral culture, with the lone written text of the Bible (and sometimes also a song collection). Beliefs were remembered, and practices were given meaning, by the formulation of theology into oral types—songs, stories, stock narratives, proverbs, epigrams, sermon styles, and the like. As individuals and communities reiterated these oral types, the culture of Folk Religion was spread and sustained. In his classic work *Orality and Literacy,* Walter Ong writes that "in an oral culture, knowledge, once acquired, had to be constantly repeated or it would be lost: fixed, formulaic thought patterns were essential for wisdom."[23]

This knowledge was formulated and repeated across a wide expanse, but it was limited to the South and to the impoverished class of the region: tenants and sharecroppers, coal miners and textile workers, remote-area small farmers, domestics. In Folk Religion the poor of the region crafted a culture that articulated their struggles and longings, giving higher meaning to the everyday, confronting phenomena like exhaustion with, as Cash put it, "songs of the spirit." Thus while Neo-Evangelicalism was propelled by an outward drive for national cultural engagement, Folk Religion was a turning in to trace and engage what one country song called "the cold hard facts" in the lives of the southern poor. Neo-Evangelicalism learned to imagine Christianity in the dominant idioms of the postwar United States (consumerist and therapeutic), but Folk Religion shaped its culture to confront poverty-based realities like confinement, insecurity, and frustration. To these everyday realities it presented both comfort and challenge. In two reflections in the 1990s, Cash expressed this dialectical identity. In liner notes to his 1996 album *Unchained,* he remembered: "The first preachers I heard at a Pentecostal church in Dyess, Arkansas, scared me. The talk about sin and death and eternal hell without redemption made a mark on me. At four, I'd peep out the window of our farmhouse at night, and if, in the distance, I saw a grass fire or forest fire, I knew hell was almost here."[24] In a very different spirit, he reflected in his 1997 memoir, "I'm remembering my childhood again. I'm back on the front porch . . . with my mom and dad and brothers and sisters, all of us together, while my mother sings her sacred songs and plays her guitar, banishing fear and loneliness, bringing the black dog [Cash's phrase for the darkness in the soul] to heel, drowning out even the screams of panthers from the brush."[25]

With this dialectical mixture of comfort and challenge, Folk Religion imagined human beings as fragile creatures, subject to the terror of death at any moment, open to the possibility of receiving mystical visions from God. Time gained heightened meaning as a ripe moment when the Word might break in or Death might make its awful appearance. All human beings were insecure and confined, Folk Religion taught in a body of Death songs and a catalogue of vision accounts. Thus was the insecurity and confinement of the poor imbued with higher meaning. Similarly, Folk Religion emphasized the ever-present capacity for perverse evil in each human soul (Cash's "black dog"), and it confronted the possibility of social dissolution with an ethos of communal neighborliness. People needed to work together to fight the possibility of violence and despair, and they needed to be vigilant against their own darkness in the soul. The Devil always stalked the Christian, from the inside, and threatened to destroy both individuals and the communities that sustained life. Tales and lore of the Devil and sermons and songs articulating an ethos of neighborliness taught these ideas, challenging the frustration and anger that the poor could easily be consumed by in their everyday struggles.

Struggle—both the everyday struggles that the poor confronted and the struggle for Christian living that they were beckoned to—was the defining element in Folk Religion. A Georgia farm laborer explained what Folk Religion meant to him, emphasizing its difference from easy alternatives:

> A lot of people, they're wanting an easy drive up there to Heaven, that's what. . . . They think an hour or two on Sunday, or around Christmas and Easter, and when they die, they'll see a sign, and it'll say: Heaven, and the Lord will be yonder, on the hill, waiting, with a smile on his face. That's soft religion; that's faking. It's no good religion. It's a waste of time. Our religion is hard; it's a hard, hard religion. We're in trouble, and we may not get where we want to be going, but we're going to try, oh we are![26]

Folk Religion was a "hard, hard religion" for the "cold hard facts of life." After coalescing as a form in the 1880s and 1890s, it thrived in the first four decades of the twentieth century. As families like the Cashes migrated to frontier areas of the New South like Mississippi County in the 1930s, they brought their religion with them, and it continued to inform their lives as it spoke (literally, in its orality) to their struggles in poverty.

In the very decade that Cash was born and his family came to the Delta, though, forces were set in motion that would radically transform the South. The region was "the Nation's No. 1 economic problem," Franklin Roosevelt famously wrote in 1938, and New Deal policy and World War II militarization brought capital, industry, and migrants to the South.[27] Change happened much more quickly in some places than in others—in Mississippi County, Cash was still picking cotton by hand with his family as an eighteen-year-old in 1950. For him the decisive personal break with the older South came that year, when he joined the U.S. Air Force. After four years of service, he returned to the Mississippi River region, but to the expanding metropolis of Memphis, not the cotton patch.

Here, as noted, he began his career as a professional musician. As also noted, Cash's music in his first dozen years showed the religious imprint of his youth, but in a nostalgic fashion. The nostalgia makes sense as a way in which migrants out of the impoverished rural South tried to hold onto the religion they had grown up with, but only succeeded in a vestigial way. The context that Folk Religion originated in and spoke to, the impoverished New South, was radically different from the Sunbelt that supplanted it, and the shock of transformation was borne out in the lives of those who lived through the cultural passage. While they gained many things their parents had lacked—prosperity, security, optimism—they often displayed the pathos of culture shock in pathologies like diabetes, obesity, alcoholism, and in Cash's case, drug addiction.[28] Folk Religion as a coherent culture survived only in the most unchanged parts of the region, like areas of the Delta, Appalachians, and Ozarks into the 1960s and 1970s. There, impoverished communities continued to practice its wisdom by telling its stories and singing its songs.

In the 1980s Cash began to return to the Folk Religion of his youth. Neither tangible local communities of folk believers nor the pre-mechanized, labor-intensive rural South still existed, but remembered oral forms—especially a body of songs—did. Beyond personal memory, the old songs survived through commercial and folk recordings, some dating back to the 1920s. Through the songs, more than anything else, Cash made an imaginative return to his roots. In various interviews he described the presence and persistence of the old songs, never more succinctly than a few months before his death, when he told a journalist that they were "powerful songs . . . my magic to take me through the dark places."[29]

Appropriately, Cash conveyed his return to Folk Religion primarily in song, a striking contrast to his Neo-Evangelicalism, which he publicized largely in personal appearances, testimony, memoir, and film. In the volley of music he recorded in his last decade, but most overtly in his final year, Cash sang old songs from received tradition, wrote new ones in the traditional idiom, and refashioned the songs of contemporary musicians into a folk religious frame and thereby made them his own. The packaging of the music was intentionally archaic and mysterious. On the cover of 1994's *American Recordings*, Cash stood as a dark figure against a moody sky, flanked by two dogs whose names, he explained in supporting press material, were "Sin" and "Redemption." On 1996's *Unchained*, he stood against the unpainted wood of a weather-beaten barn, and on the posthumously released *Ain't No Grave* (2010), a grainy black-and-white photograph of Cash at age twelve was the entire cover. In album liner notes Cash wrote in a reflective, ruminating style, taking the album listener back to Mississippi County in story and anecdote.

The songs spoke of the struggle for faith, of epiphanies in crisis moments, of the dark side of human beings, of the pervasive limit of death. Enigmatic imagery and mystical visions appeared in many of the songs, and Jesus was a "ragged stranger" ("The Mercy Seat," 2000) who brought both consoling comfort ("Spiritual," 1996) and cataclysmic judgment ("The Man Comes Around," 2002). Deliverance was less a possession realized in the present believer's pietistic soul than a longed-for, hoped-for reality of which the present believer caught only glimpses ("Redemption," 1994; "Unchained," 1996), and the struggle against evil in oneself was palpable and perpetual ("The Beast in Me," 1994; "I See a Darkness," 2000; "Hurt," 2002). Human incapacity and limitation were accentuated ("Why Me Lord," 1994; "Personal Jesus," 2002; "Help Me," posthumously released in 2006), and the helpless believer hoped for Jesus' help rather than making a willful decision for Christ.

In addition to the posthumously released *My Mother's Hymn Book*, Cash in these recordings suggested their folk religious background. He reworked "Wayfaring Stranger" (2000), a somber mid-nineteenth-century dirge that imagined the Christian as a "poor wayfaring stranger / traveling through this world of woe." He did artful interpretations of "God's Gonna Cut You Down" (posthumous, 2006) and "Ain't No Grave" (posthumous, 2010), songs of New South vintage that spoke of God's power over death and in resurrection. One of the last songs that he wrote, "Like the 309" (posthumous, 2006), narrated his own funeral, with the hope that his "box" would be "loaded on the 309" and carried away on the chugging train of ultimate redemption. With Cash's weathered voice cracking at points in the song, it was both poignant and a masterful example of creating within a received idiom, the Folk Religion of his youth.

But the *coup de grace* was the majestic, booming Cash composition "The Man Comes Around." Opening with Cash's voice reading from the book of Revelation, with scratchy sound like an old radio, the song moved with sparse instrumentation into a series of visions of the apocalypse. Its opening lines, "There's a man goin' round takin' names," were lifted from a New South folk song, and the volley of cryptic, arresting lyrics that followed drew freely from the rich symbolism of biblical prophets. "The whirlwind is in the thorn tree," Cash sang in the chorus (a striking image that came to him in a dream, he wrote in the liner notes), and "it's hard for thee to kick against the pricks," he continued in the language of the King James Bible. "Til Armageddon" there would be "no shalom," and God's order would be realized only when, at a cataclysmic point, "the Man comes around." The song then concluded with Cash continuing the passage from the book of Revelation. In its rich, mystical symbolism, sense of human fragility, and stark message of impending cataclysm, the song could have come right out of the Folk Religion of Cash's youth. Coupled with "Hurt," which came next on the album and, with its evocative video, displayed Cash's struggle against the darkness in his own soul, "The Man Comes Around" imbued Cash's life and musical career with the distinct religious aura of Folk Religion. On the heels of the songs he had recorded since the early 1990s, and given a definitive imprint as his last word when he died the following year, the folk religious narrative of Cash came to compete with the Neo-Evangelical one.

Many commentators noted Cash's paradoxical Christianity and how he did not fit into available religious categories. In the *Atlantic Monthly* Francis Davis called him "God's lonely man" and noted that, unlike so many in 2004, he was "a Christian who didn't cast stones, a patriot who didn't play the flag card."[30] Benjamin Hedin in the *Nation* praised "The Man Comes Around" as "arguably his greatest original song," and Nicholas Kulish in the *New York Times* traced Cash's "journey through the other side of virtue" and wished for a paradoxical figure like Cash "in a world increasingly reduced to good and evil."[31] Audiences eagerly received Cash's folk religious presentation of his persona, as they demonstrated by making his late recordings some of the best-selling of his career. This acclaim made Cash's own ultimate narrative of his life, for which he used the frame of his inherited Folk Religion, a powerful presence that left a deep impression. As this acclaim came forth from centers of national culture and from mass audiences, it suggests that Cash, in drawing on the seemingly forgotten backwater of Folk Religion, more successfully engaged with the dominant culture than the Neo-Evangelicals—though ironically, Folk Religion's drive had been limited and not expansive, and its actual, tangible presence was a chapter in the more-removed past.

It is too early to say if this heightened public interest in Cash's end-of-career work, with analogues in the *O Brother, Where Art Thou?* phenomenon, indicates the stirrings of new developments in American religion, perhaps some search for roots, tradition, and particularity in the forgotten cultural backwaters and eddies outside the mainstream. Consumers of popular culture are too disparate to be called a community or movement, pop culture and fashion are notably evanescent, and listeners and viewers can hear and see a multiplicity of things in a given work of art. Still, some judgments can be made about the appeal of southern Folk Religion for Cash in his later life and (through the medium of Cash's later music) for the audiences who listened to it.

When Cash returned imaginatively to the Folk Religion he had absorbed in his Mississippi County youth, it was to a religious form that articulated struggle and that de-centered the individual believer in favor of local communities, inherited tradition, and God's mysterious purposes. The folk religious sense of the Christian life as a "hard, hard" struggle in which "we may not get where we want to be going" resonated with Cash as his life experiences, particularly his relapse and continued battle with drug addiction, belied the Neo-Evangelical promise of utter newness. As he saw his own failings and stumbles, the notion of an inner, pietistic guarantee of self-evident knowledge seemed like less and less of a solid rock amidst "the vortex of a sometimes chaotic whirl." A received tradition from the past, one that Cash had personally seen embodied in people he had grown up with, with an elaborate body of varied oral forms, came to seem like a much more durable basis for faith. Appropriately, Cash in his last decade was also writing a novel/memoir called *The Hoxie Rock*. It was set in the year 1944, when he was baptized and when his brother was killed, and its title came from a large rock he picked up on a boyhood trip past Hoxie, Arkansas, and placed by his family's farmhouse as a striking contrast to the flat, muddy, rock-free soil of Mississippi County.[32] Through this novel (as yet unpublished), and publicly through the music of his last decade, Cash sought a stable basis for religious understanding in the past. Only what was received and transcended the lone individual would withstand the ravages of time, would endure amidst shifting ground, like the durable Hoxie rock (still at the decaying, sinking Cash family farmhouse as of this writing).

Cash's listeners and viewers also participated in this phenomenon, but their route to it was surely different. The majority of his late-career audience was middle class, college educated, and alien to country music and to the hard world of the cotton patch. They lived in metropolises and suburbs, not in agricultural areas like Mississippi County. They were of the same type of background as those most likely to swell the ranks of Neo-Evangelicalism. What differed was their response to the changes that Neo-Evangelical converts also felt. In the 1980s and 1990s the forces of globalization and the information revolution accelerated, and macroeconomic change seemed more rapid, even as an ever-dizzying array of virtual imagery came streaming through the latest technology. People experienced an overload of cultural messages without any obvious center, even as global capitalism seemed to override anything given and transform everyday patterns at a revolutionary pace. In this context, Cash's artistic evocations of Folk Religion presented him as a figure who was authentic, not virtual, who was historical and grounded amidst dizzying change and transformation. Standing out from the visual overload and panoply of cultural messages, he articulated matters of substance by singing candidly of the "cold hard facts of life," and in a revolutionary world lacking a grounded center, he was a time-weathered persona who sang out of a particular, specific, inherited tradition. In U2's "The Wanderer *Starring* Johnny Cash" (a song they wrote about him, for him to sing on their 1993 album *Zooropa*), Cash was a religious wanderer, a wayfaring stranger who trod through cities "without a soul," amidst "the capitals of tin," down "that old eight-lane." He carried "a Bible and a gun," and everywhere he went, he was looking, searching for "one good man," for an elusive figure who would "sit at his father's right hand." Like the mighty Mississippi, Cash in this song and his late-career art was elemental, pushing past ephemera in his search for religious truth. His way led back, imaginatively, to the world of the river—not the swelling main stream symbolized in the Neo-Evangelicals' 1942 St. Louis meeting, but a much more hidden backwater, in which Cash had been baptized in 1944, near which he had placed the Hoxie rock. It was a countercurrent that carried considerable power for the folk of the New South, for Cash himself as a youth and as an older man, and for his listeners in an anomic, ahistorical, virtual age.

Notes

1. Joel Whitburn, *Billboard Hot Country Songs, 1944 to 2008* (Menomonee Falls, WI: Record Research, 2008), 84–86.
2. Benjamin Hedin, "JC's Resurrection," *Nation*, March 8, 2004, 33–36.
3. Greil Marcus, *Invisible Republic: Bob Dylan's Basement Tapes* (New York: Owl, 1997).
4. Richard Corliss, "The Man in Black," *Time*, September 22, 2003.
5. Kris Kristofferson, "The Pilgrim, Chapter 33."
6. Bill Malone, *Don't Get Above Your Raisin': Country Music and the Southern Working Class* (Urbana: University of Illinois Press, 2002), 116.
7. *Music City News*, March 1970, 32.
8. For a terse, helpful summary of Neo-Evangelicalism's history, see Christian Smith, *American Evangelicalism: Embattled and Thriving* (Chicago: University of Chicago Press, 1998), 9–13.
9. *Life*, June 30, 1972, 43.
10. Charles Paul Conn, *The New Johnny Cash* (Old Tappan, NJ: Fleming H. Revell, 1973), 12, 91, 93.
11. Martin Marty, "The Revival of Evangelicalism and Southern Religion" in *Varieties of Southern Evangelicalism*, ed. David Harrell (Macon, GA: Mercer University Press, 1981), 15.
12. Malone, *Don't Get Above Your Raisin'*, 111.
13. Johnny Cash, *Man in Black* (Grand Rapids, MI: Zondervan, 1975), 153–54.
14. Conn, *New Johnny Cash*, 29.
15. John Egerton, *The Americanization of Dixie: The Southernization of America* (New York: Harper's, 1974), 192–95.
16. Ted Olson, "Johnny Cash's Song of Redemption," *Christianity Today*, November 2003, 60–62.
17. Steve Turner, *The Man Called Cash: The Life, Love, and Faith of an American Legend* (Nashville: W Publishing Group, 2004), 187, 230.
18. Walker Percy, *The Moviegoer* (New York: Ivy, 1961), 9, 86, 146.
19. Cash, *Man in Black*.
20. Marshall Grant with Chris Zar, *I Was There When It Happened: My Life with Johnny Cash* (Nashville: Cumberland House, 2006), 278, 283.
21. Johnny Cash with Patrick Carr, *Cash: The Autobiography* (New York: Harper, 1997), 16.
22. For a sketch of some of the practices that characterized this interracial folk religion, see Paul Harvey, *Freedom's Coming: Religious Culture and the Shaping of the South from the Civil War through the Civil Rights Era* (Chapel Hill: University of North Carolina Press, 2005), 109–26.
23. Walter Ong, *Orality and Literacy: The Technologizing of the Word* (London: Routledge, 1982), 24.
24. Johnny Cash, liner notes to *Unchained* (American 43097–2, 1996).
25. Cash with Carr, *Cash*, 58–59.
26. Robert Coles, *Flannery O'Connor's South* (Athens: University of Georgia Press, 1980), 61.
27. David Carlton and Peter Coclanis, eds., *Confronting Southern Poverty in the Great Depression: The Report on Economic Conditions of the South with Related Documents* (Boston: Bedford/St. Martin's, 1996), 42.

28. Michael Streissguth, *Johnny Cash: The Biography* (Cambridge, MA: Da Capo, 2006), 85.

29. Johnny Cash, liner notes to *Unearthed* (American B0001679–02, 2003), 84.

30. Francis Davis, "God's Lonely Man," *Atlantic Monthly,* March 2004, 141–45.

31. Hedin, "JC's Resurrection"; Nicholas Kulish, "Johnny Cash's Journey through the Other Side of Virtue," *New York Times,* November 27, 2005, 4:9.

32. Nick Tosches, "Chordless in Gaza: The Second Coming of John R. Cash," *Journal of Country Music* 17, no. 3 (1995): 29.

AFTERWORD

◆

"No Home Like a Raft"

REPOSITIONING THE NARRATIVES OF
U.S. RELIGIOUS HISTORY

Thomas A. Tweed

"I never felt easy till the raft was . . . out in the middle of the Mississippi," the narrator of *The Adventures of Huckleberry Finn* says as he and the escaped slave traveling with him set out on their aquatic journey. After Jim and Huck hung up their "signal lantern" and let the currents carry them, they felt "powerful glad to get away." "We said there warn't no home like a raft, after all. Other places do seem so cramped up and smothery."[1] For those characters in the novel by Mark Twain, who grew up on the river where he later piloted boats, being on the raft was exhilarating because it put distance between them and the immorality, hypocrisy, and suffering on the "sivilized" shore.[2]

Readers of this collection of historical essays are "powerful glad" for other reasons. The contributors to this book—a rather different mode of transport—also tell their stories from the Mississippi, following the currents from its source in northern Minnesota to its destination in the Gulf of Mexico. This aquatic vantage allows for more expansive vistas. By contrast, the usual historical surveys, which have been set in the woodlands and cityscapes farther east, "do seem so cramped up and smothery." Yet positioned along the Mississippi River more characters enter the complex plot as the settings shift, moving up and down the major artery dividing the terrain that came to be called the United States. Taken together, in other words, the essays move us toward richer narratives. We might just leave it at that and conclude, as Huck does at the end of his fictional journey, "there ain't nothing more to write about, and I am rotten glad of it."[3] Postponing our delight, however, it might help to write just a *little* more—about where these essays have taken us and where we might go next.

So where are we as we reach the end of this book? Michael Pasquier says that he and his collaborators hope the book will contribute "to the ongoing conversation about how historians tell stories about religion in America," and the volume succeeds in that task in several ways.[4] First, the contributors employ and imply organizing motifs that allow us to notice the movement of people, things, and practices up and down the Mississippi—and not just the settlements along the bank. Second, those kinetic themes are especially helpful in emphasizing the valley's heterogeneity: an exceptionally diverse cast of characters enters these stories. As Jon Sensbach notes, the Mississippi was a site that witnessed the "confluence" of many cultures and religions, and his focus on the "Black Atlantic," for example, brings Muslims into the story. The diversity of "sovereign Indian nations," a point emphasized in Sylvester Johnson's chapter, also emerges clearly, as does the history of African American Christianity (Giggie). Especially but not only in the colonial period, Catholicism moves toward the center of the plot when narrators situate themselves in the Mississippi basin, a region once part of New France; varied Protestants receive significant attention here, too, as do the Latter-day Saints and other new religious movements (Smith, Perry). Finally, the contributors also challenge the predominant plot of "western expansion by white Protestants" by highlighting the watery boundary that divides eastern and western terrain and by reorienting the narrative in terms of a north-south axis.[5] Chapters about the northern headwaters (Remillard) and Lower Mississippi (Greene, Poché, Hayes), remind us to think about locales at and beyond the U.S. border. In particular, as the contributors note that the river flows toward the Caribbean and the Atlantic World, they expand the spatial limit of the usual historical narratives.

As exhilarating journeys prompt travelers to imagine their next trip, this collection of essays provokes further reflection and points to future research.[6] First, by situating us along the Mississippi River, the authors provide a vantage from which to think about how to further expand the narrative's spatial and temporal frame. Johnson maps the precolonial boundaries and considers indigenous communities that inhabited those lands, but much of the action in the stories collected here begins with European colonization. Yet at the time the Vikings sailed for the North American coast—and centuries before Columbus first crossed the Atlantic—cultures that scholars now call "Mississippian" flourished in lands up and down the river between 1000 and 1350 CE.[7] At Cahokia, across the Mississippi from St. Louis, ten to twenty thousand people lived surrounding the central earthen mound that served religious and political functions, a site where chiefs displayed and solidified their power and priests conducted rituals organized according to solar cycles and seasonal shifts. From the Great Lakes to the Gulf of Mexico, chiefdoms up and down the river flourished a thousand years ago. Beginning our stories then—and thereby bringing archeologists into the conversation about narratives—might offer an even more textured account of religious life throughout that basin— and the territory that later became the United States.

We can also expand our narratives' spatial scope. The Mississippian basin was the setting for contact between Europeans and Indians after Christian missionaries, slave traders, and imperial representatives arrived in the sixteenth century and people, things, and practices traveled up and down that aquatic pathway. We know more about that segment of the story, however. Less often emphasized—but just as important—are the contacts that come into view if we follow the river beyond its northern and southern limits: we notice that the Mississippi opens out to global cultural flows.

Turning to one helpful source—nineteenth-century census records—allows us to trace the flow of migrants across the northern U.S. border and from the north Atlantic Ocean.[8] Consider the residents of Little Falls, Minnesota, a small town established in 1848 not far from the Mississippi's northern headwaters. As we position our historical narrative there, some familiar characters come into view, like Sister Mary Francis and the other Canadian-born Francophone and Anglophone nuns at St. Francis Convent.[9] Taking notice of those Catholic nuns reminds us, however, that some looked down toward the headwaters from beyond the United States' northern boundary. Further, the convent's residents also included European-born migrants—and by the late nineteenth century, so did the area's homes, hotels, and boarding houses. The upper Mississippi region opened out toward the North Atlantic World—and not only France and Britain. In 1880, the 508 residents in Little Falls included immigrants such as Simon Bach, a German-born shoemaker, and Ammond Holden, a Norwegian livery stable worker.[10] Each lived in a "hotel" or boarding house, and their fellow renters included many foreign born—not only the French Canadian widow who supervised Bach's hotel and the lumberman from English-speaking Canada who boarded with Holden, but Protestants and Catholics who had left central and northern Europe to make a new life in America. For example, other town residents hailed from Finland and Sweden, and a thirty-four-year-old Irish mason lived with Bach while a Swiss-born father of seven collected Holden's rent.

The flows went in other directions, too. That Gilded Age town included newcomers who had traveled up the river from as near as Iowa and Illinois and as far downstream as Mississippi and Louisiana, and surviving records contain the traces of transnational migrants along the lower Mississippi who had journeyed from Africa and the Caribbean, including New Orleans' Creoles of color who practiced Spiritualism and Vodou.[11] In that way, as the contributors to this volume have noted, the lower Mississippi opened out to the circum-Atlantic World. Yet some living along the river had been born in Asia, and the global flow of trade and travel extended to the Indo-Pacific World.[12] In the colonial period, Filipino Catholics were among the first Asians to stop or stay in southern Louisiana, and, after the U.S. abolition of slavery, planters along the lower Mississippi imported Chinese-born horticultural workers from Cuba—Havana is less than seven hundred miles from New Orleans—or recruited them from coastal California or southern China. Consider Ham Chang, a thirty-year-old migrant, who in 1870 lived in cramped quarters with ten other Chinese laborers on a plantation rented by an Episcopalian planter in northeastern Louisiana's Carroll Parish, a rural area along the Mississippi River.[13] The records don't reveal much about Chang. We don't know if he ever visited his boss's congregation—or any of the Protestant and Catholic churches that dotted the racially segregated landscape. We can say with some confidence, however, that even though there was no Chinese temple in Carroll Parish, it is likely that he continued to be shaped by the mix of Buddhist, Daoist, and Confucian traditions popular among others in his native region of China. Remembering Chang—and the more than six hundred other Chinese migrants who lived in Louisiana by 1875—illustrates that the religious, ethnic, and linguistic diversity of the Mississippi basin was even greater than we sometimes assume and that the cultural flows connected the U.S. South to the Indo-Pacific World.[14]

The American-born residents of the lower Mississippi—and those living farther north—could not agree about whether the Chinese migration was a good thing or not; but after the Civil War many southern planters, officials, and ministers took a global view that extended eastward. *The Louisiana Planter and Sugar Manufacturer* noticed the "extraordinary improvement in Cane Mills in Cuba," where more than a hundred thousand indentured Chinese laborers toiled, and farmers worried about the economic threat of "coolie grown wheat from India" and "coolie grown rice" from various places.[15] Ministers living along the southern Mississippi also opined about the spiritual state and moral qualities of the Chinese. An 1872 letter by a Protestant preacher in Mississippi published in *American Missionary,* for example, saw "the hand of God in this Chinese immigration"; another Protestant contributor, who complained that those Asians were "lazy, turbulent, and unmanageable" unless they were whipped "within an inch of [their] life," pronounced "the experiment of introducing Chinese labor to Louisiana . . . a decided failure."[16] Like that critic, many other American observers reported that the Chinese who grew rice and harvested sugar cane in the U.S. South, Peru, and Cuba were "in a state of chronic sullenness."[17]

But nineteenth-century American assessments of the Chinese ignored the spiritual sources of the exiles' grief. In their Confucian worldview, personal identity and moral value were linked with the extended family, especially descendants who must ritually establish the ancestors' place in the lineage; yet the displaced Chinese who had imagined a temporary stay came to realize they would suffer the ultimate indignity of never returning. As one Chinese cane worker told officials investigating abuses in Cuba, "It is certain for us that there will be neither coffin nor grave, and . . . neither our sons nor our sons' sons will know what we have endured."[18] That might have been why many of the seventy-nine Chinese migrants in Carroll Parish attended a public funeral procession in Providence, about four miles from Chang's plantation, but failed to perform traditional mortuary rituals or go to the gravesite. The 1876 newspaper story about the death of that "heathen Chinee" noted that "a John Chinaman died in the fisherman's shanty, on the river bank, Saturday night, and was buried in the public cemetery on Sunday. Quite a concourse of Chinamen attended the funeral, in carriages, getting all the public conveyances in town." But the journalist's report continued, "We learned that they would not go through the Chinese ceremonies, and did not go out to the burial."[19] We can't know if Chang was there or why those Chinese mourners didn't go to the grave. But attending the interment of their friend—whom the reporter described only as "John Chinaman," as if he lacked any distinguishing human traits—might have only reminded the displaced workers about where they weren't and who wouldn't mourn them. They were not home. And no matter how many carriages their compatriots hired for their funeral procession, when they died, their descendants couldn't ritually emplace them in their native soil and ancestral lineage.

American Protestant missionaries—some of whom understood the centrality of family in Chinese religion—generally ignored the migrants in the

U.S. South and Latin America. They focused instead on saving "heathen" souls in East Asia. At the same time, as Twain pointed out in "The United States of Lyncherdom," U.S. Protestants often ignored or minimized injustice at home. Twain had been reared on what he called the religion of "fire and brimstone," but he came to challenge racial injustice and lampoon religious intolerance.[20] Pointing to the brutal lynching of African Americans in the South, Twain attacked anti-Chinese sentiment and condemned evangelical hypocrisy by offering a plea of his own: "O kind missionary, O compassionate missionary, leave China! Come home and convert these Christians!"[21]

Like many of the Christian missionaries he condemned, Twain sailed the Pacific and Indian Oceans; he also traveled some of the world's great rivers, including the Ganges. While he accurately reported the local Hindu view that "the Ganges itself and every individual drop of water in it are temples," Twain also dismissed India's sacred stream as "the river of their idolatry."[22] As he noted after that world tour, however, it was not only the Mississippi River that had taken on symbolic value as well as material significance. In this way, too, *Gods of the Mississippi* suggests another area of future research: it invites us to compare the Mississippi basin with other riverine environments. How does the Mississippi compare with other great waterways of the world, whether or not they have been imagined as sacred? What might we learn about U.S. religious history by comparing the Mississippi with the Nile, the Yangtze, or the Amazon?

Comparisons with the Amazon, the second longest river in the world and the largest in the Americas, might prove especially illuminating. Actually, Twain himself had an early interest in that South American river. While in Cincinnati in 1857, he'd been reading an explorer's account that praised the Amazon and the medicinal powers of the coca plant that flourished there. "I made up my mind," Twain reported decades later, "that I would go to the head-waters of the Amazon and collect coca and trade in it and make a fortune. I left for New Orleans with this great idea filling my mind."[23] American literary history might have been different if, after traveling down the Mississippi River, Twain had been able to find a ship departing for South America. He couldn't. Out of necessity, he then turned to a career as a pilot on a Mississippi riverboat instead: "so there I was. I couldn't get to the Amazon. I had no friends in New Orleans and no money to speak of. I went to [the captain] and asked him to make a pilot out of me."[24] Twain later went on to write a great deal about his beloved Mississippi but never did reach the Amazon or compare it with the U.S. river he came to know so well.

Appealing to racial, geographical, or religious factors to explain the differences, some of his contemporaries in North and South America did make those comparisons, however. Theodore Roosevelt, whom Twain found "impulsive" but "likeable," offered a racialized account of the difference in cultural "progress" along major rivers in the two regions. In his five-volume *Winning of the West*, he argued, "Temperate South America is as fertile and healthy for the white man as temperate North America, and is so much less in extent as to offer a far simpler problem of conquest and settlement."[25] Further, Roosevelt pointed out that the Spanish and Portuguese reached South America's rivers "two centuries before the American backwoodsman reached the Mississippi" yet "scarcely made as much progress in a decade as his northern rival did in a year." That mainline Protestant observer, who traveled both the Mississippi and the Amazon, implied that Catholicism's deficiencies played a role, but he most directly attributed the variation to the Anglo-Saxon race's superiority. "If a race is weak," President Roosevelt reasoned, "if it is lacking in the physical and moral traits which go to the makeup of a conquering people, it cannot succeed."[26]

The Peruvian historian and essayist Víctor Andrés Belaúnde, who minimized Roosevelt's Anglo-Saxonism but praised his account of "the basin of the Mississippi and its tributaries," proposed an alternative explanation that attributed agency to landscape rather than race.[27] In his lecture "The Frontier in Hispanic America," Belaúnde acknowledged multiple factors, including "race, climate, religion, and the system of government during the colonial regime."[28] However, endorsing Frederick Jackson Turner's thesis that "the dynamic element par excellence in the development of Anglo-Saxon America has been the frontier," that Peruvian interpreter suggested the cultural variations in the northern and southern cultural regions developed because of differences in accessible and arable land.[29] The Andes are a much more formidable barrier than the Alleghenies, he pointed out, and "the Mississippi, theater of the Saxon-American frontier, and the valley of the Amazon, theatre of the possible Hispanic American frontier," were vastly different. The fertile lands of the Mississippi, Belaúnde proposed, were not owned by the church or state and could be reached by individual migrants with sufficient initiative, "whereas the territories of the valley of the Amazon consisting of tropic forests could not be converted into arable land and access to them from the region of the Andes was most difficult."[30] These geographical differences yielded cultural variations, since the Mississippi allowed—even generated—the individualist temper and democratic impulse that came to define U.S. religion and culture.

The result, that Peruvian concluded, was the difference between the cultural "stagnation" and "rigidity" along the Amazon and the "fluidity" and "vitality" along the Mississippi.[31]

Whether contemporary historians accept Belaúnde's geographical explanation or suggest that some other factor provides the best starting point for cross-cultural analysis, the attempt to compare the Mississippian region with other places promises to reveal more about what's distinctive—and what's not so exceptional—about religious life throughout that valley, just as these essays also remind us that the story of U.S. religion shifts as our vantage does. By repositioning narrators along the Mississippi, this collection has performed a great service for readers. We find ourselves less "cramped up and smothery," as the historical accounts collected here carry us toward new stories that reorient the plot on a north-south trajectory and trace movements up and down the nation's aquatic center—and even beyond its political borders to the farther reaches of the Western Hemisphere, the Atlantic World, and the Pacific Rim.

NOTES

1. Mark Twain, *The Adventures of Huckleberry Finn* (New York and London: Harper and Brothers, 1899), 163–64. The novel originally appeared in 1884.

2. Twain, *Huckleberry Finn*, 35, 411. For autobiographical accounts of the early life and riverboat experience of Mark Twain (Samuel L. Clemens), see Harriet Elinor Smith and the other editors of the Mark Twain Project, *Autobiography of Mark Twain*, vol. 1 (Berkeley: University of California Press, 2010), 209, 444, 589, 646–47.

3. Twain, *Huckleberry Finn*, 411,

4. For another attempt to shift narratives by positioning the narrator near the Mississippi, see Richard J. Callahan Jr., "Introduction: A Reorienting View from the Center of the Country," in *New Territory, New Perspectives: The Religious Impact of the Louisiana Purchase*, ed. Callahan (Columbia: University of Missouri Press, 2008), 1–15. For my own account of the history of the subfield and my attempt to contribute to this conversation about the narratives of U.S. religion, see Thomas A. Tweed, ed., *Retelling U.S. Religious History* (Berkeley: University of California Press, 1997), and Thomas A. Tweed, "Expanding the Study of U.S. Religion: Reflections on the State of a Subfield," *Religion* 40 (2010): 250–58.

5. The phrase is from Sensbach's contribution to this volume.

6. The suggestions I make here and below—that we expand the chronological and geographical scope of our narratives and engage in more transnational and comparative studies—I offered in Tweed, "Expanding the Study of U.S. Religion."

7. Daniel K. Richter, *Facing East from Indian Country: A Narrative History of Early America* (Cambridge, MA: Harvard University Press, 2001), 3–7. See also Joel W. Martin, "Indians, Contact, and Colonialism in the Deep South: Themes for a Postcolonial History of American Religion," in *Retelling U.S. Religious History*, ed. Tweed,

149–80. There is a vast literature about Cahokia and what archeologists call the Mississippian Ideological Interaction Sphere (MIIS). For a brief and accessible overview of Cahokia, see William Iseminger, *Cahokia Mounds: America's First City* (Charleston: History Press, 2010). On Mississippian religion, see James A. Brown, "The Archeology of Ancient Religion in the Eastern Woodlands," *Annual Review of Anthropology* 26 (1997): 465–85; F. Kent Reilly III and James F. Garber, eds., *Ancient Objects and Sacred Realms: Interpretations of Mississippian Iconography* (Austin: University of Texas Press, 2007); and John E. Kelly and James A. Brown, "In Search of Cosmic Power: Contextualizing Spiritual Journeys between Cahokia and the St. Francois Mountains," in *Archaeology of Spiritualities,* ed. Kathryn Rountree, Christine Morris, and Alan A. D. Peatfield (New York: Springer, 2012), 107–29.

8. Those government records also reveal the ethnic, linguistic, and religious heterogeneity of the population and enrich what we already know from other sources—that those who claimed tribal identities settled near their historic homelands or moved up and down the river; former slaves from southern states traveled up the Mississippi to seek fewer constraints or more humane labor; American-born migrants traveled south on the water or along the land to seek work.

9. Sister [Mary] Francis, Little Falls, Morrison County, *Minnesota Territorial and State Censuses, 1849–1905,* Provo, Utah: Ancestry.com, Original data: Minnesota Historical Society, *Minnesota State Population Census Schedules, 1865–1905,* St. Paul. On Canadian views of U.S. religious history, see William Westfall, "Voices from the Attic: The Canadian Border and the Writing of American Religious History," in *Retelling U.S. Religious History,* ed. Tweed, 181–99.

10. The information in the rest of this paragraph is derived from the original census documents for Simon Bach and Ammond Holden and the neighbors who appear on the same form: Little Falls, Morrison County, Minnesota, *Tenth Census of the United States, 1880,* Records of the Census Bureau, Record Group 29 (Washington, D.C.: National Archives).

11. On the "dissident religious culture" of Creoles of color, who were culturally situated between black and white, see Shirley Elizabeth Thompson, *Exiles at Home: The Struggle to Become American in Creole New Orleans* (Cambridge, MA: Harvard University Press, 2009), 157–60, 243–51.

12. For recent reflections on the "Atlantic World," see Bernard Bailyn and Patricia L. Denault, eds., *Soundings in Atlantic History: Latent Structures and Intellectual Currents, 1550–1830* (Cambridge, MA: Harvard University Press, 2009); and Jack P. Greene and Philip D. Morgan, eds., *Atlantic History: A Critical Appraisal* (New York: Oxford University Press, 2009). On the underemphasized connections between the Atlantic and the Pacific, see Reed Ueda, "Pushing the Atlantic Envelope: Interoceanic Perspectives on Atlantic History," in *The Atlantic in Global History, 1500–2000,* ed. Jorge Cañizares-Esguerra and Erik R. Seeman (Upper Saddle River, NJ: Pearson, 2007), 163–75.

13. Ham Chang, Carroll, Manning Place, Ward 2, Louisiana, *The Ninth Census of the United States, 1870* (Washington, DC: National Archives and Records and Records Administration, n.d.). Like other Chinese in the region, Chang most likely signed a multi-year contract to work in the fields in exchange for food rations and a monthly salary. Chang's boss was E. C. Manning (1839–1914), and the plantation was called Manning Place. On Manning, his wife, Mattie, and their denominational affiliation, see Georgia Payne Durham Pinkston, *A Place to Remember: East Carroll Parish, LA, 1832–1976* (Baton Rouge: Claitor's Publishing, 1977), 222. Most nineteenth-century

migrants to the Americas originated in southern China, near Canton or Macau. The latter was settled by the Portuguese in the sixteenth century, so there was a Catholic presence. Protestant missionaries arrived by 1807. So it is possible that a small proportion of the laborers in the Americas had been exposed to Christianity in some way. Yet during the years of significant Chinese migration (1847–86) the overwhelming majority of indentured laborers abroad would have been influenced in childhood by the usual blending of Buddhist, Daoism, Folk, and Confucian traditions. On this, see the map (13) and analysis (19–20) in Denise Helly, "Introduction," in *The Cuba Commission Report: A Hidden History of the Chinese in Cuba: The Original English-Language Text of 1876* (Baltimore: Johns Hopkins University Press, 1993), 3–30.

14. The figures about the number of Chinese in Carroll Parish (79) and the state (619) are from 1875 and are cited by Moon-Ho Jung, *Coolies and Cane: Race, Labor, and Sugar in the Land of Emancipation* (Baltimore: Johns Hopkins University Press, 2006), 198. Jung points out that those figures are probably too low. For the wider context of Chinese migrants in the South, see also Lucy M. Cohen, *Chinese in the Post–Civil War South: A People without a History* (Baton Rouge: Louisiana State University Press, 1984).

15. "Double Cane Mills," *The Louisiana Planter and Sugar Manufacturer,* 1, no. 4 (July 28, 1888): 33–34, and "John Foos and the Tariff," ibid., 34. This periodical was a weekly newspaper published in New Orleans and "devoted to the sugar, rice, and other agricultural industries of Louisiana." The English noun *coolie* (which has rough equivalents in several languages, including Portuguese, Dutch, Gujarati, and Tamil) is now mostly a derogatory historical term. It has been used at least since the seventeenth century to refer to "an Asian laborer working abroad." Coolie, n. *Oxford English Dictionary,* 3rd ed., September 2008, online version March 2011, http://www.oed.com .ezproxy.lib.utexas.edu/Entry/40991, accessed 5 May 2011.

16. "Mississippi: Letter from Mr. H. S. Beals," *American Missionary,* 16, no. 3 (March 1872): 50, and "Chinese Labor," ibid., 54.

17. W. M. L. Jay [Julia Louisa Matilda Woodruff], *My Winter in Cuba* (New York: E. P. Dutton, 1871), 221–22. Obviously, Woodruff (1833–1909) used a pseudonym.

18. The quotation from the Chinese laborer is included in *The Cuba Commission Report: A Hidden History of the Chinese in Cuba,* 110. Approximately 250,000 Chinese migrated to Cuba and Peru in the middle of the nineteenth century. On that migration and the laborers who were interviewed as part of the 1876 report, see Lisa Yun, *The Coolie Speaks: Chinese Indentured Laborers and African Slaves in Cuba* (Philadelphia: Temple University Press, 2008).

19. This account was originally published in the Providence, Louisiana, newspaper, the *Carroll Watchman,* January 29, 1876. It was reprinted in Sandy L. Schmitz, ed., *Murder, Mayhem, and Misc. of Carroll Parish, La., 1866–1876* (Berryville, AR: S & S Press, 2001), 301.

20. *Autobiography of Mark Twain,* 188, 313–15.

21. Mark Twain, "The United States of Lyncherdom," in *Asian Religions in America: A Documentary History,* ed. Thomas A. Tweed and Stephen Prothero (New York: Oxford University Press, 1999), 121–22. Twain also advocated for the Chinese in other ways, including by collaborating with Chinese diplomats and appealing to U.S. leaders to support Chinese pupils studying in the United States. On this, see *Autobiography of Mark Twain,* 71–73.

22. Mark Twain, *Following the Equator: A Journey around the World* (Hartford, CT: American Publishing, 1897), 482, 497. Twain's world tour was in 1895–96.

23. *Autobiography of Mark Twain,* 461. Two U.S. naval officers penned the account Twain was reading in Ohio: William Lewis Herndon and Lardner Gibbon, *Exploration of the Valley of the Amazon, Made under Direction of the Navy Department* (Washington, DC: Robert Armstrong, 1853).

24. *Autobiography of Mark Twain,* 461.

25. Twain's assessment of Roosevelt is found in *Autobiography of Mark Twain,* 259.

26. All three quotations in this paragraph are from Theodore Roosevelt, *Winning of the West: An Account of the Exploration and Settlement of Our Country from the Alleghenies to the Pacific* (New York and London: G. P. Putnam's Sons, 1907), 5:118. For Roosevelt's travels on rivers in South America, and his mention of both the Mississippi and the Amazon, see Theodore Roosevelt, *Through the Brazilian Wilderness,* reprint of 1914 edition (New York: Greenwood, 1969), 53–55, 96–98, 271–72, 312–13, 321. Roosevelt called the Mississippi "the white man's highway" (53).

27. Víctor Andrés Belaúnde, "The Economic Basis of Politics in Latin America," *Annals of the American Academy of Political and Social Science* 342 (July 1962): 55. Volumes 3 ("La Realidad nacional") and 4 ("Peruanidad") of his collected works also include passages that display his hemispheric perspective and comparative analysis. Víctor Andrés Belaúnde, *Obras completas* (Lima: Comisión Nacional del Centario, 1987).

28. Víctor Andrés Belaúnde, "Lectures" [Section III: "The Frontier in Hispanic America"], *Rice Institute Pamphlets* 10, no. 4 (October 1923): 202–13. This quotation is from page 202, and the lecture was originally delivered in 1922 to the American Historical Association.

29. Belaúnde, "Lectures," 202, 206.

30. Ibid., 206.

31. Ibid., 208, 213.

CONTRIBUTORS

John M. Giggie is Associate Professor of American History and African American Studies at the University of Alabama. He is author of *After Redemption: Jim Crow and the Transformation of African American Religion in the Delta, 1875–1915* and editor of *Faith in the Market: Religion and the Rise of Urban Commercial Culture.*

Alison Collis Greene is Assistant Professor of American History at Mississippi State University and author of "No Depression in Heaven: Religion and Economic Crisis in Memphis and the Delta."

John Hayes is Assistant Professor of American History at Augusta State University and author of "Hard, Hard Religion: Faith and Class in the New South."

Sylvester Johnson is Associate Professor of African American Studies and Religious Studies at Northwestern University and author of *The Myth of Ham in Nineteenth-Century American Christianity: Race, Heathens, and the People of God.*

Michael Pasquier is Assistant Professor of Religious Studies at Louisiana State University. He is author of *Fathers on the Frontier: French Missionaries and the Roman Catholic Priesthood in the United States, 1789–1870* and co-editor of the *Journal of Southern Religion.*

Seth Perry is a PhD candidate in Divinity (expected 2013) at the University of Chicago, where he is writing a dissertation entitled "The Endless Making of Many Books: Bibles and Religious Authority in Early-National America."

Justin D. Poché is Assistant Professor of History and Alexander F. Carson Faculty Fellow in the History of the United States at the College of the Holy Cross and author of "Religion, Race, and Rights in Catholic Louisiana, 1938–1970."

Arthur Remillard is Assistant Professor of Religious Studies at Saint Francis University and author of *Southern Civil Religions: Imagining the Good Society in the Post-Reconstruction Era.*

Jon F. Sensbach is Professor of History at the University of Florida and author of *Rebecca's Revival: Creating Black Christianity in the Atlantic World* and *A Separate Canaan: The Making of an Afro-Moravian World in North Carolina, 1763–1840.*

Thomas Ruys Smith is lecturer in American Literature and Culture at the University of East Anglia and author of *River of Dreams: Imagining the Mississippi before Mark Twain* and *Blacklegs, Card Sharps, and Confidence Men: Nineteenth-Century Mississippi River Gambling Stories.*

Thomas A. Tweed is Gwyn Shive, Anita Nordan Lindsay, and Joe and Cherry Gray Professor of the History of Christianity at the University of Texas and author of *America's Church: The National Shrine and Catholic Presence in the Nation's Capital* and *Crossing and Dwelling: A Theory of Religion.*

INDEX